KU-044-315

STUDY GUIDE

FOR ATKINSON, ATKINSON, SMITH, AND HILGARD'S

INTRODUCTION TO

Psychology

NINTH EDITION

Rita L. Atkinson

HARCOURT BRACE JOVANOVICH, PUBLISHERS

San Diego   New York   Chicago   Austin   Washington, D.C.
London   Sydney   Tokyo   Toronto

Copyright © 1987, 1983, 1979, 1975, 1971 by Harcourt Brace Jovanovich, Inc.

All rights reserved. No part of this publication may be reproduced or transmitted in any form or by any means, electronic or mechanical, including photocopy, recording, or any information storage and retrieval system, without permission in writing from the publisher.

Requests for permission to make copies of any parts of the work should be mailed to: Permissions, Harcourt Brace Jovanovich, Publishers, Orlando, Florida 32887.

ISBN: 0-15-543685-6

Library of Congress Catalog Card Number: 85-82651

Printed in the United States of America

Cover: "Head No. 56" by Italo Scanga, 1985, oil on wood (28½ × 15½ × 11). Private collection. Courtesy of Susanne Hilberry Gallery.

Tables on pages 155 and 156 from Reese, Ellen P., Jane Howard, and T. W. Reese, *Human Behavior Analysis and Application*, 2nd ed. © 1966, 1978 by Wm. C. Brown Company Publishers, Dubuque, Iowa. Reprinted by permission.

To the Instructor

The *Study Guide* is designed to assist students in mastering the content of the introductory course. In the preparation of the *Study Guide,* consideration was given to four major difficulties students often encounter: First, they may be uncertain about what to learn from each chapter—how to distinguish crucial material from less important details. Second, they may fail to learn the meanings of specific psychological concepts and terms. Third, they may have no satisfactory way of knowing how well they have mastered the material until after an examination (which often is too late). Fourth, they frequently find it difficult to understand or appreciate the role that research plays in psychology.

The five sections of each chapter in this *Study Guide* have been designed to help students in each of these areas. The first section is a list of *learning objectives* to help students focus on what they should learn from the chapter. Next is a *programmed unit,* which gives students a preliminary acquaintance with some of the terms and ideas covered in the chapter. Students should work on this unit *before* reading the corresponding text chapter. Next is a list of the important *terms and concepts* in the chapter. After reading the programmed unit and the text, students should be able to provide brief identifications for each of these. Items missed then become an object for further study. Next is a multiple-choice *self-quiz,* which provides students with an opportunity to practice taking exams and, at the same time, points out their areas of weakness. Finally, there are *individual and class exercises,* which give students a closer look at one or more of the concepts discussed in the chapter, a chance to explore some interesting aspects of human behavior, and a feeling for the way information is derived from research. A few of the exercises must be done in class, but most have been planned so that students can carry them out on their own if the instructor does not want to take class time. The usual procedure is for each student to collect data, which he or she can then analyze or bring to class; each student's data can then be combined with those of other students for analysis and discussion.

To the Student: How to Use This Guide

The *Study Guide* is designed to help you in several ways: It tells you what you should learn from each chapter; it introduces the concepts and terms you will encounter in the text; it provides examination questions that will enable you to determine just how much you have learned; and, finally, it suggests exercises that will give you an understanding of the interests of the psychologist and, in most cases, a look at psychological research methods.

Each chapter in the *Study Guide* parallels one in the text, and there are five sections for each chapter. The first section of each chapter in the *Study Guide* lists the *learning objectives*—the ideas and facts you should learn from the chapter. Look them over before you start to read the chapter. You may want to refer back to each objective after you have covered the appropriate section in the text. Or you may prefer to complete the chapter and then see if you have mastered all the objectives. In any event, the learning objectives cover the important ideas in each chapter; they include topics you will probably be expected to know on an examination.

The second section of each chapter uses a technique of learning called *programmed instruction,* a method of self-instruction. This technique, based on certain principles of learning, aids in the understanding and mastery of material.

These programmed units are intended as *previews* of the corresponding chapters in your textbook. From each programmed unit you will acquire an acquaintance with *some* of the key ideas and concepts presented in the text; as a result, you should be able to read the text chapter with increased understanding. Although the programmed units are meant to be completed before you read the text, they also may be profitably used later as a review before examinations.

A word of warning: The programmed units cannot serve as a substitute for the text chapters. They do not treat all the ideas presented in the text—for the programmed units to do so would require a book many times the size of this one. Even the ideas they do cover are treated in greater detail in the text. If you work through a programmed unit, however, and then go on to study the text, you will master the text treatment more easily than if you had not gone through the programmed material.

The programmed unit consists of a series of short steps called "frames." Each frame requires you to make a *response*—either by filling in a blank or by circling one of two words. To the left of the frame, on the same line as the blank, is the correct response.

Use a paper or cardboard strip to cover the answer column to the left of the program. After you have written your answer in the appropriate blank in the frame, move the strip down only far enough to reveal the correct answer. If you have made a mistake, cross out your answer and write the correct one above it.

Once you have completed the programmed unit, read the corresponding chapter in the text. After you study the text chapter, turn to the *terms and concepts* section of the *Study Guide* and see how many you can identify correctly. If you have trouble, consult the appropriate section of the chapter or look in the glossary. The list of terms and concepts may seem long for some chapters, but if you learn them all you will have a good grasp of the material that is likely to appear on an examination.

Next, turn to the *self-quiz* section of the *Study Guide* and answer all the questions. Check your answers against the answer key; for questions on which you made an error go back to the text and review the appropriate material.

The final section of each *Study Guide* chapter presents one or more *exercises* designed to illustrate various aspects of psychological research. A few of the demonstrations require special equipment and must be presented by the instructor in class, but most are designed so that you can carry them out on your own. Sometimes you may be asked to do an exercise on your own but to bring the data to class so that the data from all students may be combined for analysis and discussion. The exercises in the *Study Guide* are designed to give you a better understanding of scientific methodology, some interesting insights into human behavior, and a feeling for how psychologists investigate the types of problems presented in the chapters.

To summarize, there are five sections in each chapter of the *Study Guide:* learning objectives, programmed unit, terms and concepts, self-quiz, and individual or class exercises. First look over the learning objectives and complete the programmed unit for a chapter, read the chapter, and then proceed to the terms and concepts for identification, the self-quiz, and the exercises. These sections are designed to help you understand the concepts in the text, to allow you to evaluate your learning, and finally, to introduce you to the methods of psychology. It is important to remember, however, that the *Study Guide* is designed as a supplement, not a substitute, for the text. Used properly, the *Study Guide* will enhance your comprehension of the text's contents.

Contents

Each chapter in this *Guide* consists of Learning Objectives, a Programmed Unit, Terms and Concepts, a Self-Quiz, and Individual and/or Group Exercises.

1
Nature of Psychology

LEARNING OBJECTIVES

1-1. Be able to name and define the five approaches to psychology used in the text. Know what characterizes each, and how each approach differs from the other four.

1-2. Be able to state the definition of psychology given in the text. Be familiar with the several ways in which it has been defined and how the definition has changed over time.

1-3. Be familiar with the different fields of specialization within psychology.

1-4. Understand the use of the term behavioral and social sciences; also the use of the term cognitive sciences.

1-5. Know what distinguishes the experimental method from other methods of observation. Be able to define, and to differentiate between, an independent variable and a dependent variable.

1-6. Be familiar with the observational, survey, test, and case-history methods as they are used in psychology. Understand when and why each is used and the advantages and disadvantages of each.

1-7. Know what is involved in the designing of an experiment. Be able to define, and to differentiate between, an experimental group and a control group.

1-8. Understand the use of a mean in experimental design, including the use of tests of the significance of a difference between means.

1-9. Know when correlation is an alternative to experimentation and understand its advantages and disadvantages.

1-10. Know the meaning of differences in the size and arithmetic sign of a coefficient of correlation. Be able to show, with an example, why correlation does not establish cause-and-effect relationships.

1

psychology
(*or* people)

1. *Psychology* studies people from a number of different viewpoints. This book will cover five approaches to the study of _____ .

2. The *neurobiological approach* attempts to relate a person's actions to events taking place within the *nervous system.* If you measure the activity of nerve cells in different parts of the brain when a person is angry, you would be studying emotion

neurobiological

from the neuro_____ approach.

3. The neurobiological approach to psychology studies the relation between a person's

nervous

thoughts or actions and events taking place within the _____ system.

4. A study relating changes in the nerve cell structure to the learning of a new task is

neurobiological

an example of the _____ approach to psychology.

nervous

5. Instead of studying events occurring in the _____ system, we can focus on the individual's *behavior.*

6. Behavior refers to those activities of an organism that can be *observed.* When we

behavior

observe a child laughing or talking, we are observing _____ .

observed

7. Behavior refers to any action of an organism that can be _____ .

8. If we measure the neural hormones secreted when a person is angry, we are using

neurobiological

the _____ approach to study emotion. If, instead, we count the number of times the person strikes his or her fist on the table when

behavioral

angry, we are using the _____ approach.

observable
internal

9. The *behavioral approach* focuses on (*observable/internal*) events; the neurobiological approach studies (*observable/internal*) events.

10. Some behaviorists do study events occurring within the body, provided they can be objectively measured. But a strict behavioral approach, called *stimulus-response* (S-R) *psychology,* focuses on the *stimuli* that elicit behavioral *responses* and is not concerned with what goes on inside the organism. Stimulus-response psychologists

responses

study stimuli and _____ rather than internal events.

11. An experimenter studying how quickly a person can press a lever in response to the

stimulus-response

onset of a tone would probably be a _____ - _____ psychologist.

12. Strict stimulus-response psychologists are not concerned with the mental processes that intervene between hearing a tone (the stimulus) and pressing a lever (the

response

response). They are interested only in the stimulus and the _____ . *Cognitive* psychologists, on the other hand, study the way the mind *processes* sensory information.

13. A psychologist who studies how the mind processes incoming information is called

cognitive

a _____ psychologist. *Cognition* refers to those mental processes by which sensory information is transformed in various ways, coded and stored in memory, and retrieved for later use.

14. As you read this sentence your mind transforms the stimuli of "marks on paper" into visual images and compares those images with others stored in memory to arrive at meaning. The events that intervene between stimulus input and your

cognition

processes

response are what we mean by _____ . Perceiving, remembering, and thinking are all cognitive _____ .

thinking

cognitive process

15. Cognitive processes include perceiving, remembering, and _____ . Perceiving is a _____ _____ , and so is remembering.

16. Cognitive psychologists are usually interested in *conscious* mental processes, such as

remembering

perceiving, _____ , and thinking, rather than *unconscious* processes. Conscious processes are mental events of which we are *aware*. Percep-

conscious

tions, memories, emotions, and dreams are all _____ processes of which we are aware.

17. Conscious processes are those internal psychological events of which we are fully

aware

_____ . If you are angry and are aware that you are angry, this is

conscious

a _____ process.

18. Some internal events are unconscious; these are emotions, repressed memories, and desires of which we are not aware. Internal psychological events of which we are

unconscious

unaware are called _____ processes.

19. If you are angry at your mother but are not aware of this anger, then it is an

unconscious

_____ process.

20. The *psychoanalytic approach,* developed by Sigmund Freud, assumes that much of

unaware
(*or* not aware)

our behavior is influenced by unconscious processes of which we are _____ .

21. Freud believed that many of the forbidden or punished impulses of childhood are

unconscious

driven out of awareness and become _____ . He assumed that such unconscious impulses are expressed indirectly in dreams, slips of speech, and other forms of behavior.

22. The assumption that many of an individual's impulses are unconscious is basic to

psychoanalytic

the _____ approach.

23. Freud believed that unconscious impulses are usually concerned with *sex* or *aggres-*

aggressive

sion. Sexual and _____ impulses are those most often punished in

consciousness
(*or* awareness)

children, and thus those most apt to be banished from _____ .

24 A fifth approach to the study of psychology focuses on the individual's *subjective experience,* the individual's own perception and interpretation of events. This

approach is called *phenomenological* because it looks at events, or phenomena, through the eyes of the _____ .

25. The phenomenological approach is concerned with _____ experience rather than behavior. On her first day at school a little girl sits in the corner crying. If you note the frequency and loudness of her sobs, you are using the _____ approach. If, instead, you ask her to describe how she views the situation, what it means to her, you are using the _____ approach.

26. The phenomenological approach focuses on the individual's _____ _____ . Some phenomenological theories are also called *humanistic* because they emphasize those "human" qualities that distinguish people from animals—primarily their *free will* and their drive toward *self-actualization*.

27. Humanistic theories reject the idea that we are mechanically controlled either by external stimuli or by unconscious impulses. We are responsible for our own actions

and thus are said to have free _____ .

28. The psychological approach that focuses on the individual's subjective experience is called _____ . Within this approach are theories that emphasize self-actualization and free will. *Self-actualization* refers to our need to develop our potential to the fullest.

29. Our natural tendency to actualize our potential to the fullest is called _____-_____ .

30. For review, identify each of the following approaches to the psychological study of people.

a. Relates actions to events in the brain and nervous system. _____

b. Relates stimuli to observed responses. _____

c. Focuses on the way the mind processes information. _____

d. Emphasizes unconscious processes. _____

e. Emphasizes subjective experience, free will, and self-actualization.

_____

31. Because there are so many different approaches to the study of psychology, it is difficult to define the field precisely. For our purposes we will define psychology as *the science that studies behavior and mental processes*. Behavior refers to any

action of the organism that can be _____ . Mental processes are internal events that (*are/are not*) directly observable.

32. Psychology is defined as the science that studies _____ and mental processes. If we are aware of our mental processes, they are _____ . Unconscious mental processes are not available to one's _____ .

mental processes	**33.** Psychology is the science that studies behavior and _____ _____ , both conscious and unconscious.
	34. The aim of the science of psychology is to discover *relationships among variables.* A *variable* is something that changes, something that can take on different values. "To vary" means "to change"; therefore a quality that is subject to change is called a
variable	_____ .
	35. A person's rate of breathing in different situations is likely to change. Breathing
variable	rate is thus a _____ .
	36. Experiments are designed to examine how one variable affects another. If we
two	wished to discover the effect of fear upon breathing rate, we would have _____
relationship	(*number*) variables in the study. We would be trying to discover the rel_____
rate, fear	between the variables of breathing _____ and _____ .
	37. *Time* is a variable in many experiments. A psychologist who wants to determine the effect of the passage of time on forgetting might ask several subjects to memorize the same set of materials and then have them recall the materials after varying intervals of time. In this case the variable whose effect the psychologist was trying to
time	discover would be _____ .
	38. The psychologist studying the rate of forgetting by varying the passage of time is able to manipulate the time variable by deciding when he or she will test the subject's memory. A variable that is directly controlled or *manipulated* by the experimenter is called an *independent variable.* Time, in the experiment we have been
independent	describing, is a(n) _____ variable.
	39. We call such a variable independent because its value does not depend on the values
manipulated	of any other variable. Instead, it is controlled or _____ by the experimenter.
	40. The experimenter can control or manipulate time in an experiment but cannot directly control or manipulate forgetting. If the experimenter finds, however, that forgetting is affected by the passage of time, it can be assumed that forgetting is *dependent* on time. If time is called an independent variable, then forgetting can be
dependent	called a(n) _____ variable.
	41. The independent variable is the variable manipulated by the experimenter. The variable whose value may vary as a result of changes in the independent variable is the
dependent	_____ variable. In other words, the value of the dependent variable is dependent on the value of the independent variable.
	42. If we want to discover the effects of marijuana on sexual behavior, the amount of
independent	marijuana administered will be the _____ variable and sexual behavior will be the dependent variable.
	43. If we are concerned with the effect of age on the accuracy of visual perception, age

of the subject is the independent variable and the accuracy of perception is the

dependent _____ variable.

44. If an experimenter varies the temperature in a classroom to determine its effect on

independent examination grades, the temperature level is the _____ vari-

dependent able and the examination grades of the students constitute the _____
variable.

45. In a laboratory experiment the variable the experimenter manipulates, the

independent _____ variable, can be varied with precision. Similarly, the

dependent variable that is a consequence of the subject's behavior, the _____
variable, can be carefully measured. Other variables that the investigator does not
want to influence the outcome of the experiment can be *controlled.*

46. For example, if we want to study the effect of sleep loss on learning ability, we can
select subjects of the same age and intelligence, provide them with the same diet
and living conditions, and then see how their performance on a learning task (such

sleep as memorizing a poem) varies with the amount of _____ they are permitted.
In this situation, variables that we do not want to influence the results (such as age,

controlled intelligence, and diet) are con_____ . We can thus be fairly confi-

dependent dent that differences in scores on the learning task, the _____

independent variable, result from different amounts of sleep, the _____
variable.

control **47.** Laboratory experiments thus enable us to _____ variables that we do
not wish to influence our results, as well as provide the means for careful manipula-

independent tion of the _____ variable and precise measurement of the

dependent _____ variable.

48. But it is not possible to study all types of behavior in the laboratory. *Observation* in
a natural setting is another method psychologists use to study behavior. Suppose we
want to know how a child's aggressiveness on the school playground is related
to his or her behavior at home. If the mother's answers to a questionnaire indicate
that the child is quite "aggressive" at home, will the child also exhibit aggressive
behavior on the playground? We cannot answer this question in the laboratory,

controlled where variables can be precisely _____ . Instead we must deter-

observations mine how the ratings provided by the mother correspond to _____
made by trained observers who record notes on the child's behavior on the playground.

49. The relationship between home behavior and playground behavior in this case (*is/*

is not *is not*) determined by manipulating aggressive behavior at home and studying the
results on the playground; instead we observe both variables as they occur in nature
and then look for a *relationship* between them.

relationship **50.** With observational methods we seek to determine the _____
between the two variables. The relationship between two variables in situations

manipulate (*or* control)	in which we cannot experimentally _____ the variables is determined by *correlation.*

51. Suppose we want to know whether "cooperativeness" is a personality characteristic that persists throughout life. Will a child who exhibits cooperative behavior in nursery school be judged cooperative as an adult? In this case we cannot use the experimental method to answer the question. Instead we use the method of

correlation — cor _____ to determine the relationship between a measure of

cooperative — cooperative behavior in childhood and another measure of _____ behavior in adulthood.

cooperative **52.** As a measure of _____ behavior in childhood we might use judgments by nursery school teachers, who rate each child according to the degree he or she cooperates in play as opposed to being aggressive or withdrawn. As a

measure — _____ of cooperative behavior in adulthood we could look at the same individuals when they are in college and note how their classmates rate them on a scale of cooperativeness.

measures (*or* variables) **53.** The figure below shows the relationship between these two _____ for ten different young men. A rating of 1 indicates very uncooperative behavior,

cooperative — while a rating of 12 indicates extremely _____ behavior. Note

2 — that John received a rating of 2 in nursery school and the same rating of _____ in college. Thus we would say that John's behavior has been consistently (*cooperative/*

uncooperative — *uncooperative*) over the years.

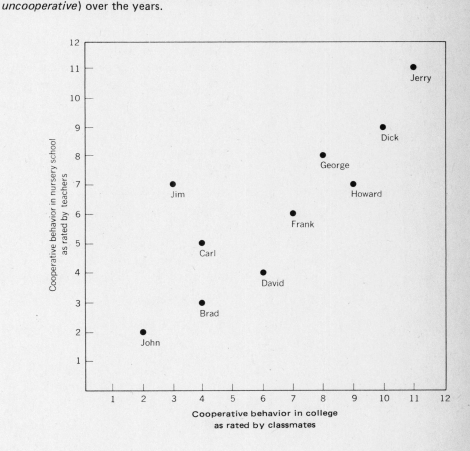

11
cooperative

7

Jim

ratings
correlation

correlation

childhood

correlation

diagonal

correlation

coefficient

correlation

increase

correlation

variable

negative

positive

54. Jerry received a rating of _____ in nursery school and also in college. His behavior appears to be consistently (*cooperative/uncooperative*).

55. What can we say about Jim and Howard? They both received the same rating of _____ in nursery school, but in adulthood Jim is rated as less cooperative than Howard. Both boys changed over the years, but the change was greater for _____ .

56. The other subjects show some discrepancy between ratings in childhood and _____ in adulthood. But their ratings are similar enough to indicate a close relationship, or cor_____ , between cooperative behavior in childhood and cooperative behavior in adulthood.

57. If the c_____ between child and adult behavior were perfect, then all the ratings would fall on a straight *diagonal* line when plotted on the graph; each person would have received the same rating in adulthood as he or she did in _____ .

58. If there were no relationship, or _____ , between adult and child cooperative behavior, then the scores would be scattered randomly all over the graph.

59. Since the scores in this hypothetical study fall very close to a straight _____ line, we can conclude that there is a close relationship, a high _____ , between child and adult behavior.

60. The actual measure in a correlational study is the *coefficient of correlation,* signified by the lower-case letter r, which expresses the degree of relationship. If there had been a perfect correlation between cooperation in childhood and adulthood in the above study, then we would have a correlation coef_____ of $r = +1.00$.

61. The plus sign signifies that the relationship is *positive,* that a child who is cooperative will tend to be cooperative as an adult. A positive coefficient of _____ , or r, indicates a positive relationship between the two variables; an increase in one variable is associated with an _____ in the other.

62. If, on the other hand, children who were cooperative in nursery school always turned out to be uncooperative adults, we would have a perfect *negative correlation.* A negative _____ of $r = -1.00$ indicates that one variable increases as the other _____ decreases.

63. Life expectancy decreases as the amount a person smokes increases. This is an example of a (*positive/negative*) correlation.

64. Life expectancy increases as the adequacy of one's diet increases. This is an example of a _____ correlation.

positive

negative

65. A correlation coefficient of +1.00 signifies a perfect (*positive/negative*) relationship between two variables. A correlation coefficient of −1.00 indicates a perfect _____ relationship.

coefficient

r = .00

66. A correlation _____ of $r = .00$ signifies no relationship at all. If we tried to determine the relationship between hair color and grades in college, we would expect a correlation of (*r = 1.00/r = .00/r = −1.00*).

67. A correlation between $r = .00$ and either +1.00 or −1.00 indicates an imperfect

correlation

relationship. The more closely the _____ approaches 1.00, either plus or minus, the greater the degree of relationship, either positive or negative. In our study on cooperativeness, for example, we might expect a correlation

r

positive, is not

in the neighborhood of ___ = +.86 between childhood and adult behavior. There is a (*positive/negative*) relationship between the two variables, which (*is/is not*) perfect.

68. Cause-and-effect relationships cannot always be inferred from high negative or high positive correlations. In laboratory experiments we can manipulate the

independent

_____ variable and measure its effect upon the

dependent

_____ variable. In correlational studies we can only note that

cannot

two variables vary together. We (*can/cannot*) say for certain that one variable *causes* the other.

69. For example, there is a positive correlation between the softness of the asphalt in city streets on a summer day and the irritability of infants on that day. We do not assume that some poisonous vapor from the soft asphalt causes infants to become irritable. Instead, we attribute the relationship to a third variable, probably

heat (*or a synonym*)

_____ .

70. Correlation implies the existence of a positive or negative relationship between two

causes

variables. It does not necessarily mean that one _____ the other.

71. Now let's review. Psychology is concerned with the study of behavior and mental activity. By "behavior" we refer to those activities of an organism that can be

observed

_____ by another person.

72. Mental activity includes internal events, such as emotions and memories, which

conscious

we are aware of and can report; these are called _____ processes.

unconscious

Internal events of which we are not aware are called _____ processes.

activity

73. In studying behavior and mental _____ psychologists often measure quantities that are subject to change. Any quantity subject to change is called a

variable

_____ .

independent

74. The variable under the control of the experimenter is called the _____ variable; by manipulating this variable the experimenter can observe its effects upon

behavior

the b_____ of the subject.

75. The variable that the experimenter observes and that depends upon the value of the

independent, dependent

_____ variable is called the _____ variable.

independent

measurement

control

76. In laboratory experiments we find careful manipulation of the _____ variable, _____ of the dependent variable, and _____ over variables that we do not wish to influence the experiment.

correlation

variables

77. In situations in which we cannot control the variables but simply make observations, we use the method of _____ to determine the relationship between the _____ .

_r_

relationship

positive, negative

causes

78. The coefficient of correlation, which is signified by the letter _____ , tells us whether there is a rel_____ between the variables, and whether the relationship is _____ or _____ . It does not necessarily imply that one variable _____ the other.

A reminder: This programmed unit is intended as an introduction to, not a substitute for, Chapter 1 of the text. If you have mastered the terms presented here, you will draw more meaning from the text itself. But you will find that the text presents more ideas, and goes deeper into the ideas presented here, than it is possible to do in this programmed unit.

TERMS AND CONCEPTS

neurobiological approach _____

_____

_____

_____

behavioral approach _____

_____

_____

_____

cognitive approach _____

_____

_____

_____

psychoanalytic approach _____

_____

_____

_____

unconscious processes _____

_____

_____

_____

phenomenological approach _____

_____

_____

_____

psychology _____

_____

_____

_____

experimental psychologist _____

_____

_____

_____

physiological psychologist _____

_____

_____

developmental psychologist _____

_____

_____

_____

social psychologist _____

_____

_____

_____

personality psychologist _____

_____

_____

_____

clinical psychologist _____

_____

_____

_____

school psychologist _____

_____

_____

_____

industrial psychologist _____

_____

_____

_____

behavioral and social sciences _____

_____

_____

_____

cognitive sciences _____

_____

_____

_____

experimental method _____

_____

_____

independent variable _____

_____

_____

_____

dependent variable _____

_____

_____

_____

observational method _____

_____

_____

_____

survey method _____

_____

_____

_____

test method _____

_____

_____

_____

case history _____

_____

_____

_____

longitudinal study _____

_____

_____

_____

experimental group _____

_____

_____

_____

control group _____

_____

_____

_____

mean _____

_____

_____

_____

correlation _____

_____

_____

_____

_____ 1. Measurements on individuals made at periodic intervals over an extended period of time characterize
a. the survey method
b. a reconstructed biography
c. the retrospective method
d. a longitudinal study

_____ 2. In an experiment involving one manipulated variable that is either present or absent, subjects who are in the "condition absent" group are called the _____ group.
a. control
b. experimental
c. independent variable
d. dependent variable

_____ 3. In the early 1900s, John B. Watson
a. introduced the "introspection" technique
b. maintained that behaviorism was futile
c. advanced a position later known as behaviorism
d. advocated examining carefully a person's mental experiences and activities

_____ 4. Psychologists may be usefully categorized by
a. the type of problems they are interested in
b. their approach to problems that interest them
c. the type of organization that employs them
d. all of the above

_____ 5. A coefficient of correlation
a. can be used only when experimental control is possible
b. can be used with large masses of data
c. is usually a good indication of cause-effect relationships
d. all of the above

_____ 6. Freud believed that
a. sex and aggression are basic instincts
b. urban life brings out the worst in people
c. people can learn to live together peacefully
d. all of the above

_____ 7. In one study, subjects were asked to memorize word lists after taking various doses of marijuana. Which statement about this study is _false_?
a. The dependent variable was the amount recalled.
b. The independent variable was the dose of marijuana.

c. The material to be memorized was different for the control group and the experimental group.
d. Subjects were tested in a laboratory.

_____ 8. The correlation between shoe size and size of vocabulary in a randomly selected group of adults would probably be
a. .50
b. −1.00
c. .00
d. −.50

_____ 9. Stimulus-response psychology focuses on stimuli that elicit
a. introspection
b. cognitive processes
c. behavioral responses
d. emotional experiences

_____ 10. The mean is
a. the arithmetic average
b. the sum of the measures divided by the number of measures
c. the most common statistic used in psychology
d. all of the above

_____ 11. Understanding of the individual's inner life and experiences, rather than prediction and control of behavior, is the goal of _____ psychologists.
a. cognitive
b. psychoanalytic
c. phenomenological
d. stimulus-response

_____ 12. In studying the influence of sleep on learning
a. the amount of learning is the independent variable
b. the amount of sleep is the dependent variable
c. the amount of sleep is the independent variable
d. sleep "is a function of" learning

_____ 13. The experimental method
a. requires the use of a laboratory
b. seeks to establish cause-and-effect relationships among variables
c. always requires precision apparatus
d. all of the above

14. A goal of cognitive psychology is to
    a. develop theories about how emotions function
    b. develop theories about how mental processes are organized
    c. conduct experimentation on behavioral data
    d. conduct psychological studies of stimuli

15. A psychologist interested in the study of problem solving works on a series of verbal problems and carefully observes and records her own thoughts as she is working. This is an example of _____ .
    a. behavioral analysis
    b. introspection
    c. the subjective approach
    d. the psychoanalytic approach

16. When the experimental method is used, only the _____ variable is allowed to vary across different groups of subjects.
    a. independent
    b. dependent
    c. quantitative
    d. observed

17. Which of the following correlations represents the *greatest* degree of relationship between two variables?
    a. $r = +.42$
    b. $r = +.07$
    c. $r = -.00$
    d. $r = -.61$

18. The text defines psychology as the
    a. science that focuses on behavioral phenomena
    b. scientific study of behavior and mental processes
    c. scientific study of human behavior, both learned and unlearned
    d. scientific study of mental activity

19. To say that a difference between two means is statistically "significant" is to say that it is
    a. trustworthy
    b. important
    c. of practical significance
    d. all of the above

20. The _____ approach to the study of human beings is particularly concerned with the relationship between behavior and experience and brain activity.
    a. behavioral
    b. cognitive
    c. psychoanalytic
    d. neurobiological

KEY TO SELF-QUIZ

1. d	6. a	11. c	16. a
2. a	7. c	12. c	17. d
3. c	8. c	13. b	18. b
4. d	9. c	14. b	19. a
5. b	10. d	15. b	20. d

INDIVIDUAL EXERCISES

PUBLISHED PSYCHOLOGICAL RESEARCH

One way to get an idea of what psychologists do is to look at their publications. Go to a library and ask where the psychological journals are located. They may be placed together in one area of the current periodical room, or they may be arranged alphabetically with the other periodicals. There are a large number of psychological journals published in the United States and in many other countries. Some, like the *Journal of Experimental Psychology,* the *Journal of Comparative Psychology,* and *Developmental Psychology,* publish primarily research reports. Others, like the *Journal of Abnormal Psychology,* the *Journal of Personality and Social Psychology,* the *Journal of Applied Psychology,* and the *Journal of Educational Psychology,* publish both theoretical and research papers. *The Psychological Review* presents original theoretical papers; *The Psychological Bulletin* publishes articles reviewing and evaluating areas of research. *The American Psychologist* publishes the official papers of the American Psychological Association, as well as articles of general interest to psychologists. *Contemporary Psychology* reviews current books in the field. These are some of the general research publications in psychology; many other publications are devoted to more specific interests, for example, *Perception and Psychophysics* and *Psychotherapy: Theory, Research, and Practice.* Appendix IV in the textbook lists the major journals of psychology and a description of the types of articles they publish.

Glancing at the index and scanning a few articles in several of these journals will give you an idea of the range of problems studied by psychologists, as well as the way in which psychological research is conducted and reported. If you are seeking particular information—whether for personal interest or for an assignment—there are numerous abstracting systems, which both index and summarize all the articles published in hundreds of journals. The professional psychology journals will be found in *Psychological Abstracts* or *Educational Index.* The *Reader's Guide to Periodical Literature* indexes general publications. Your librarian can help you learn to use these systems.

THE SCIENTIFIC METHOD

Introduction

The status of psychology as a science depends on its use of the experimental method. An experiment involves observation of some aspect of behavior (dependent variable) while one factor (independent variable) is systematically changed under certain specified conditions (controlled variables). In the experimental method all factors, except the one whose effects are being examined, are held constant. Before an experiment is performed, the experimenter generally states a hypothesis about the process that he or she believes underlies the behavior under investigation. The experimental method provides the most reliable source of scientific information and is the preferred method of science. However, difficulties may be encountered even in simple experiments where extraneous variables appear to have been well controlled. On closer examination, or with the advantage of hindsight (after the experiment has been conducted), it may turn out that certain variables were not properly controlled. Subsequent information may indicate that these variables (which seemed unimportant at the time) were confounded with variations in the independent variable; they, rather than the independent variable, may have caused the experimental outcome. Sometimes years later a re-examination of an experiment will establish confounding variables that were not properly controlled, thereby raising questions about the validity of the research findings. It is always best to be skeptical about any research finding until it has been verified by several investigators under a range of conditions.

The following experiment will provide you with an opportunity to criticize procedure and to become somewhat more familiar with the scientific method.

Procedure

The results of a fictitious experiment are given in Tables 1 and 2. Read carefully the experimental problem, the hypothesis, the procedures used, the results obtained, and the conclusions drawn. Then, using the concluding questions as an aid, make an analysis of the experiment.

1. EXPERIMENTAL PROBLEM: To investigate the effects of drinking coffee (which contains caffeine) on the achievement of college students on a final examination in general psychology.

2. HYPOTHESIS: Two cups of black coffee taken immediately before a task requiring mental exertion increase a student's academic efficiency.

3. PROCEDURE: Two groups of subjects were used. Group 1 consisted of 200 freshmen who were matched in age, intelligence, sex, and grade-point average with the 200 freshmen in Group 2. Subjects in both groups were enrolled in the elementary course in psychology. All subjects in Group 1 (experimental group) drank two cups of black coffee immediately before taking the final examination. All subjects in Group 2 (control group) were instructed not to take any stimulants during the day the final examination was to be taken. For purposes of analysis, the grades of the students of both groups were converted into the following numerical equivalents (grade points): A = 4; B = 3; C = 2; D = 1; and F = 0. The average grade-point score for each of the two groups was then computed.

4. RESULTS: The results of the experiment are summarized in the tables. Table 1 indicates the number and percentage of students in each group obtaining each of the five letter grades on the final exam in general psychology. Table 2 gives the average grade-point scores of the two groups.

These results indicate that the students in Group 1 did consistently better than the students in Group 2.

	TABLE 1			
	Group 1 (drank coffee)		Group 2 (did not drink coffee)	
Grade	Number	Percentage	Number	Percentage
A	30	15	14	7
B	46	23	24	12
C	80	40	112	56
D	36	18	40	20
F	8	4	10	5

TABLE 2	
Group	Average grade-point score
1 (coffee drinkers)	2.25
2 (noncoffee drinkers)	1.96

5. CONCLUSIONS: Comparison of the final examination grades earned in general psychology by two groups of college students (a stimulant-taking group and a non-stimulant-taking group) indicates that taking a mild stimulant, such as two cups of black coffee, immediately before an examination increases the academic efficiency and achievement of freshmen college students in a general psychology course.

Questions for Discussion

1. What is the dependent variable in this experiment?

2. What is the independent variable in this experiment?

3. What were some of the controlled variables in this experiment?

4. What are some of the limitations of the experiment?

5. Why is this procedure superior to a simple correlation that would seem to imply the same finding? Suppose, for example, you were told that coffee drinking showed a high and statistically significant correlation with exam grades. What could you conclude?

2
Biological Basis of Psychology

LEARNING OBJECTIVES

2-1. Be able to identify the major components of a neuron. Know the functions of sensory neurons, motor neurons, and interneurons and the difference between neurons and nerves. Understand the major events of neural transmission.

2-2. Be able to identify the main features of a synapse and to describe synaptic transmission. Understand the role of neurotransmitters and the difference between excitatory and inhibitory synapses.

2-3. Be able to name and to diagram the relationships among the major components of the nervous system. Be able to explain the functioning of a spinal reflex.

2-4. Know what structures comprise each of the three concentric layers of the human brain. Be able to describe, in general, the functions of these structures.

2-5. Be able to define and describe the cerebral cortex. Be able to describe its major areas and know approximately where each is located.

2-6. Be familiar with the right/left differences typically found in humans. Know what functions are usually controlled by each of the two hemispheres.

2-7. Be able to describe, in general, the differing structure and function of the two divisions of the autonomic nervous system.

2-8. Be familiar with the major endocrine glands and their hormones. Understand the interrelationships between the endocrine system and the autonomic nervous system.

2-9. Be able to define and differentiate between genes and chromosomes. Understand what is meant by dominant, recessive, and sex-linked genes. Be familiar with the several chromosomal-abnormality syndromes discussed in the text.

2-10. Understand the multiple contributions to human traits, including polygenic transmission and environmental interaction. Be familiar with the use of selective breeding and twin studies.

1. All behavior depends on the integration of bodily processes by the *nervous system.*

system   The basic unit of the nervous _____ is the *neuron,* or nerve cell, which is diagramed below. The human nervous system contains many billions of these

neurons   nerve cells, or _____ .

2. The neuron has three main parts: the *cell body,* the *dendrites,* and the *axon.* As

body   you can see from the diagram, the wide part of the neuron is its cell _____ .

3. The short, branching fibers at one end of the neuron are the *dendrites.* The den-

cell   drites and the _____ body receive messages from other neurons.

dendrites   4. A neuron receives messages by way of its cell body or its _____ .
These messages are then transmitted to other neurons by way of the *axon.*

dendrites   5. Messages are received by the cell body or the _____ of a neuron

axon   and transmitted by the _____ .

receiving   6. The dendrites are the (*receiving/transmitting*) end of the neuron and the axon is the

transmitting   (*receiving/transmitting*) end.

7. The junction between the axon of one neuron and the cell body or dendrites of the

synapse   next neuron is called a *synapse.* This junction, or _____ , is not a direct connection. There is a slight gap across which the message must be transmitted.

synapse   8. Neural transmission across this gap, or sy_____ , is usually by means of a chemical intermediary. The axon of one neuron releases a chemical, called a *neuro-*

neuron   *transmitter,* into the synapse, stimulating the dendrites of the next _____ .

9. Neural transmission at the synapse is in one direction only. The axon sends the

synapse   message and the dendrites receive it. The signal is transmitted across the _____

axon, dendrites   from the _____ of the first neuron to the _____ or cell body of the next neuron.

10. The chemical intermediary that transmits the signal across the synapse is called a

neurotransmitter   _____ .

11. To review: The three main parts of the neuron are the _____ _____ ; the

cell body

dendrites, axon

synapse

11. To review: The three main parts of the neuron are the _____ _____ ; the
_____ , which receive(s) messages; and the _____ , which
transmit(s) messages across the _____ .

12. While all neurons have these general features, they vary in size and shape, depending
on the particular function they perform. Neurons that carry messages to the brain
or spinal cord about what is going on in the environment or within the body are

neurons

called *sensory* _____ .

brain

13. Sensory neurons carry messages to the _____ or spinal cord about what is

environment, body

going on in the _____ or within the _____ .

14. For example, neurons that inform the brain that your skin is being pierced by a

sensory

needle would be called _____ neurons.

15. Sensory neurons receive their input from *receptors,* which are specialized cells
in the sense organs, skin, muscles, and joints. Receptors detect changes in the
environment and translate these events into messages that are transmitted, via

sensory, spinal

_____ neurons, to the brain and _____ cord.

16. Special cells in the inner ear translate sound waves into signals that are transmitted
to the brain via sensory neurons in the auditory nerve. These cells would be called

receptors

re_____ .

changes

17. Receptors detect _____ in the environment or within the body and

sensory

signal the brain by means of _____ neurons.

18. Specialized cells within the joints tell us about the position of our arms and legs.

receptors

These cells would also be called _____ .

brain, spinal

19. Sensory neurons carry messages to the _____ or _____

cord

_____ . *Motor neurons* convey signals from the brain or spinal cord to
the muscles that control our movements as well as to those that control some of the
internal organs.

motor

20. When your brain signals your hand to move, the message is carried by _____

motor

neurons. Contraction of the heart muscles is also controlled by _____

neurons

_____ .

sensory

21. Information from the environment is carried to the brain by _____

motor

neurons. Signals to action are transmitted by _____ neurons.

22. *Interneurons* receive signals from sensory neurons and send impulses to other

interneuron

interneurons or to motor neurons. Thus, the _____ is the
connecting link between sensory and motor neurons. Interneurons are found only
in the brain and spinal cord.

23. A *nerve* is a bundle of axons belonging to many neurons. The axons of hundreds of

nerve

neurons joined together form a _____ .

sensory
24. Some nerves are composed mainly of the axons of incoming, or _____ ,

motor

neurons; some contain mainly outgoing, or _____ , neurons; and some

axons

are composed of _____ from both types of neurons.

25. The *central nervous system* is composed of the brain and the spinal cord. The spinal
cord provides connections for simple reflexes (such as the knee jerk) and for the
passage of messages to and from the brain. Together, the brain and spinal cord

central nervous system

constitute the _____ _____ _____ .

spinal cord
26. The central nervous system consists of the brain and the _____ _____ .

sensory
27. The incoming, or _____ , neurons and the outgoing, or

motor

_____ , neurons form connections with interneurons in the brain and
spinal cord. Since these are the chief centers in which junctions between neurons
occur, you might expect the brain and spinal cord to contain large numbers of

interneurons

_____ .

28. Nerves that are not part of the brain and spinal cord form the *peripheral nervous
system.* Some of these nerves carry incoming messages from specialized cells,

receptors

called _____ , that detect changes in the environment. Others carry

nervous

messages from the central _____ system to the muscles that control
movement of the body.

29. Nerves connecting the brain and spinal cord with the sense receptors, skeletal
muscles, and body surface are part of the peripheral nervous system; they form the

nervous

somatic division of the peripheral _____ system.

peripheral
30. Another part of the p _____ nervous system is the *autonomic system,* which includes nerves running to the *glands* and *smooth muscles* (those found
in the stomach, intestines, and other internal organs). We would expect the nerves

autonomic

leading to the salivary glands to be part of the (*somatic/autonomic*) system.

peripheral
31. The somatic and autonomic systems together make up the _____

nervous system

_____ _____ . The brain and the spinal cord form the

central nervous system

_____ _____ _____ . The division into systems
helps in anatomical discussions; in actuality, however, all parts of the nervous
system function in a highly integrated manner.

brain
32. Let's review. The central nervous system consists of the _____ and the

spinal cord

_____ _____ . All nerves outside of the brain and spinal cord are

peripheral

grouped into the _____ nervous system, which has two divisions:

somatic

the _____ division consists of nerves running to and from sense organs,

autonomic

skeletal muscles, and the body surface; the _____ division consists
of nerves running to the glands and smooth muscles.

Since the brain is the most important part of the nervous system, we will need to look at it in more detail. The illustration of the human brain on page 22 is an adaptation of the illustration you will find in the text. In this programmed unit you will begin to learn the names of the parts of the human brain. Note that the text illustration, in addition to listing the labels shown here, provides lists of the various functions of each part of the brain. (These functions are also described in the text.) You will not learn all these functions from this programmed unit, but you will become acquainted with some of them. Now look at the illustration and go on to the next question. Refer to the illustration as necessary.

33. As the spinal cord enters the brain it enlarges to form the *brain stem* (not labeled on the illustration). The lower portion of the brain, connecting with the spinal

brain stem

    cord, is the _____ _____ .

34. An important structure within the brain stem is the *medulla.* The medulla regulates breathing and controls some of the reflexes that help us maintain an upright pos-

medulla

    ture. Some very basic life processes are regulated by the _____ .

35. Attached to the rear of the brain stem, just above the medulla, is a convoluted structure known as the *cerebellum*; it regulates intricate motor coordination. The complex movements involved in such activities as walking, dancing, speaking, and

cerebellum

    playing a musical instrument are controlled by the _____ .

36. Starting in the brain stem and extending upward is a system of neural circuits called

system

reticular

system

    the *reticular system.* The reticular _____ controls our state of *arousal* or

    alertness. When we change from sleep to wakefulness, nerves in the _____

    _____ are involved.

alertness

37. The reticular system controls our state of arousal or _____ .

38. The convoluted structure to the rear of the brain stem that controls complex motor

cerebellum

    skills is the _____ .

39. Now locate on the diagram a small but vital structure in the center of the brain called the *hypothalamus.* The hypothalamus plays an important role in *motivation* and *emotion.* It helps regulate hunger, thirst, and sex; it influences our feelings of pleasure, fear, and anger. When we experience pangs of hunger, the brain structure

hypothalamus

    involved is the _____ .

motivation

40. The hypothalamus plays an important role in _____ and emotion.

41. By regulating hunger and thirst the hypothalamus attempts to maintain *homeostasis,* a level of functioning characteristic of the healthy organism. If the blood-sugar level gets too low, the hypothalamus signals the organism to start eating.

homeostasis

    Ingested food raises the level of sugar in the blood, thus restoring homeo_____ .

42. The hypothalamus attempts to maintain the body in a state of normalcy or con-

homeostasis

    stancy. This optimal level of functioning is called _____ .

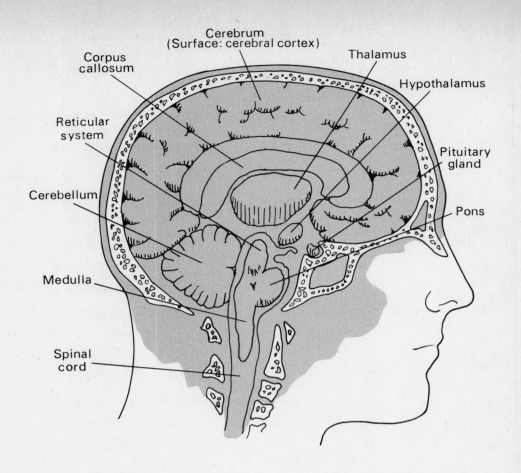

Cerebrum
(Surface: cerebral cortex)

Corpus
callosum

Thalamus

Hypothalamus

Reticular
system

Pituitary
gland

Cerebellum

Pons

Medulla

Spinal
cord

43. When the concentration of salt and certain other chemicals in the blood becomes too great, the hypothalamus signals the organism to start drinking water. Water intake dilutes the blood chemicals to the proper concentration. This is another

homeostasis

example of _____ .

44. The brain structure that maintains homeostasis and plays an important role in

hypothalamus

motivation and emotion is the _____ .

45. Now locate another part of the brain stem, the *thalamus*. This portion serves as a sensory relay station for impulses coming up from the spinal cord and down from the higher brain centers. In any activity that requires the coordination of informa-

thalamus

tion from several receptors, the (*hypothalamus/thalamus*) is likely to be involved.

spinal

46. The thalamus is a sensory relay station for impulses coming up from the _____

cord

_____ and down from the higher brain centers.

47. For a review of the brain areas discussed so far, identify the structures involved in each of the following functions.

cerebellum

a. Controls body coordination, as in walking or dancing. _____
b. Maintains homeostasis and plays important role in motivation and emotion.

hypothalamus

_____

thalamus

c. Serves as a sensory relay station. _____

reticular
system

d. Controls state of arousal, as from sleep to wakefulness. _____

_____

medulla

e. Regulates basic body processes such as breathing and postural reflexes.

_____

48. The large mass of brain tissue that surrounds the brain-stem structures is the *cerebrum*—the most highly developed portion of the human brain. The surface of the cerebrum is highly wrinkled, or convoluted. The fact that this surface, known as the *cerebral cortex*, has so many wrinkles, or convolutions, means that the total

greater

surface area is much (*greater/smaller*) than it would be if the surface of the cerebrum were smooth.

49. Since the cerebral cortex, or surface, of the cerebrum is so large, it provides room for many interconnections of neurons. Thus the cerebral cortex makes it possible for us to learn, remember, think, and carry on many of the activities that distinguish us from the lower animals. You might expect the cerebral cortex of a fish to

less

be (*more/less*) wrinkled, or convoluted, than that of a human being.

cerebrum, cerebral

50. The _____ , with its wrinkled surface, the _____ cortex, is the part of the human brain that makes possible thinking and reasoning.

51. A top view of the brain, as distinguished from the side view shown here, would show that the cerebrum is divided into two halves, or hemispheres. (Your text will make this clear.) Now locate the *corpus callosum,* which contains fibers connecting the two cerebral hemispheres. The two cerebral hemispheres are connected by the

corpus callosum

_____ _____ .

52. Now locate the *pituitary gland,* a small structure below the hypothalamus. The pituitary gland is *not* a part of the nervous system; it is an important *endocrine gland.* Endocrine glands secrete special chemical messengers, called *hormones,* into

endocrine

the bloodstream. The pituitary gland is one of the most important _____ glands.

hormones

53. The chemical messengers, or _____ , secreted by the endocrine glands help the hypothalamus maintain its normal level of functioning, called

homeostasis

homeo _____ . They also play an important role in growth, sexual and maternal behavior, emotions, and reactions to stress.

pituitary

54. The endocrine gland located just below the hypothalamus is the _____ gland. It is often called the "*master gland*" because it secretes the largest number of

hormones

h _____ and also controls the secretion of several other endocrine

glands

_____ .

pituitary, master

55. The _____ gland is often referred to as the " _____ gland" because its influence on the body is so pervasive. One of the pituitary hormones controls the timing and amount of *body growth.*

56. If an individual develops into a giant, we can suspect that a malfunctioning of the

pituitary

_____ gland is involved. Other hormones secreted by the pituitary gland trigger the action of the sex glands, or *gonads,* which, in turn, influence *mating* and *reproductive behavior.*

BIOLOGICAL BASIS OF PSYCHOLOGY

master gland

body, mating
(*or* reproductive)

57. We can see why the pituitary gland is called the "_____ _____," since it influences such important functions as _____ growth and _____ behavior.

gonads

58. In addition to triggering the action of the sex glands, or _____ , pituitary hormones also influence the secretion of the *adrenal glands.*

59. One adrenal gland is located just above each kidney. The adrenal glands secrete

endocrine

hormones into the bloodstream, as do other _____ glands. Two important hormones secreted by the adrenal glands are *epinephrine* (also known as adrenalin) and *norepinephrine* (noradrenalin).

adrenal

60. Epinephrine and norepinephrine are secreted by the _____ glands. They act in a number of ways to prepare the organism for an emergency.

61. We noted earlier that the autonomic nervous system consists of nerves running to the smooth muscles (such as line the stomach and other internal organs) and the

glands

g_____ . It should not be surprising to learn, therefore, that there is a close

autonomic

interrelationship between the endocrine glands and the _____

nervous

_____ system.

62. The secretion of the adrenal glands is regulated by the autonomic nervous system. The autonomic nervous system controls many activities that are "autonomous" or "self-regulating." The process of digestion, for example, goes on autonomously without any conscious willing on our part. Digestion is controlled by the

autonomic

(*autonomic/central*) nervous system.

63. The self-regulating activities controlled by the autonomic nervous system can go on while a person is asleep or unconscious, that is, without the individual being

aware
(*or* conscious)

_____ of them.

64. The autonomic nervous system has two divisions: the *sympathetic* and the *para-sympathetic* divisions. These two divisions are often opposite, or *antagonistic,* in

smooth

their actions. Both divisions control the glands and the _____ muscles,

antagonistic

but their actions are often an_____ .

65. The sympathetic division of the autonomic nervous system operates to *dilate* the blood vessels of the heart, while the parasympathetic division operates to *constrict* these blood vessels. This is an illustration of the fact that the two divisions are often

antagonistic

opposite, or _____ , in their action.

66. The sympathetic division tends to be active in *excited* states, while the parasympathetic division tends to be more important in *quiescent* states, or those activities that conserve and protect bodily resources. If you observe that a man's heart rate has speeded up, that he is perspiring profusely, and that his pupils are dilated, you

sympathetic

might expect that the _____ division of the autonomic nervous system is playing a part in these responses.

67. Since the adrenal gland is dominant in excited states, it would be logical to con-

parasympathetic

clude that the _____ division has no connection to this gland.

sympathetic

parasympathetic, sympathetic

parasympathetic

68. The two divisions of the autonomic nervous system are the _____ and the _____ divisions. The _____ division tends to be active during excited states, whereas the _____ division tends to take over during quiescent states.

autonomic

antagonistic

69. The _____ nervous system has two divisions, the sympathetic and parasympathetic divisions, which are often _____ in their action.

autonomous

aware

antagonistic, sympathetic

parasympathetic, sympathetic

parasympathetic

quiescent

70. Let's review. The *autonomic nervous system* derives its name from the fact that many of its activities are _____ , or self-regulating, and occur without our being _____ of them. It has two divisions that are often _____ in their action: the _____ division and the _____ division. The _____ division tends to be active in excited states, whereas the _____ division tends to take over during _____ states.

peripheral

central

somatic

71. The autonomic nervous system is one division of the (*central/peripheral*) nervous system. Its nerves are outside of the brain and spinal cord, which constitute the (*central/peripheral*) nervous system. The other part of the peripheral nervous system is the _____ system, which consists of nerves running to and from the sense receptors, body surface, and skeletal muscles. All these systems coordinate in a complex manner to provide for the smooth functioning of the organism.

characteristics

genetics

72. Many of our *physical characteristics* are inherited from our parents. *Genetics,* the science of heredity, shows how physical ch_____ such as eye and hair color are transmitted from one generation to the next. Psychological characteristics—ability, temperament, and emotional stability—may also depend to some extent on heredity. As you might guess, the branch of genetics that studies the inheritance of psychological or behavioral characteristics is called *behavior* g_____ .

inherited (*or* hereditary)

73. Behavior genetics studies the degree to which psychological characteristics are _____ .

chromosomes

74. The *hereditary units* that individuals receive from their parents and transmit to their offspring are carried by microscopic particles known as *chromosomes,* found within each cell of the body. Each human body cell has 46 chromosomes. At conception the human being receives 23 chromosomes from the father's sperm and 23 _____ from the mother's ovum. These 46 chromosomes form 23 *pairs,* which are duplicated in every cell of the body as the individual develops.

chromosomes

75. A fertilized ovum contains 46 _____ , 23 of its own and 23 received from the sperm.

76. The chromosomes are duplicated in every cell of the body as the individual develops. Thus every body cell contains _____ chromosomes arranged in 23 _____ .

46, pairs

77. The chromosomes carry the basic units of heredity, which are called *genes.* Each chromosome carries many of these hereditary units, or _____ . Like chromosomes, the genes occur in pairs; one gene of each pair comes from the sperm chromosome and one gene from the ovum _____ .

genes

chromosome

78. Chromosomes occur in pairs, and each chromosome pair contains many pairs of _____ .

genes

79. In human beings each chromosome carries more than 1,000 genes. Since the fertilized ovum has _____ pairs of chromosomes, the number of genes is high enough to make it extremely unlikely that any two persons would have the same heredity. The exception would be individuals who develop from the same ovum; such individuals are called *monozygotic twins.*

23

80. Monozygotic twins develop from the same _____ . They are also called identical twins; since they share the same heredity, they are alike in many respects.

ovum

81. Fraternal or *dizygotic twins* develop from two separate ova fertilized by two separate sperm cells. Thus they (*do/do not*) share the same heredity and are no more alike than ordinary siblings.

do not

82. Because _____ twins have exactly the same heredity, differences between them are attributed largely to differences in environment.

monozygotic
(*or* identical)

83. Genetic studies frequently compare the similarities between monozygotic twins and those between dizygotic twins to determine the extent to which a psychological characteristic is influenced by heredity. For example, monozygotic twins are much more similar in intelligence test scores than dizygotic twins. This finding suggests that (*heredity/environment*) influences intelligence.

heredity

84. If one monozygotic twin develops a mental illness called schizophrenia, there is a 46 percent chance that the other twin will be schizophrenic. Among dizygotic twins there is only a 14 percent chance that if one twin is schizophrenic the other will be also. This indicates that there is a(n) _____ component in the susceptibility to some forms of schizophrenia.

hereditary
(*or* genetic)

TERMS AND CONCEPTS

neuron _____

_____

_____

_____

dendrite _____

_____

_____

_____

axon _____

_____

_____

axon terminal _____

_____

_____

_____

synapse _____

_____

_____

_____

sensory neuron _____

_____

_____

_____

motor neuron _____

_____

_____

_____

interneuron _____

_____

_____

_____

nerve _____

_____

_____

_____

depolarization _____

_____

_____

_____

all-or-none principle _____

_____

_____

_____

neurotransmitter _____

_____

_____

_____

central nervous system _____

_____

_____

_____

peripheral nervous system _____

_____

_____

_____

somatic nervous system _____

_____

_____

_____

autonomic nervous system _____

_____

_____

_____

cerebrum _____

_____

_____

_____

central core _____

_____

_____

_____

cerebellum _____

_____

_____

_____

thalamus _____

_____

_____

_____

hypothalamus _____

_____

_____

_____

homeostasis _____

_____

_____

_____

reticular system _____

_____

_____

_____

limbic system _____

_____

_____

_____

cerebral cortex _____

_____

_____

_____

motor area _____

_____

_____

_____

somatosensory area _____

_____

_____

_____

association areas _____

_____

_____

_____

Broca's area _____

_____

_____

_____

corpus callosum _____

_____

_____

_____

split brain _____

_____

_____

_____

sympathetic division _____

_____

_____

_____

parasympathetic division _____

_____

_____

_____

endocrine system _____

_____

_____

_____

hormones _____

_____

_____

_____

pituitary gland _____

_____

_____

_____

adrenal glands _____

_____

_____

_____

behavior genetics _____

_____

_____

_____

chromosome _____

_____

_____

_____

DNA _____

_____

_____

_____

gene _____

_____

_____

_____

dominant gene _____

_____

_____

_____

recessive gene _____

_____

_____

_____

sex-linked trait _____

_____

_____

_____

polygenic trait _____

_____

_____

_____

fraternal twins _____

_____

_____

_____

identical twins _____

_____

_____

_____

_____ 1. Which of the following is a specialization of the right hemisphere of the brain?
   a. understanding spatial relationships
   b. understanding speech
   c. producing speech sounds
   d. controlling the right side of the body

_____ 2. If you are a female with blue eyes, we know that
   a. your father had blue eyes
   b. one of your parents had blue eyes
   c. both of your parents had blue eyes
   d. none of the above

_____ 3. The human brain may be thought of as being composed of three concentric layers. Of these the _____ is on the outside, while the earlier evolutionary development, the _____ , is concealed within it.
   a. limbic system, central core
   b. cerebrum, limbic system
   c. limbic system, cerebrum
   d. cerebral hemispheres, cerebrum

_____ 4. The _____ gland has been called the "master gland" because it _____ _____
   a. pituitary, controls the secretion of several other glands
   b. adrenal, produces the largest number of hormones
   c. pituitary, produces epinephrine
   d. adrenal, controls the secretion of several other glands

_____ 5. Drugs such as LSD and chlorpromazine alter moods by changing the
   a. thickness of the myelin sheath
   b. size of the action potential
   c. synaptic gap distance
   d. neurotransmitter activity at the synapse

_____ 6. In sorting out the effects of environment and heredity, one ideally should study
   a. monozygotic twins
   b. dizygotic twins
   c. both of the above
   d. neither of the above

_____ 7. The effect of injury to the left side of the brain will manifest itself on the

   a. spinal cord
   b. thalamus
   c. control of visceral functions
   d. right side of the body

_____ 8. The sympathetic and parasympathetic systems
   a. typically act in an antagonistic fashion
   b. are divisions of the autonomic nervous system
   c. may be involved in the same behavior via sequential action
   d. all of the above

_____ 9. Damage to the _____ results in jerky, uncoordinated movements, because of its central role in coordinating complex motor activity
   a. cerebrum
   b. cerebellum
   c. medulla
   d. limbic system

_____10. The amount of somatosensory or motor cortex associated with a particular part of the body appears to be directly related to
   a. the optic chiasma
   b. its sensitivity and use
   c. its frequency in higher mammals
   d. the visual and auditory areas

_____11. When release of a neurotransmitter at a synapse produces a change in permeability in the direction of depolarization, the synapse is
   a. an excitatory one
   b. an inhibitory one
   c. becoming polarized
   d. in a refractory phase

_____12. The many large areas of the cerebral cortex not directly concerned with sensory or motor processes have been called
   a. projection areas
   b. organization areas
   c. association areas
   d. thinking areas

_____13. Homeostasis is maintained by the _____ , which also plays an important role in motivation.
   a. hypothalamus
   b. thalamus
   c. limbic system
   d. reticular system

_____14. In a test of a split-brain patient, if the name of an object is briefly flashed on the left half of the screen, he or she can
   a. describe the use of the object
   b. pick out the object from a pile of others
   c. write down what the object is
   d. say the word

_____15. The simplest reflex may involve
   a. a sensory neuron and a receptor
   b. an interneuron
   c. only a sensory neuron and a motor neuron
   d. a three-neuron reflex arc

_____16. The speech centers for left-handed people are
   a. usually in the left hemisphere
   b. usually in the right hemisphere
   c. typically in both hemispheres
   d. about evenly divided, with some left-handers having centers in the left hemisphere and some in the right hemisphere

_____17. Each neuron in the nervous system consists of three main parts: the _____ , the _____ , and the _____ .
   a. glia, cell body, dendrites
   b. axon, nerve, cell body
   c. glia, axon, cell body
   d. dendrites, cell body, axon

_____18. The _____ nervous system includes both the _____ system and the _____ system.
   a. peripheral, central, autonomic
   b. somatic, autonomic, peripheral
   c. peripheral, autonomic, somatic
   d. autonomic, somatic, peripheral

_____19. A normal male child has received
   a. an X chromosome from his mother and a Y from his father
   b. a Y chromosome from each parent
   c. a Y chromosome from his mother and an X from his father
   d. an X chromosome from each parent

_____20. In a resting nerve cell, the cell membrane keeps out _____ ions.
   a. uncharged
   b. chloride
   c. potassium
   d. sodium

KEY TO SELF-QUIZ

20. d	15. c	10. b	5. d
19. a	14. b	9. b	4. a
18. c	13. a	8. d	3. b
17. d	12. c	7. d	2. d
16. a	11. a	6. c	1. a

INDIVIDUAL EXERCISE

REACTION TIME

Introduction

Every voluntary motor act takes time, not only to perform, once movement begins, but to initiate. Because we do not easily sense small time increments, we normally assume that a movement occurs as soon as we think about it. While this is an acceptable approximation for ordinary daily activity, it is an oversimplification when movements are judged with respect to small time intervals. We typically encounter such intervals in relation to rapidly moving objects: tennis balls, hockey pucks, and other objects outside us, or automobiles and airplanes, with us inside them. As various organizations concerned with automotive safety often tell us, a major portion of the distance needed to stop a car is covered between the time the stimulus for stopping occurs and the time when the brakes are applied. Although your braking may seem "immediate" to you, the time needed to register the stimulus, interpret it, decide on action, signal that action, and operate the muscles allows your car to cover a substantial distance.

The time between the onset of a stimulus and the subject's response is called the _reaction time._ Obviously we cannot have our readers running down hapless pedestrians in demonstrations of their reaction time. This exercise, however, is designed to demonstrate a similar phenomenon: movement past you while you take time to react. It provides you with a scientific approach and, for the less inhibited among you, a party trick.

Equipment Needed

Ruler (preferably a yardstick)

Procedure

While this exercise can be attempted by one person, it is really necessary for one person to test another.

1. Have your subject stand and hold out either hand with the thumb about an inch in front of the index finger and the fingers set to quickly squeeze together (see right photo). Hold the yardstick between the subject's fingers and thumb, and tell him or her to grasp the yardstick when you drop it. The subject is to watch your hand so that as soon as you release the yardstick,

he or she is prepared to grasp it. Both of you may be surprised to seé that it drops several inches no matter how quickly the subject tries to react.

2. Make your procedure more precise by specifying the subject's finger-to-thumb gap each time and by starting with one of the inch markers of the yardstick opposite his or her middle finger so that you can measure the distance it falls.

3. An even better technique is to have your subject stand by a doorway, with his or her palm by the jamb and the fingertips curved loosely around the doorjamb (see

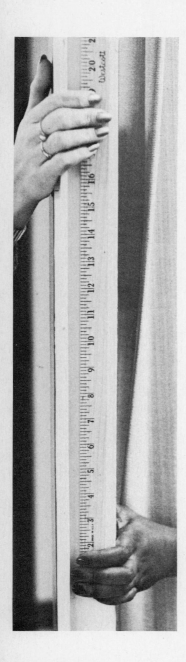 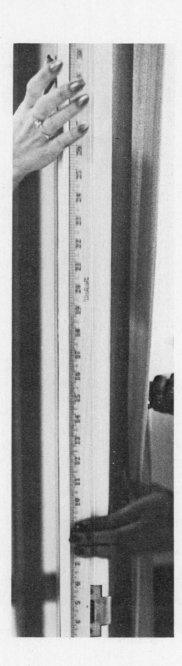 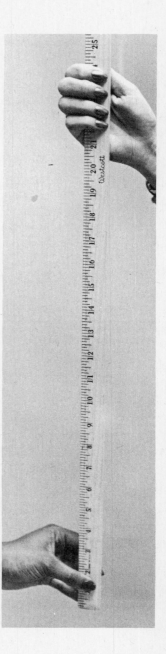

left photo). Begin with the yardstick held flat against the jamb and the zero mark beneath the subject's middle finger. This procedure helps assure a vertical fall of the yardstick and allows measurement directly from zero.

4. The number of inches the yardstick falls can be translated into seconds. For our purposes we can use the following equation for estimating the number of seconds it takes a falling body to move a certain distance:

$$seconds = \frac{\sqrt{inches}}{13.9}$$

A nine-inch fall thus represents a reaction time of

$$\frac{\sqrt{9}}{13.9} = \frac{3}{13.9} = .216 \ seconds$$

Using the table below you can convert inches to reaction time in seconds.

Inches		Seconds
1	=	0.072
2	=	0.102
3	=	0.125
4	=	0.144
5	=	0.161
6	=	0.176
7	=	0.190
8	=	0.203
9	=	0.216
10	=	0.227

For greater precision, give five trials and use the average distance in calculating the reaction time. Reaction-time data are usually presented in milliseconds (msec) rather than as fractions of a second (1,000 msec = 1 sec); thus .216 seconds would be 216 msec.

5. The basic procedure can now be used to study other variables. Some possibilities include comparing the reaction times of males and females, right hands and left hands, subjects suffering from lack of sleep and normal subjects, and so forth.

6. Other important variables that can be examined involve attention and expectation. You might try varying the cues: sometimes say "Get ready," and other times drop the yardstick without warning. To note the effects of distractions, use a confederate or take advantage of naturally occurring distractions; your distracted subject may feel he or she is paying attention, yet miss the yardstick completely.

7. A different demonstration based on the same principle does not yield measurements but is nonetheless dramatic and may serve to impress your friends—provided you do it right. Suggest that you are going to drop a dollar bill through your friends' fingers and that anyone who can catch it may keep it. Armed with your research data, you can arrange the procedure so that no one is likely to do so. (If your subjects always took six inches or more to catch the yardstick and the bill is held halfway through your friends' fingers, you can see that you are pretty safe.) If you want to be sure, control not only the finger gap and the length of bill left to catch, but also take advantage of the distraction effect. Under these circumstances you should be able to use the same bill all evening.

Questions for Discussion

1. Why is it necessary that one person drop the ruler for another? Try catching the ruler yourself. Can you catch the ruler sooner than your subjects? Why? (Hint: your reflexes are *not* that fast!)

2. Is this a good test to compare reaction times for different individuals? Could the experimenter unintentionally bias the results? (Hint: if you wanted to make one person do better than another at the task, how could you use the variables noted earlier to ensure it?)

3
Psychological Development

LEARNING OBJECTIVES

3-1.   Understand how heredity and environment interact in human development. Be able to define the concept of maturation and show how it relates to this interaction, using motor development as an example.

3-2.   Be able to discuss the influences of environmental events on early development, including the consequences of restricted or enhanced sensory-motor stimulation.

3-3.   Know the sequence of Piaget's stages of cognitive development and the major developments that characterize each stage.

3-4.   Be familiar with the research on attachment, including experiments with artificial monkey mothers. Be able to describe how parental responsiveness influences attachment and the relationship between early patterns of attachment and later behavior.

3-5.   Be able to describe Kohlberg's stages of moral development. Be familiar with criticisms of his theory, including the relationship between moral thought and moral behavior.

3-6.   Understand what is meant by sex roles or sex-typed behavior and be able to describe some of the influences that create and maintain them.

3-7.   Be familiar with the concept of identification and some of the factors that influence its development.

3-8.   Be able to specify when the adolescent growth spurt and puberty occur. Be familiar with the problems faced by early or late maturers and with data concerning sexual behavior of adolescents.

3-9.   Understand the problems and confusion involved in the adolescent's search for personal identity.

3-10.   Be familiar with Erickson's psychosocial stages and how they relate to the problems faced by people at different times in their lives.

1. Human development is determined by a continuous *interaction between heredity and environment.* The *genetically specified characteristics* we inherit from our parents and the *experiences* provided by the environment in which we are raised both influence the way we develop. Our behavior at any stage in life results from

interaction

the continuous _____ between them.

heredity

2. Most of our abilities are not determined solely by environment or by h_____ , but by the interaction between the two.

3. For example, all human infants are born with the ability to learn a spoken language. Other species are not so endowed. Thus, language ability depends on certain charac-

are

teristics that (*are/are not*) inherited.

4. The language the child learns to speak, however, will be that of the culture in which he or she is raised. Language development depends on both heredity and

environment (*or* experience)

_____ .

characteristics

5. The genetically specified _____ with which we are born express themselves through the process of *maturation.* Maturation refers to innately determined sequences of growth or bodily changes that are relatively independent of learning or experience. If all members of the same species develop certain behavior at about the same time, without special training, we may suspect that the

maturation

behavior is largely the result of _____ .

6. Some species of birds reared in isolation, so that they never hear the song characteristic of their species, are still able to reproduce it fairly well at the appropriate stage of development. Thus we can reasonably say that singing in these birds is controlled

maturation

largely by _____ rather than by learning.

7. When behavior depends more on physical *growth* processes than on *learning,* the

maturation

process controlling the behavior is said to be _____ .

8. Maturation refers to growth processes that produce behavior changes that are rela-

learning (*or* experience)

tively independent of _____ . If the behavior change is due to training

learning

or experience, the process is called _____ rather than maturation.

9. The development of the fetus within the mother's body, which follows a fixed time schedule, provides a clear picture of what we mean by maturation. Fetal behavior, such as turning and kicking, follows an orderly sequence depending on the growth

maturation

stage of the fetus; fetal behavior is thus a result of _____ .

10. Growth, of course, is not complete at birth. The physical skills of the infant after birth develop in such an orderly sequence (rolling over, sitting, standing, walking)

growth

that these behaviors appear to be the result of continuing _____ processes,

maturation

or _____ , rather than learning.

11. Maturation provides the readiness to learn, and most behavior depends on both learning and maturation. Children will learn to talk only after they have reached the

maturity (*or synonym*)

proper stage of _____ . The language they will speak is the one they

learning (*or* experience)

hear, thus indicating the role of _____ .

12. We noted earlier that human development is determined by a continuous inter-

heredity

action between _____ and environment. We can state this principle more specifically by saying that behavior during the early years of development frequent-

maturation, learning

ly reflects an interaction between m_____ and l_____ .

13. Physical skills, such as reaching for objects or walking, develop without special

maturation

training because they are primarily the result of _____ . But environmental conditions can affect the *rate of development.*

14. Infants raised in very restricted environments—confined in cribs for most of the day with little opportunity to move about freely—will learn to sit up, stand, and walk

rate

much later than normal. A restricted environment retards the _____ of development.

15. Thus, although physical skills are primarily dependent on maturation, the rate at

environment

which they develop can be influenced by the quality of the _____ .

16. The development of many behaviors follows an *orderly sequence,* usually proceeding from *simple* behaviors to those that are *more complex.* Children learn to walk before they run, to speak words before they speak sentences, to count by rote before they understand the concept of numbers. Their behavior proceeds in an

sequence, complex

orderly _____ from simple to more _____ actions.

orderly

17. Some psychologists view this _____ sequence of development as a con-

learning (*or* experience)

tinuous process in which maturation interacts with _____ to produce a smooth and continuous change in behavior. Other psychologists see development as a series of *stages* through which individuals pass as they grow up.

18. When we talk about infancy, childhood, adolescence, and adulthood, we are talking

stages

broadly about successive _____ of development.

19. Psychologists have defined the concept of developmental stages more precisely. For example, the Swiss psychologist Piaget has proposed that children progress through a fixed sequence of stages in their *cognitive development.* The first stage, from

cognitive

birth to two years, is called the *sensorimotor stage* of _____ development.

sensorimotor

20. During the sensori _____ stage children do not use language or symbols but explore the environment by means of the senses and motor activity. At first they can study objects only visually, but they soon learn to reach for and explore them with the fingers and mouth.

stage | **21.** One of the many things the child learns during the sensimotor _____ is that an *object* is *permanent*; that is, it continues to exist even when it is not present to the senses. The rattle does not disappear forever when hidden by a blanket but is

object | a permanent _____ that will reappear when the child lifts the blanket.

22. The concept of object permanence is achieved, according to Piaget, during the

sensorimotor | _____ stage of development, which occurs in the first

two | _____ years of life.

development | **23.** A later stage in cognitive _____ , called the *preoperational stage,* occurs between the ages of two and seven years. The child now possesses language and can begin to deal with problems by means of symbols and concepts. Objects become symbols that represent classes of things.

preoperational | **24.** During the pre_____ stage, the child begins to use

symbols, stage | sym_____ to conceptualize the environment. The preoperational _____

seven | covers the period from two to _____ years.

preoperational | **25.** One of the concepts developed toward the end of the pre_____ stage is that of *conservation.* The child learns that the amount of a substance does not change—that is, it is conserved—when the substance is divided into parts or placed in different-sized containers. If a four-year-old is shown two identical short jars containing what he or she acknowledges to be an equal amount of beans and watches while the contents of one jar are poured into a tall, cylindrical jar, the

has not | child will say that the tall jar contains more beans. The four-year-old (*has/has not*) attained the concept of conservation.

26. A six- or seven-year-old presented with the same situation will say that the contents of the short and tall jars are equal. The child has attained the concept of

conservation | _____ .

27. If a child says that a ball of clay contains the same amount of material when it is rolled into a sausage shape as when it is a sphere, he or she has achieved the concept

conservation | of _____ .

28. The development of the concept of conservation occurs during the

preoperational, two | _____ stage, which covers the ages of _____ to

seven | _____ . Later stages of cognitive development during which the child's thought processes gradually approach those of an adult are discussed in the text.

29. The infants' tendency to *seek closeness* to the individuals who care for them and to *feel more secure* in their presence is known as *attachment.* Babies at the crawling stage follow their mothers from room to room as they move about the house. This

attachment | is an example of _____ .

30. A toddler clings to mother's skirt in an unfamiliar situation and cries when sepa-

attachment | rated from her. This is another example of _____ .

31. It seems reasonable to assume that attachment to the mother, the tendency to seek

closeness, secure   _____ to her and feel more _____ in her presence, develops because she is the source of food and thus satisfies a basic need. But experiments with infant monkeys cast doubt on this assumption. If a monkey is raised from birth in a cage containing two artificial "mothers," one constructed of wire but with a nipple providing milk and the other covered with soft terry cloth but no milk supply, the monkey will spend most of its time clinging to the terry cloth "mother."

32. The infant monkey will show greater attachment to the cuddly, terry cloth

food
is not   "mother" despite the fact that she is not a source of _____ . These results indicate that attachment to the mother (*is/is not*) solely dependent on the fact that she provides food.

33. With human infants, distress at separation from the mother (or primary caregiver),

attachment   which is one indication of _____ , begins around 8 months of age and reaches a peak at about 18 months.

34. Attachment to the mother reaches a peak at about _____ months; from then

18   on, the child becomes progressively more willing to be separated from the mother. But attachment to the parents and other family members still remains close during the preschool years. Because the parents are the dominant figures in children's lives, they serve as models for children to copy. When we say that children *identify* with their parents, we mean that they assume many of the parents' values and patterns of behavior as their own.

35. When Sarah bathes and diapers her doll using the same mannerisms and tone of voice that her mother uses in caring for her baby brother, we may assume that

identifies   she _____ with her mother.

36. When Tommy staggers around in his father's fishing boots casting an imaginary

identifies   line into the bathtub, we may assume that he _____ with his father.

37. When we say that a person is identifying with another person, we mean that

like (*or a synonym*)   whether the individual knows it or not, he or she is trying to become_____ the other person.

38. One of the major ways in which parents influence their children is in the area of

typing   *sex typing.* Sex ty_____ refers to the acquisition of those characteristics and behaviors that one's culture considers appropriate for females or males.

39. Sex-typed behaviors are those that one's culture considers appropriate for

males, females
(*either order*)   _____ and _____ .

40. Beth plays with dolls; David plays with trucks and soldiers. These are examples

sex typing   of _____ _____ .

sex-typed   **41.** Children acquire many of their _____ - _____ behaviors by observing their parents.

42. We should not confuse sex typing, which refers to the acquisition of characteristics and behaviors that one's _____ considers appropriate for males and females, with *gender identity*.

culture (*or* society)

43. Gender _____ refers to the degree to which one regards oneself as female or male.

identity

44. A girl may have a firm view of herself as female (a clear _____ identity) yet still not adopt all of the behaviors that her culture considers feminine, nor avoid all behaviors labeled masculine.

gender

45. Gender _____ and _____ _____ are not the same, although parents play an important role in both.

identity
sex typing

46. To the extent that a girl identifies with her mother, she will have a clear _____ identity, a firm view of herself as _____ .

gender
female

47. To the extent that both parents encourage behaviors the culture considers appropriate for females and discourage those considered appropriate for males, the girl will be strongly _____ _____ .

sex typed

48. *Adolescence,* the transitional period from childhood to adulthood, is a period of development marked by *changes.* The most striking of these _____ are physical changes in the *sex characteristics* and *rate of growth* that culminate in *puberty.*

changes

49. Mary is a typical 12-year-old adolescent girl. We would expect her to experience striking physical changes in _____ characteristics and in _____ of growth, culminating in _____ .

sex, rate
puberty

50. Puberty, which is marked by menstruation in girls and the appearance of live sperm cells in the semen of boys, is reached at different ages by different youngsters. There is a wide variation in the age at which boys and girls reach _____ .

puberty (*or* maturity)

51. In general, however, girls attain puberty two years earlier than boys. Thus, girls, on the average, mature (*earlier/later*) than boys.

earlier

52. Girls generally reach _____ before boys.

puberty

53. On reaching sexual maturity, or _____ , adolescents are faced with decisions about sexual behavior. Since society's attitudes toward sexual activities are much more *permissive* today than in the past and guidelines for "appropriate" behavior are less clear, adolescents may experience *conflict.*

puberty

54. Because current attitudes toward sexual behavior are (*more/less*) permissive than in the past, parental standards of sexual morality may differ markedly from the standards of the adolescent's peers. These differing values may be a source of con_____ for the adolescent.

more

conflict

55. Surveys indicate that today's adolescents are engaging in sexual intercourse at an earlier age than did their parents. These data undoubtedly reflect the fact that

permissive   society's attitudes concerning sex are now more _____ .

56. While adolescents and parents may agree on many of their values, they are most apt

sexual   to have different views about appropriate _____ behavior.

57. The adolescent, in addition to deciding on standards for sexual behavior, must formulate *standards of conduct* for other areas of life. This is part of developing a

identity   sense of *personal identity*. A sense of personal _____ involves decid-

conduct   ing what is worth doing and formulating standards of _____ . It also involves feelings about one's own competence.

58. A major task facing the adolescent is to develop a sense of _____

personal

identity   _____ . We noted earlier that young children assume many of their

identify   parents' values as their own; that is, they _____ with their parents.

59. As children grow toward adolescence, the values of peers and of teachers and other adults become increasingly important. When parental views differ markedly from those of peers and other adults, the adolescent may have difficulty developing a

personal identity   sense of _____ _____ ; he or she may experience *role confusion.*

confusion   **60.** Role _____ means that the young person tries out one role after another and has difficulty synthesizing the different roles into a single identity.

61. Margaret's parents expect her to be docile and submissive to their values. Her teachers encourage independent thinking and self-direction. Her friends tend

role   to rebel against any adult authority. Margaret will probably experience _____

confusion, personal identity   _____ in her search for _____ _____ .

inconsistent   **62.** Role confusion is apt to occur when parental values are (*consistent/inconsistent*) with the views of peers and other adults.

63. We have looked at some aspects of development from infancy through adolescence, but development does not end with the attainment of physical maturity, or

puberty   _____ . It is a continuous process extending from birth to old age. Erik Erikson has proposed a series of eight *psychosocial stages* to characterize develop-

psychosocial   ment throughout life. He calls them psycho_____ stages because he believes that psychological development depends on the social relations established at various points in life.

cognitive (*or* intellectual)   **64.** Whereas Piaget's stages are concerned with _____ development,

psychosocial   Erikson's focus on problems of _____ _____ development. For example, Erikson claims that during the *first year of life* infants learn to *trust or mistrust* other people, depending on how well their needs are attended to at a period when they are helpless and totally dependent.

65. Infants' first social contacts occur while they are being fed. If the experience is pleasant and their needs are satisfied, they learn to associate mother with satisfaction and relaxation. They learn that they can tr_____ other people to satisfy their needs.

trust

66. If, on the other hand, the feeding situation is unpleasant and hurried, so that the infants remain hungry and uncomfortable, they may learn to mis_____ others as a source of satisfaction. We can see how these experiences during the _____ year of life might well lead to a basic attitude of _____ or _____ toward people later in life.

mistrust

first, trust

mistrust (*either order*)

67. During the second year of life, children have their first real encounter with discipline and self-control, in connection with toilet training and in learning not to touch forbidden or dangerous objects as they begin walking. According to Erikson the psycho_____ problem at this stage is one of *autonomy* versus *doubt*.

psychosocial

68. The psychosocial stage during the second year of life concerns autonomy and _____ . If parental discipline is warm but firm, children learn pride in controlling their own impulses. If the parents try to discipline by shaming the child and making the child feel that he or she does not live up to their expectations, the child is likely to develop feelings of self-_____ .

doubt

doubt

69. Erikson has proposed a number of later stages that are concerned with _____ problems. You might expect that the major problem during the adolescent stage is developing one's personal _____ in relation to parents, peers, and other people important in one's life.

psychosocial

identity

TERMS AND CONCEPTS

maturation _____

_____

_____

_____

developmental stages _____

_____

_____

_____

critical period _____

_____

_____

_____

sensorimotor stage _____

_____

_____

_____

object permanence _____

_____

_____

_____

preoperational stage _____

_____

_____

_____

principle of conservation _____

_____

_____

concrete operational stage _____

_____

_____

formal operational stage _____

_____

_____

attachment _____

_____

_____

stages of moral reasoning _____

_____

_____

_____

identification _____

_____

_____

_____

sex typing _____

_____

_____

_____

gender identity _____

_____

_____

_____

adolescent growth spurt _____

_____

_____

_____

secondary sex characteristics _____

_____

_____

_____

puberty _____

_____

_____

role confusion _____

_____

_____

psychosocial stages _____

_____

_____

_____ 1. Maturation
    a. is influenced primarily by variations in the environment
    b. is relatively independent of experience
    c. depends on cultural influences
    d. ends by the age of 20 or 25

_____ 2. Children who are born with cataracts which are not removed before age 7 will suffer permanent disability. These first 7 years are described as a _____ for development of vision.
    a. sensitive time
    b. critical period
    c. hierarchical stage
    d. maturational sequence

_____ 3. The concept of developmental stages
    a. implies that behaviors at a given stage are organized around a dominant theme
    b. concerns only cognitive development
    c. emphasizes the smoothness and continuity of development
    d. all of the above

_____ 4. Parents who are affectionate but not very controlling or demanding tend to have children who are
    a. especially mature
    b. unusually self-controlled
    c. both mature and self-controlled
    d. immature and lacking in self-control

_____ 5. According to the text, puberty is defined by the
    a. adolescent growth spurt
    b. development of secondary sex characteristics
    c. onset of menstruation or appearance of live sperm in the semen
    d. all of the above

_____ 6. Piaget's concept of the _____ is demonstrated when a child systematically investigates the variables involved in the oscillation period of a pendulum.
    a. formal operational stage
    b. conservation of energy
    c. sensorimotor stage
    d. concrete operational stage

_____ 7. In developing a sense of identity, adolescents
    a. find parental values of increasing importance
    b. invariably reject earlier beliefs
    c. may experience role confusion
    d. all of the above

_____ 8. Linda is tempted to cheat on a test but does not because she fears the disapproval of her teacher if she is caught. Kohlberg would place her moral reasoning at the _____ level.
    a. preconvental
    b. conventional
    c. postconventional
    d. ethical principle

_____ 9. Erikson proposed eight stages of _____ development.
    a. psychosexual
    b. psychoanalytical
    c. psychosocial
    d. cognitive

_____ 10. Current data show a definite change in adolescents' sexual behavior; adolescents are
    a. behaving more promiscuously
    b. more open in their discussion of sex, although their actual behavior differs little from their parents' generation
    c. engaging in sexual activity at an earlier age than their parents
    d. beginning to have sex at the same age as their parents did, but with more partners

_____ 11. When young monkeys were reared with access only to artificial "mothers,"
    a. the females grew up to be unusually affectionate mothers
    b. they preferred the terry cloth "mothers"
    c. they used the wire "mothers" for security when exploring strange objects
    d. the females made poor mothers as adults, although their social relationships with peers were nearly normal

_____ 12. The acquisition of characteristics and behaviors that one's culture considers appropriate for females or males is known as
    a. gender identification
    b. sex typing
    c. sex-role stereotyping
    d. sexual androgyny

_____ 13. According to the psychoanalytic view, identification with a parent provides a child with
    a. a source for feelings of strength and adequacy
    b. self-control and a conscience

c. the appropriate sex role
d. all of the above

_____14. Which of the following areas of development is *least* apt to be affected by a deprived environment during the first two years of life?
    a. motor skills
    b. language skills
    c. social skills
    d. emotional stability

_____15. According to Erikson, the most important period for the development of basic trust in other people occurs
    a. during the first year of life
    b. between the ages of 2 and 3, concurrent with speech development
    c. sometime during the fifth year or when the child begins school
    d. during the adolescent years when opposite-sex attraction intensifies

_____16. On tests of memory, 6-year-olds usually do worse than 11-year-olds. The poorer performance of the younger children is probably due to their
    a. limited memory capacity
    b. limited knowledge of memory strategies
    c. inability to conserve number and mass
    d. immature hippocampus

_____17. According to Piaget, a child who can correctly predict that a ball of clay and a similar ball rolled out to a long sausage will balance on a scale must have achieved
    a. conservation of weight
    b. object permanence
    c. conservation of mass
    d. all of the above

_____18. Which of the following summarizes best the problems of development over a lifetime?

a. Developmental problems continue throughout life, but are different at the different stages of life.
b. Developmental problems are most severe during adolescence and diminish thereafter, as life becomes more stable.
c. Biological problems become more severe as people age, even though psychological development has stopped.
d. Much of life has its problems, but middle adulthood does not, since vocational status is established, income is at its maximum, and family life is stabilized.

_____19. When mothers are insensitive or unresponsive during the first year, their babies
    a. come to depend more on others
    b. cry less often
    c. show insecure attachment in the "strange situation"
    d. show aggressive behavior in the "strange situation"

_____20. Child-rearing methods in the United States
    a. differ from one social group to another
    b. differ little from those in other countries
    c. have changed very little over the past 50 years
    d. are now pretty much the same from one social class to the next

KEY TO SELF-QUIZ

20. a	15. a	10. c	5. c
19. c	14. a	9. c	4. d
18. a	13. d	8. b	3. a
17. d	12. b	7. c	2. b
16. b	11. b	6. a	1. b

INDIVIDUAL EXERCISE

SEX DIFFERENCES IN BEHAVIOR

Psychologists have for many years investigated behaviors that differ by sex. Where once it was assumed that differences in male and female behavior reflected biological differences, the common assumption now is that most such differences (other than those directly related to reproduction) reflect cultural training. For many sex-differentiated behaviors, however, it is not readily apparent whether biological factors, cultural factors, or both, are involved. A report in the journal *Science* described one such behavior. Female college students carry their books differently than males do, reported the authors; the former cradle them in both arms, the latter hold them at their sides. While this particular behavior is not of earthshaking importance, it illustrates the complexity of trying to understand sex-differentiated behaviors.

What do you think? First of all, do you agree that book-carrying behavior is sex differentiated? Look around you, preferably following a defined procedure for sampling and scoring a reasonable number of subjects of both sexes. If you observe a sex difference in book-carrying behavior, what do you think is its cause? Remember, as you consider the problem, the kinds of variables involved: (1) physical variables such as arm length, arm strength, hip shape, or breast development; (2) cultural training, for example, modeling the carrying styles of adults; (3) other cultural variables that may differ by sex, such as clothing, size of typical books for classes taken more frequently by males or females. The problem is not as simple as it seems at first. To compare the authors' logic and conclusions with your own, consult the original report, which should be available in most libraries: Jenni, D. A., and Jenni, M. A. (1976) Carrying behavior in humans: Analysis of sex differences. *Science*, 194:859-60.

INDIVIDUAL AND CLASS EXERCISE

BIRTH ORDER AND PERSONALITY CHARACTERISTICS

Introduction

Research has shown that some aspects of an individual's personality are related to order of birth. First-born or only children, in particular, tend to differ from other children. The text discusses several factors that make the first-born or only child's position in the family unique. This exercise will show whether personality differences among your acquaintances bear any relationship to birth order.

Procedure

In the spaces provided at the left of the data sheet (p. 47), write the names of ten people of your own sex whom you know quite well. Now rate each person on the personality traits listed at the bottom of the data sheet. Note that a rating of 1 means that the person possesses the trait to only a slight degree, while a rating of 5 indicates that he or she possesses the trait to a high degree. For example, a rating of 5 on the trait "aggression" indicates a very dominant, aggressive person; a rating of 1 would describe someone who is quite meek and unassertive. After deciding which number best describes the aggressive or nonaggressive nature of your first subject, enter this number in the first column next to his or her name. Now rate the subject according to the remaining three traits. Carry out the same procedure for each acquaintance. Try to avoid the common tendency of rating everyone toward the middle of the scale.

Treatment of Data

After you have rated each of your ten acquaintances on all four traits, find out their birth order (if you do not already know it) and turn to the data tabulation sheet on page 48. List the name of all first-born or only children in the appropriate column and enter their ratings for each trait. Do the same for those who were later born. Add the ratings for each trait and enter the total at the bottom of each column. Divide each total by the number of subjects in the column to find the average rating.

If this is to be done as a class exercise, bring this sheet with you to class. Your instructor will tabulate the average ratings obtained by each class member for the four traits.

Questions for Discussion

1. Is there any difference in the average ratings for first-born or only children as compared to those for the later born? If so, which traits are most affected by birth order?

2. How do the circumstances of the study limit interpretation of the results? That is, might different results have been obtained if the subjects had been selected from the population at large rather than from a group of college students?

3. What are some of the factors relevant to the individual's position in the family that might explain the results?

Name	Personality traits			
	Aggression	Conscientiousness	Intellectual ability	Sociability
1.				
2.				
3.				
4.				
5.				
6.				
7.				
8.				
9.				
10.				

Aggression	Conscientiousness	Intellectual ability	Sociability
1. Very meek	1. Careless in attention to responsibilities	1. In lower 10% of class	1. Withdrawn; a loner
2.	2.	2.	2.
3. Moderately aggressive	3. Moderately conscientious	3. Average	3. Moderately sociable
4.	4.	4.	4.
5. Very aggressive	5. Very conscientious	5. In upper 10% of class	5. Very outgoing and sociable

DATA TABULATION FOR BIRTH-ORDER STUDY

First-born or only child

Name	Aggression	Conscientiousness	Intellectual ability	Sociability
Total				
Average				

Later-born child

Name	Aggression	Conscientiousness	Intellectual ability	Sociability
Total				
Average				

4
States of Consciousness

LEARNING OBJECTIVES

4-1.   Be able to define consciousness in terms of its function in monitoring information and controlling our actions.

4-2.   Know what is meant by the terms subconscious processes, preconscious memories, and the unconscious. Be familiar with the phenomenon of dissociation as illustrated by multiple personalities.

4-3.   Be able to discuss in some detail sleep schedules, stages of sleep depth, and sleep disorders.

4-4.   Be familiar with Freud's theory of dreams and what research says about it. Know the answers to the questions about dreams discussed in the text.

4-5.   Know what is meant by the term psychoactive drug and be able to give examples of each of the subcategories of psychoactive drugs discussed in the text. Be familiar with typical pattens of use of these drugs.

4-6.   Be able to define physical dependence and psychological dependence. Know the stepping-stone theory of drug usage and some of the reasons people take drugs.

4-7.   Be able to define meditation and describe the various techniques used to induce a meditative state. Be familiar with the research findings on meditation.

4-8.   Be able to describe the procedure and typical effects of a hypnosis session. Be familiar with the phenomena of posthypnotic amnesia and other posthypnotic suggestions; understand the questions of conscious control that these phenomena raise.

4-9.   Be familiar with the phenomena of hypnotic age regression, automatic writing and other dissociated tasks. Understand what is meant by the "hidden observer" and how it is studied.

4-10.   Know the difference between unusual but scientifically demonstrable phenomena and other claimed phenomena that either cannot be demonstrated or have been demonstrated to be fraudulent. Be able to discuss the role of psychology in the study of both types of phenomena.

1. A person's state of consciousness changes from moment to moment. Right now your attention is focused on this book; in a few minutes you may be absorbed in a reverie, or daydream. An *altered state of consciousness* exists whenever there is a change in pattern of mental functioning that *seems* different to the person experiencing the change. If you shift from studying to daydreaming, you experience an

    altered   _____ state of consciousness.

2. Since our pattern of mental functioning changes when we are asleep or dreaming,

    consciousness   sleep and dreams are altered states of _____ .

3. A person meditating or in a hypnotic trance experiences a change in mental func-

    states   tioning; hence meditation and hypnosis are also altered _____ of

    consciousness   _____ .

4. Consciousness is difficult to define. The term usually refers to the individual's perceptions, thoughts, feelings, and memories that are active at a given moment. In this sense consciousness is synonymous with *awareness.* But there are *degrees of awareness* within consciousness. While reading this page you may be only dimly aware of sounds outside the room until something (a sudden noise, your name spoken) attracts your attention. This illustrates the fact that there are degrees of

    awareness   _____ within consciousness.

5. You drive your car to work, engrossed in thought. On arriving you realize that you recall nothing about the actions you performed while driving or the street corners

    degrees   you passed. Again, we see that there are _____ of conscious awareness.

6. You may have memories and thoughts that are not part of your consciousness at this moment but can be brought to consciousness if you wish to retrieve them.

    consciousness   Memories that are available to _____ are called preconscious memories.

7. You may not be aware right now of the trip you took last weekend, but this

    preconscious   _____ memory can be brought to consciousness if you wish to retrieve it.

    preconscious memories   8. We have said that _____ _____

    consciousness   can be retrieved and become part of _____ when needed. However, according to psychoanalytic theory, still other memories are in the *unconscious.* These are said to be memories that are so emotionally painful that

    consciousness   they are not retrievable and therefore not available to _____ .

9. Freud believed that, for emotional reasons, some of our experiences are driven out

    unconscious   of consciousness and repressed to the un_____ .

10. A young boy has strong feelings of hostility toward his newborn sister, who has usurped his place as the center of parental affection; but whenever he expresses such feelings, he is punished. According to Freud, the angry feelings may then be

repressed   re_____ to the unconscious.

11. In later life the boy may show, in various indirect ways, that he resents his sister. If he is not aware of any feelings of resentment, such feelings may be said to be

unconscious (*or* repressed)   _____ .

consciousness   **12.** Preconscious memories can be brought to _____ ; emotionally charged memories that we cannot recall (or can recall only with great

unconscious   difficulty) are said to be part of the _____ .

13. Perhaps the most familiar altered state of consciousness, one that we experience

sleep   every 24 hours, is sl_____ .

14. Scientists have discovered that there are *five stages* of sleep—four stages of *depth* and a fifth stage known as *rapid-eye-movement (REM) sleep,* during which dreams

five   commonly occur. One method of studying the _____ (*number*) stages of sleep is by using the *electroencephalogram* (abbreviated *EEG*), which records the electrical activity of the brain.

15. When we record the electrical activity of the brain with the electroencephalogram

EEG, depth   (abbreviated _____) we find that the four stages of d_____ of sleep are characterized by different *brain waves*.

waves   **16.** We can tell how deeply a person is sleeping by the kind of brain _____

electroencephalogram   recorded by the electro_____ .

four   **17.** There are _____ (*number*) stages of depth of sleep. Stages 1 through 4 represent a scale of increasing depth of sleep, with Stage 1 the lightest sleep and Stage 4 the deepest.

easier   **18.** You would expect it to be (*easier/more difficult*) to arouse a person from Stage 1 sleep than from Stage 4.

19. During a fifth stage of sleep, rapid movements of the eyes occur. This stage is

REM   known as rapid-eye-movement, or _____, sleep. It is this stage of sleep that is

dreams (*or* dreaming)   associated with d_____ .

20. Since rapid eye movements are not observed during the other four stages of sleep, they are known collectively as non-REM, or *NREM,* sleep. Dreams usually take

REM   place during (*REM/NREM*) sleep.

21. During REM sleep the EEG pattern is similar to that of Stage 1 sleep. (Recall that

brain   the EEG is a method of measuring the electrical activity of the _____ .) The EEG pattern during REM sleep indicates that it should be easy to arouse the

1   person, since it is similar to Stage _____, which is light sleep. But actually it is as difficult to arouse a person from REM sleep as it is from Stage 4 NREM sleep.

22. When a person is in REM sleep there is a *decrease in muscle tone* of the body muscles. This may be one reason why it is (*easy/difficult*) to awaken someone from REM sleep.

difficult

23. The stage of sleep during which dreams occur can be distinguished from the other four stages by the presence of rapid _____ _____ .
The stages of sleep vary throughout the night, but REM sleep tends to be more prominent during the second half of the night.

eye movements

24. Does everyone dream? If we accept REM sleep as evidence, then it is true that *everyone* dreams, though some people recall very few dreams. Thus we can say that (*everyone/not everyone*) dreams.

everyone

25. Both *sleeptalking* and *sleepwalking* occur primarily during NREM sleep and probably not in relation to dreaming, which occurs during _____ sleep.

REM

26. Occurring primarily in NREM sleep are two phenomena, sleep_____ and sleep _____ .

sleepwalking

sleeptalking (*either order*)

27. The most influential theory of dreams has been that of Freud. He believed that *unconscious* impulses were responsible for dreams; the aim of the dream was the fulfillment of an unconscious wish or need. Jane, who has been married two years, dreams that she is single. According to Freud, Jane has an _____ wish to be single.

unconscious

28. According to Freud, dreams express _____ impulses and provide the _____ of a wish or need.

unconscious

fulfillment

29. According to Freud's analysis, the *remembered* aspects of a dream constitute the *manifest content* of the dream. However, the *real meaning* of the same dream, or the *latent content,* is not directly expressed but is instead dramatized in *disguised form*; even the dreamer cannot readily discern its hidden meaning. If Bob recalls that he dreamed last night that he was flying over the campus grounds, this would be the dream's _____ content, since it is the remembered content of the dream.

manifest

30. The real meaning of Bob's dream may be incomprehensible to him; it is the _____ content of the dream.

latent

31. Freud believed that dreams serve to *protect sleep.* In dreams, unfulfilled impulses appear in dis_____ form; thus the dreams prevent the sleeper from being awakened by the disturbing impulses. In this sense, dreams serve to _____ sleep.

disguised

protect

32. Profound changes in conscious awareness can also be produced by the use of drugs. Drugs that affect behavior and conscious experience are called *psychoactive drugs.* Alcohol reduces anxiety, produces relaxation, and releases some of our social inhibitions; it is one kind of psycho_____ drug.

psychoactive

psychoactive

33. Alcohol and barbiturates, such as Seconal, form one group of _____ drugs that are called *depressants.* They vary in their effects, but all slow down the activity of the *central nervous system.*

34. Alcohol in small quantities may make a person more talkative and sociable, because it inhibits some of the restraints on social behavior. But several drinks produce slowed reaction times and drowsiness. Therefore, alcohol is classed as a

depressant

_____ .

psychoactive

nervous system

35. Another group of psycho_____ drugs are called *stimulants* because they speed up the activity of the central _____ _____ .

36. Amphetamines and cocaine increase alertness and wakefulness. They are classed as

stimulants

_____ .

depressants

stimulants (*either order*)

37. Two classes of psychoactive drugs are _____ and

_____ .

behavior

experience (*or* awareness)

38. Psychoactive drugs are drugs that affect a person's _____ and

conscious _____ .

39. A third class of psychoactive drugs are called *hallucinogens* or *psychedelic drugs* because they produce profound alterations in one's perceptions and conscious experience. LSD may produce serious distortions of consciousness, including

psychedelic

hallucinations; it is therefore classed as a hallucinogen or _____ drug.

40. PCP (phencyclidine) makes the user feel dissociated from the environment and may

hallucinogen

cause hallucinations. Consequently, it is also classed as a(n) _____ gen.

psychoactive

41. Drugs that affect behavior and conscious experience are called_____ drugs. (The text discusses two additional classes of drugs [opiates and cannabis] as well as the risks of drug use.)

42. Sleep is an altered state of consciousness that occurs naturally, whereas altered states occurring as a result of drugs are usually self-induced. *Meditation* is yet

altered

another _____ state of consciousness that is self-induced. It is achieved by performing certain exercises and rituals that involve regulating breathing, sharply restricting one's field of attention, assuming yogic body positions, and forming mental images of events and symbols.

43. The result is a somewhat "mystical" state in which the individual loses self-awareness and gains a sense of being involved in a wider consciousness, however defined.

meditation

The fact that _____ causes a change in consciousness goes back to ancient times and is represented in every major world religion.

44. Zen Buddhism, yoga, and Transcendental Meditation all prescribe certain

exercises

_____ , or rituals, that must be followed to achieve a state of consciousness characterized by relaxation, peace of mind, and a sense of well-being.

meditation

45. While these approaches to _____ all involve mystical, or spiritual, associations, laboratory studies have shown that a similar state of consciousness can be attained by following a simple procedure of relaxation. Whatever procedure is used, meditation reduces arousal, especially in easily stressed individuals, and may be valuable for those suffering from anxiety and tension.

are not

46. Mystical, or spiritual, associations (_are/are not_) necessary to achieve the benefits of meditation.

consciousness

sleep

meditation, drugs
(_either order_)

47. We have discussed three altered states of _____ . These include the natural state of _____ , as well as self-induced states attained through the use of _____ and _____ . A fourth state of altered consciousness is _hypnosis._

48. To induce hypnosis, the hypnotist uses a number of methods to lead the person to _relinquish some control of behavior_ and to _accept some reality distortion._ Hypnosis was once believed to be similar to sleep, but EEG measures taken during hypnosis

stages

are like those of waking rather than any of the five _____ of sleep.

is not

49. While hypnosis (_is/is not_) similar to sleep, it differs from the normal waking state in several ways. An individual in a _hypnotic state_ relinquishes some control of

behavior

_____ to the hypnotist; he or she does not like to make plans and would rather wait for the hypnotist to suggest what to do.

50. A _decreased interest in planning_ or initiating activity is thus one characteristic of

hypnotic

the _____ state.

51. Another characteristic of the hypnotic state, in addition to a decreased interest in

planning

p_____ , is a _reduction in reality testing._ A hypnotized individual will readily accept reality distortion or hallucinated experiences (for example, petting an imaginary rabbit that the person has been told is sitting on his or her lap). The same person in the normal waking state would usually reject such a distortion of

reality

_____ .

52. The hypnotic state thus differs from the normal waking state in (1) a decrease in

planning, reality

_____ and (2) a reduction in _____ testing.

testing

53. Closely related to the reduction in reality _____ under hypnosis is an increase in _suggestibility._ The hypnotized person will readily accept suggestions. If the hypnotist says, "You are very warm," the subject may begin to perspire. If the hypnotist says, "You are angry," the subject may show signs of irritability.

suggestibility

54. Another characteristic of the hypnotic state is increased sug_____ .

planning

testing, suggestibility

55. Three characteristics of the hypnotic state are a decrease in _____ , a reduction in reality_____ , and increased _____ .

suggestibility

56. Several of the phenomena that can be demonstrated with deeply hypnotized individuals are related to increased _____ . For example, the hypnotist may suggest that the subject will forget all that transpired during the hypnotic session. This is called _posthypnotic amnesia._

57. | amnesia — In posthypnotic am_____ the memories are not "lost"; when the hypnotist gives a prearranged signal, the subject recalls what took place during the hypnotic state.

58. | amnesia — The temporary loss of memory for events during hypnosis is called posthypnotic _____ . Amnesia is one form of *posthypnotic suggestion.* The hypnotist may make other suggestions while the subject is in the hypnotic state—for example, suggesting that after coming out of hypnosis the subject will open the window when the hypnotist pulls out a handkerchief but will not remember being so instructed. This is called a *posthypnotic response.*

59. | posthypnotic — If the subject opens the window at the prearranged signal but does not recall that the act was suggested by the experimenter, this is an example of a post-_____ response.

60. | amnesia / response (*either order*) — Two forms of posthypnotic suggestion are posthypnotic _____ , and posthypnotic _____ .

61. | hallucinations — Hallucinations can also occur as the result of posthypnotic suggestion for subjects who are highly responsive. These include positive hallucinations (petting an imaginary rabbit) or negative h_____ (*not* perceiving something that would normally be perceived).

62. | negative hallucination / pain — A patient with a severe injury may be told while hypnotized that she will feel no pain on arousal from the hypnotic state. If the suggestion is effective and pain is reduced, this would be an example of a _____ _____ , failing to perceive something (_____) that is normally perceived.

63. | posthypnotic / pain — Negative hallucinations created by post_____ suggestion are useful in the relief of _____ .

TERMS AND CONCEPTS

altered state of consciousness _____

_____

_____

_____

consciousness _____

_____

_____

_____

subconscious processes _____

_____

_____

_____

preconscious memories _____

_____

_____

_____

the unconscious _____

_____

_____

_____

sleep schedules _____

_____

_____

_____

REM sleep _____

_____

_____

_____

NREM sleep _____

_____

_____

_____

narcolepsy _____

_____

_____

sleep apnea _____

_____

_____

_____

manifest content _____

_____

_____

_____

latent content _____

_____

_____

_____

dissociation _____

_____

_____

_____

multiple personality _____

_____

_____

_____

psychoactive drugs _____

_____

_____

_____

physical dependence _____

_____

_____

_____

psychological dependence _____

_____

_____

_____

depressants _____

_____

_____

opiates _____

_____

_____

stimulants _____

_____

_____

hallucinogens _____

_____

_____

cannabis _____

_____

_____

meditation _____

_____

_____

mantra _____

_____

_____

hypnosis _____

_____

_____

posthypnotic amnesia _____

_____

_____

age regression _____

_____

_____

"hidden observer"* _____

_____

_____

*Indicates term used in Critical Discussion

_____ 1. The four stages of NREM sleep are defined according to
   a. subjective ratings of depth of sleep
   b. the amount of dreaming per stage
   c. the duration of each stage
   d. EEG patterns

_____ 2. The general term for drugs that produce subjective changes in consciousness is
   a. psychoactive
   b. hallucinogenic
   c. psychedelic
   d. tranquilizing

_____ 3. A mantra is a key element in
   a. Zen Buddhism
   b. Benson's relaxation technique
   c. Transcendental Meditation
   d. yoga

_____ 4. According to most psychologists, an altered state of consciousness exists whenever
   a. EEG patterns change markedly
   b. there are observable autonomic nervous system changes
   c. a person senses a change in his or her mental functioning
   d. an observer notes a change in the individual's behavior

_____ 5. In studying who can be hypnotized, it has been found that
   a. anyone can be hypnotized if enough attempts are made
   b. childhood experiences can be important in determining whether a person can be hypnotized
   c. studies of twins show no evidence of a hereditary factor in susceptibility
   d. measures of susceptibility are useful at the time given, but do not predict hypnotic performance at a later age

_____ 6. A mantra is
   a. an Eastern meditation cult
   b. a special picture used in meditation
   c. a special sound used in meditation
   d. used in opening-up meditation

_____ 7. Which of the following is *not* a characteristic of the hypnotic stage?
   a. The subject loses the sense of his or her own identity.
   b. Attention is redistributed.
   c. The subject ceases to make plans.
   d. Reality testing is reduced.

_____ 8. The relaxation technique developed by Benson does *not* make use of
   a. a comfortable sitting position
   b. a sound specially chosen for each individual
   c. a focus on breathing
   d. daily practice

_____ 9. Alcohol is classified as a
   a. depressant
   b. stimulant
   c. hallucinogen
   d. narcotic

_____ 10. Adverse LSD reactions (that is, "bad trips")
   a. occur only in those who have such reactions outside the drugged state
   b. occur only in the first few uses of the drug
   c. can occur in any user
   d. tend to be brief and transient

_____ 11. The EEG pattern of REM sleep is most similar to which one of the following stages of sleep?
   a. 1
   b. 2
   c. 3
   d. 4

_____ 12. Freud used _____ himself and treated others with it, but later realized that the drug could cause some serious addiction problems.
   a. cocaine
   b. LSD
   c. heroin
   d. alcohol

_____ 13. Studies of sleepwalking and sleeptalking have shown that
   a. sleeptalking is primarily associated with NREM sleep, although 20-25 percent is associated with REM

b. sleepwalking is primarily associated with REM sleep, although 20-25 percent is associated with NREM

c. sleepwalkers believe they are dreaming, since their reports of dreams match what they were doing while sleepwalking

d. sleepwalking only occurs during REM sleep

_____ 14. If a sleeper's EEG shows a slow regular pattern (8–13 Hz) and rapid eye movements are also recorded, he or she is probably in what stage of sleep?
a. Stage 1
b. Stage 2
c. Stages 3 and 4
d. REM

_____ 15. A person who must awaken repeatedly during the night in order to breathe suffers from
a. narcolepsy
b. alcoholic hallucinosis
c. delirium tremens
d. apnea

_____ 16. Which of the following has been experimentally verified as possible?
a. psychic surgery
b. walking barefoot on hot coals
c. fixing watches through mental processes
d. reincarnation

_____ 17. The typical dream lasts
a. only a few seconds
b. a few minutes
c. about as long as it would take for the events to occur when awake

d. an undetermined amount of time, since we have no way of measuring dream duration

_____ 18. Some people say they seldom dream. They probably _____ than those who report frequent dreams.
a. sleep less soundly
b. are more emotionally disturbed
c. dream less often
d. have more difficulty remembering dreams

_____ 19. The modern induction of hypnosis often involves
a. convincing subjects that they are going to sleep
b. authoritarian commands by the hypnotist
c. asking a subject to concentrate on a visual target
d. hypnotizing an uncooperative subject

_____ 20. Flashbacks are commonly associated with _____ and probably due to _____ .
a. LSD; restoration of LSD memories
b. LSD; lingering LSD in the body
c. alcohol; restoration of alcohol memories
d. alcohol; lingering alcohol in the body

KEY TO SELF-QUIZ

20. a	15. d	10. c	5. b
19. c	14. d	9. a	4. c
18. d	13. a	8. b	3. c
17. c	12. a	7. a	2. a
16. b	11. a	6. c	1. d

INDIVIDUAL EXERCISES

THE CHEVREUL PENDULUM

Introduction

While psychologists differ in their conception of an "unconscious" portion of the mind, most would agree that some of our thoughts, motives, and emotional responses are more available for self-inspection than others. A variety of techniques have been developed to aid us in better understanding such "unconscious" mental activity. These range from Freud's free association to Zen and other forms of meditation. The Chevreul Pendulum* technique falls into this spectrum. However, it is not an accepted research technique, as are most of the other procedures in this

*Named after the Frenchman, Michael Chevreul, who investigated the phenomenon in 1883, relating it to the use of a divining rod to discover water or precious metals beneath the earth.

Study Guide. (The Chevreul Pendulum has been widely used in the manner to be described below, but rarely as part of a carefully controlled scientific study.) It is presented as a possible way for getting more in touch with ourselves or perhaps contacting our "hidden observer."

Equipment Needed

A pendulum, made up of a small weight on 6 to 10 inches of string or fine chain. A locket on a chain will do. Or make a pendulum from a fishing weight, an eraser, etc., tied to a length of string.

Procedure

1. The Chevreul Pendulum is a device for what hypnotists term "ideomotor answering." The "answering" refers to the subject's answering questions, while "ideo-motor" means doing so by a special kind of motor performance, one that reflects a thought yet is different from normal, deliberate body movements. The hypnotists who use the "unconscious" as an explanatory system say this device allows the unconscious to answer. Others, less convinced of an unconscious "mind" lurking in our heads somewhere, still agree that such answering may yield responses different from simple verbal replies.

2. The pendulum works by allowing very fine muscular movements to provide answers to questions, movements so fine as to seem to happen by themselves. To help this happen, sit down, hold the string of the pendulum between your index finger and your thumb, and rest your elbow on a table. Pick a comfortable angle of the arm and let the pendulum hang to within an inch or two of the table. You will find that you can cause the pendulum to oscillate along a line, forward and back or left and right, and to rotate in either direction, by very small, almost imperceptible, movements.

3. In order to answer questions, you should have pendulum movements for "yes," "no," "maybe," "I don't know," and perhaps "I don't want to answer." A typical setup could be right-left for "yes," forward-back for "no," an indeterminate movement for "maybe," a circle one way for "I don't know," and the other way for "I don't want to answer." But don't just use these movements; let the pendulum tell you. Rest your elbow comfortably with the pendulum motionless and tell yourself, out loud or silently, that the pendulum

will soon move appropriately for "yes." The movement may be uncertain at first, but don't force it. Just keep thinking "yes" and expecting some movement. If all goes well the pendulum will slowly begin to move. Use the same procedure for the other answers.

4. If you can get the answering to work, then ask yourself questions—ones, for example, about which you are confused. You may get a "maybe" or "I don't know" answer, but you may be surprised to find a definite answer forthcoming.

5. You might also let someone else try the pendulum while you ask the questions.

6. Note that there is no suggestion of magic, spirits, or other psychic causation in this procedure. The answers come from you. But normal verbal consciousness is not the totality of all our thoughts and desires. The pendulum may simply allow you to listen to parts of yourself usually overridden or overlooked.

Questions for Discussion

1. Do you think that the pendulum might react differently when you use your left hand than when you use your right? (Try it.)

2. If you observe differences between the right and left hands, might they be related to the differences between the two hemispheres of your brain, as discussed in Chapter 2 of the text? If so, why?

OBSERVING REM SLEEP

Defining the REM sleep cycle and relating this phase of sleeping to dreams has probably been the most significant finding in the study of sleep and dreams. There are two ways you can study the process of REM sleep: by observing its outer signs in animals or other people and by observing your own dreams.

It is part of our folklore that when Rover whimpers and twitches while sleeping, he is dreaming of chasing cats. Based on the similarity of the sleep cycles across a variety of species and on interviews with human subjects, we now presume that something of the sort really is going on, not only in sleeping dogs, but in a variety of other species. Researchers studying cats' sleep have noted, for example, that it is difficult for even an expert to tell the difference in the EEGs of a sleeping cat and a sleeping human.

The signs of REM and the cycles into and out of it can be observed in a sleeping pet or zoo animal; for example, a pet cat sleeping on your lap. As the cat goes deeper asleep, it still occasionally shifts position. But after a while, it will be quite still. Often, however, heavy breathing or twitching of the limbs will occur as signals from the aroused brain overcome the limb paralysis of REM. At these times the eye movements themselves will be quite noticeable beneath the closed eyelids; the eyelids may even open a bit, allowing the eye movements to be seen directly. After some minutes, the REM period will end; eye movements will cease and the cat will yawn, stretch, change position, and settle down for another cycle. Similar behavior can be seen in other pets and often in wild animals at the zoo, especially the various great cats, who sleep a great deal during the day. If you observe a sleeping human, the same pattern will also be seen.

While you cannot observe your own sleep cycles without the aid of videotape or film, you can make some observations of your dreams. One way is via a dream diary. Put writing materials beside your bed, so that they can be easily reached, and leave on a very dim light. As you go to sleep, remind yourself that you are interested in your dreams and really want to write them down. At first you may only write down a few fragments recalled in the morning, after the last sleep cycle. But if you keep at it, you may find that you are able to take advantage of that brief semi-waking at the end of a REM period (when the cat stretches and yawns) to write down your dream. Some people find, on awakening in the morning, that they have written at length about dreams that are now remembered only poorly, if at all. Even the act of writing may be forgotten, the result of an amnesia barrier that normally helps us keep dream events from intruding into daytime memories.

If you do get useful reports with this procedure, you may wish to analyze them for content—not with the intent of "interpreting" them, but simply for scientific curiosity. Much of what we believe about dreams is probably a result of the amnesia barrier. For example, we tend to remember unusual and vivid dreams, but most dreams reported in the laboratory are about everyday events. Although we may not remember color or detail from our dreams, laboratory results suggest both are common. How do your dreams compare?

As you keep your diary and focus attention on your dreams, you may find yourself experiencing one of the most striking of dream phenomena, the so-called "lucid dream." In a lucid dream, the setting and your actions seem so vivid and undreamlike that you question whether you are dreaming. You may "see" your surroundings (sometimes the room in which you are sleeping) so clearly that you feel certain you are awake. Only on actually awakening are you convinced that you were indeed dreaming.

You may also be able to specify a topic for a night's dreaming by setting it as a "program" as you go to sleep; some people claim to be able to do so regularly.

Observing your own REM sleep and that of others should provide you with a better understanding of the processes involved as well as some insight into the excitement of sleep research that motivates people to give up their own sleep to study that of others.

EXPERIMENTAL MEDITATION

There are a number of ways of attaining a sense of detachment or meditation. The text describes Benson's technique, derived from Transcendental Meditation (p. 135), and two other techniques are noted below: the first is a form of what has been termed "concentrative meditation," similar to Zen, while the second is a form of "opening-up meditation," more akin to yoga. Try each of these three techniques to see which helps you best to free your mind from extraneous thoughts while expanding your awareness. For each procedure you should choose a time when you are not sleepy, sit relaxed in a comfortable chair or on the floor supported by pillows.

For the concentrative procedure put an object such as a vase or a bowl on a table about eight feet in front of you, keeping the background as simple as possible. Now concentrate all your attention on the object, excluding all other thoughts or feelings or body sensations. Do not try to analyze the object or associate ideas with it; simply concentrate on it as it is. After a few minutes you will find that it will be difficult to keep your eyes in proper focus. Do not try to retain a sharp focus; let your eyes unfocus but continue to concentrate on the object for at least five minutes.

How did you feel? Were you able to avoid being distracted by events going on around you? Did you have a feeling of detachment, of being able to step aside and watch your feelings and ideas flow by without getting involved in them? Were there any perceptual distortions of the object being viewed? Did you have a feeling of more intense perception of the object? Was the state a pleasurable one?

Now try the opening-up technique and see if you get the same results. Again sit in a comfortable position, but do not be so relaxed that you will go to sleep. Breathe naturally and focus your attention on your breathing: the movements of your chest and stomach, not the sensations in your nose and throat. Try to avoid being distracted by extraneous thoughts or stimuli. Keep your attention on your breathing, turning aside all other thoughts.

What are your feelings? Are they similar to, or different from, those elicited by the first technique? How do the sensations in both cases differ from those you experience while drowsy or in a half-asleep state?

Now try Benson's technique. How do the effects compare to those of the other procedures? (Note that this technique has similarities to both of the others; it focuses on breathing, as does the general opening-up technique, and the repeated use of the word "one" is somewhat similar to the concentration on the vase of the general concentrative technique.)

5
Sensing

LEARNING OBJECTIVES

5-1. Know what is meant by a sensory filter and the specific neuron code hypothesis. Understand how psychologists use the terms perception and sensory processes.

5-2. Be familiar with the procedures for measuring the absolute threshold and the difference threshold. In this regard, know what is meant by psychometric function, *jnd*, and Weber's law.

5-3. Be able to specify the main parts of the visual system, and the sequence by which light passes through them and is transformed into visual information in the brain.

5-4. Understand the phenomena of color mixing, color deficiency, color appearance, and the four basic color sensations. Be able to discuss these phenomena from the perspective of trichromatic theory, opponent-color theory, and two-stage color theory.

5-5. Be familiar with procedures to measure spatial resolution and the concept of a pattern filter. Be able to describe the setup for a single-cell recording experiment and what is meant by a feature detector.

5-6. Be able to specify the main parts of the auditory system, and the sequence by which sound passes through them and is turned into auditory information in the brain.

5-7. Understand the place theory of pitch perception. Be familiar with some of the problems with the theory, and the alternative explanations that have been offered, namely, temporal theories and duplicity theory.

5-8. Be familiar with the mechanisms of smell and taste.

5-9. Be familiar with the separate senses involved in what is commonly called the sense of touch. Know what research shows about these receptors and how they interact to produce a variety of sensations.

5-10. Be prepared to discuss the question "How do we sense stimuli?" from the viewpoint of Helmholtz's hypothesis of a specific neuron code.

1. All of our information about the world comes to us by way of stimuli impinging on

sense

our *sense organs.* Without our eyes, ears, nose, and other _____ organs, we would know nothing about the people, objects, and events that make up our world.

sense

2. We gain information about the world in which we live by way of our _____

organs

_____ . But a certain *minimum* of sense-organ *stimulation* is required before any sensory experience will be evoked. The minimum physical energy neces-sary to activate a given sensory system is called the *absolute threshold.* To put it

absolute

another way, the _____ threshold is the intensity at which a stimulus is just noticeable.

3. A spot of light in a dark room must reach some measurable intensity before an individual can distinguish it from darkness. In other words, the degree of intensity

threshold

necessary for the spot of light to be seen is its absolute _____ for that individual.

4. Likewise, a sound emitted in a soundproof room must reach a certain intensity before it can be heard. The intensity at which it can be heard by someone is its

absolute

_____ threshold.

5. In both the instances mentioned above, we see that a certain minimum of sense-organ stimulation is required before any sensory experience will be evoked. This

absolute threshold

minimum is called the _____ _____ .

6. A pin prick cannot be felt unless the pressure of the pin on the skin reaches a cer-tain intensity. The intensity of pressure necessary for the pin prick to be felt is its

absolute threshold

_____ _____ .

7. We can see from these examples that whether the stimulus is light, sound, or touch,

minimum, stimulation

a certain _____ of sense-organ _____ is required before any sensory experience will be evoked. This minimum is called the

absolute threshold

_____ _____ .

8. There must also be a certain magnitude of difference between two stimuli before one can be distinguished from the other. The minimum amount of difference neces-sary to tell two stimuli apart is known as the *difference threshold.* Thus, two tones must differ to some degree before one is heard as higher than the other. The point

difference

at which they can be told apart is the _____ threshold.

9. The transition between no sensory experience and some sensory experience is the

absolute

_____ threshold; the transition between no difference and some

difference

difference in stimuli is the _____ threshold.

10. Thresholds *vary* from one person to the next and may even *fluctuate* over time within one individual. Therefore, we should think of a threshold measurement as a statistical average. If a psychologist were interested in measuring your

difference   dif_____ threshold for discriminating between two tones, he or she would probably not get identical results at each testing. Likewise, your threshold for discriminating between the two tones would probably not be the same as someone else's threshold.

vary   **11.**   Thresholds not only _____ from one individual to the next but may even fluctuate within one individual from time to time.

12.   Threshold measurement should be thought of as a statistical average. That is, for

fluctuate   the same person thresholds may _____ from one time to the next,

individual *(or a synonym)*   and thresholds also vary from one _____ to another.

absolute   **13.**   The two kinds of thresholds we have discussed are the _____ threshold, which is the transition between no sensory experience and some sensory

difference   experience, and the _____ threshold, which is the transition between no difference and some difference in stimuli.

sense   **14.**   The human eye is one of the most complex _____ organs. Note the drawing of the human eye and as you proceed, consider the location and functions of its different parts. To begin, locate the *cornea,* where light *enters* the eye.

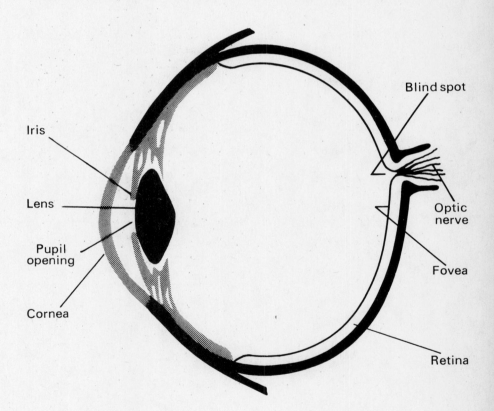

cornea   **15.**   Light enters the eye through the _____ ; the amount of light is *regulated* by the size of the *pupil opening,* which is an opening in the *iris.*

enters   **16.**   The cornea is the portion of the eye through which light _____ ; the

pupil   amount of light entering the eye is regulated by the size of the _____ opening.

cornea

pupil opening

17. After light has entered the eye through the _____ and its amount has been regulated by the _____ _____, the *lens* then *focuses* the light on the receptor surface, the *retina*.

cornea

pupil, iris

18. The parts of the human eye we have identified thus far are the c_____ , the p_____ , the i_____ , and the lens, which focuses light on the retina.

enters

regulated

focuses

19. Light _____ the eye through the cornea; the amount of light is _____ by the size of the pupil opening, which is an opening in the iris. The lens then _____ the light on the receptor surface, the retina.

lens, retina

20. The _____ focuses the light on the receptor surface, the _____ .

retina

21. The lens focuses the light on the _____ , which is made up of a number of specialized cells. Two of these specialized types of cells (not shown in the drawing) are of particular interest. These are the *rods* and *cones*, which have different functions. (In the text you will find a diagram showing the rods and cones.)

22. *Rods* and *cones* are specialized cells with *different* functions and are found in the

retina

_____ .

different

23. Rods and cones, which have _____ functions, are found in the receptor surface, the retina.

rod, cone *(either order)*

24. Two specialized types of cells in the retina are _____ and _____ .

25. *Cones* are active primarily in *daylight* vision and permit us to see both *achromatic* colors (white, black, and the intermediate grays) and *chromatic* colors (red, green,

different

blue, and so on). The rods and cones are specialized cells with _____

retina

functions and are found in the _____ .

cones

26. The _____ of the retina permit us to see white, black, and the intermediate grays (the achromatic colors), and red, green, blue, and the other chromatic colors.

rods

27. The _____ , in contrast to the cones, enable us to see only *achromatic* colors. The rods function mainly in vision under *reduced* illumination, as in twilight or *night vision*.

28. The cones function in normal daylight vision, whereas the rods function under

reduced

_____ illumination, as in night vision.

29. Rods enable us to see only achromatic colors and function in vision under

reduced

_____ illumination.

daylight

30. Cones function in normal _____ vision, whereas the rods function in

night

_____ vision.

31. When you enter a dark room your eyes gradually become more sensitive to light, so that after a while you are able to see more than when you first entered. This experience is known as *light adaptation.*

adaptation

32. The experience of light _____ shows how the rods and cones differ in their functions. When you first enter a dark room, the cones in your retina become more sensitive to light. Stated another way, their absolute threshold is (*raised/lowered*).

lowered

33. After about five minutes in the dark, the sensitivity of the cones has increased as much as it will. The rods, however, continue to adapt to the dark and become appreciably more sensitive for about half an hour. You can see better after twenty minutes in the dark than after five minutes because of the functioning of the

rods

_____ .

cone

34. The _____ cells no longer increase their sensitivity to light after a few minutes

daylight

in a dark room because they function best in normal _____ vision.

rod

35. The _____ cells function in night vision and enable us to see only achromatic colors.

cones

36. In the experience of light adaptation the _____ increase their sensitivity for

rods

the first few minutes, but the _____ become increasingly more sensitive over a longer period.

37. The most sensitive portion of the eye in normal *daylight* vision is a small area of the retina called the *fovea,* on which light that comes from the center of the visual field

cone

is focused. The fovea must contain _____ cells because these function in normal daylight vision.

fovea

38. The most sensitive portion of the eye in normal daylight vision is the _____ ; it contains *only cone* cells, which are packed closely together in a small area.

Rod

_____ cells are found only *outside* the fovea.

rod

39. The portion of the retina outside the fovea contains *both* _____ and cone cells.

rod, cone *(either order)*, cone

40. Outside the fovea are _____ and _____ cells. Within the fovea are only _____

daylight

cells, which are closely packed together and function best in _____ vision.

41. Not far from the fovea, on the surface of the retina, is an insensitive area, the *blind spot,* where nerve fibers from the retinal cells come together in a bundle to form the *optic nerve,* which carries impulses from the eye to the brain. The area where

nerve

the optic _____ leaves the eye is called the blind spot because it contains neither rods nor cones.

fovea

42. The most sensitive portion of the eye in normal daylight vision is the _____ ,

blind

which contains only cone cells; the insensitive area is the _____ spot, where the nerve fibers from the cells of the retina come together in a bundle to form the

optic

_____ nerve.

43. Without looking at the earlier drawing you should be able to label the parts of the eye in the drawing presented here. Check your results with the labeled drawing of

cone

the eye. (Rod and cone cells are not shown, but you should remember that _____

fovea, rod

cells are concentrated in the _____ , whereas both _____ and

cone *(either order)*

_____ cells are found outside the fovea.)

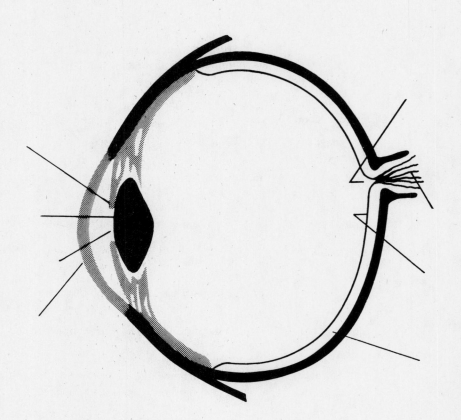

44. Let us now discuss color vision. We can produce the colors that are familiar to us in a *rainbow* by passing sunlight through a prism, which breaks it into a band of vari-

light

colored _____ .

45. When sunlight is passed through a prism, it breaks into a band of varicolored light

rainbow

that is familiar to us in the _____ . The colors correspond to *wavelengths,* the *red* end of the rainbow being produced by the *long* light waves, the *violet* end by the *short* light waves.

46. Sunlight sent through a prism produces a rainbow effect. This band of varicolored

wavelengths

light is called a *solar spectrum.* The colors correspond to _____ , the red end of the spectrum being produced by the long light waves and the violet

short

end by the _____ light waves.

47. The colors of the solar spectrum can be arranged in the form of a *color circle*. The

solar

_____ spectrum is bent back around itself to form a circle as shown below. The break in the color circle between red and violet (shown as a dashed line in the figure below) contains colors that do not appear in the solar spectrum but can be produced by mixtures of other colors. The colors *opposite* each other on the

color circle

_____ _____ are called *complementary colors*. Note that blue and yellow, red and blue-green, are found opposite each other. They are

complementary

_____ colors.

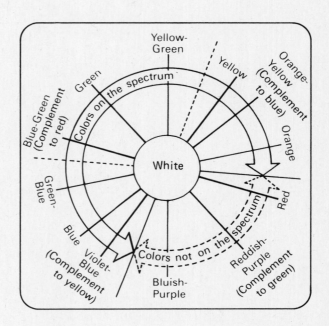

48. Blue and yellow, red and blue-green, are complementary colors, since they appear

opposite

_____ each other on the color circle. When complementary colors are mixed as *lights* (*not as pigments*), they cancel each other and will look white. *Spectral colors* (the colors of the solar spectrum) must be opposite each

color circle

other on the _____ _____ in order to be considered complementary colors.

spectral

49. The s_____ colors resemble a rainbow. When they are opposite each

complementary

other on a color circle, they are called _____ colors.

50. Green-blue and orange are complementary colors. If mixed together as *lights*, the

white

resulting color would be _____ .

51. Complementary colors are opposite each other on a color circle; when mixed to-

lights

gether as _____ , they cancel each other and appear white.

52. The combination of colored lights is called an *additive mixture.* An additive mixture of two colors that are not complementary yields a color that falls somewhere between the two on the arc of the _____ circle.

color

orange

additive

53. The additive mixture of red and yellow yields a shade of _____ .

The exact shade of color obtained with an _____ mixture will depend on the respective energy levels of the two light sources.

additive mixture

yellow

54. The _____ _____ of green and orange yields a shade of _____ .

purple

solar

55. The additive mixture of red and blue yields a shade of _____ , a color not found in the _____ spectrum.

color

56. With additive mixing, almost the entire _____ circle can be produced with just three colors.

three

additive mixture

57. Any _____ widely spaced colors on the solar spectrum can be used to provide all the other colors by _____ _____ .

58. Color television provides an example of additive mixing. Examination of the TV

three

screen with a magnifying glass will reveal that there are tiny dots of only _____ (*number*) colors (red, green, and blue). Additive mixing occurs because the dots are so close together that the eye cannot separate them, so their retinal images overlap.

59. The *complementary afterimage* is an interesting phenomenon in color perception. If you stare at a red circle and then look at a plain gray surface, you will have the experience of seeing a blue-green circle on it; that is, you experience a complementary afterimage. You recall that blue and yellow are complementary colors. Were you to stare at a yellow circle and then look at a plain gray surface, you would have

blue

the experience of seeing a _____ circle on it.

60. If you stare at a green circle and then look at a plain gray surface, you are likely to

reddish-purple

complementary

see a _____ - _____ circle on it; that is, you experience a _____ afterimage.

complementary afterimage

61. A _____ _____ is so named because after staring at a particular color, one usually sees its complementary color on a gray surface.

62. Vision is, of course, only one of several human senses. In everyday language, most

five, taste

smell *(either order)*

people speak of our having _____ senses: sight, hearing, _____ , _____ , and touch.

63. Students of psychology are expected to be more precise in defining the senses. As you will see shortly, the sense of touch is not one sensation but four. In addition, there are two special senses that provide information about body position and body movement and enable us to keep our balance. Therefore it is inaccurate to say that

senses

humans have only five _____ . (Hearing and the senses dealing with body position and movement and balance are treated in the text.)

64. Taste, smell, and the skin sensations are important in everyday life, but they do not provide us with the rich patterns and organization that vision and audition do. Vision and audition are spoken of as the "higher senses"; taste, smell, and the skin

lower   sensations are therefore thought of as the "_____ senses."

65. From an evolutionary point of view, the sense of *smell* is one of the most primitive

senses   and most important of the _____ . Smell has more direct neural pathways to the brain than any other sense.

smell   **66.** The sense of _____ has more direct neural pathways to the brain than any other sense. It plays a more important role in the life of the lower animals than in humans.

67. Psychologists have identified four primary taste qualities: *sweet, sour, salty,* and *bitter.* But most taste experience is brought about by a fusion of these qualities with other sense experiences. As you might guess, the "taste" of strong cheese is

smell   considerably affected by our sense of _____ .

taste, bitter **68.** The four primary _____ qualities are *sweet, sour, salty,* and _____ . But taste is also affected by other senses. If you were blindfolded and your nostrils

smell   were pinched together so that you could not _____, you would have trouble distinguishing between the taste of an apple and a raw potato.

TERMS AND CONCEPTS

filter _____

_____

_____

_____

specific neuron code hypothesis _____

_____

_____

_____

absolute threshold _____

_____

_____

_____

psychometric function _____

_____

_____

_____

difference threshold _____

_____

_____

_____

jnd _____

_____

_____

_____

sensitivity _____

_____

_____

single-cell recording _____

_____

_____

_____

ROC curve* _____

_____

_____

retina _____

_____

_____

_____

rod _____

_____

_____

_____

cone _____

_____

_____

_____

fovea _____

_____

_____

_____

Weber's law _____

_____

_____

_____

Fechner's law _____

_____

_____

_____

additive color mixture _____

_____

_____

complemetary colors _____

_____

_____

_____

color anomalous _____

_____

_____

*Indicates term used in Critical Discussion

hue _____

_____

_____

_____

brightness _____

_____

_____

_____

saturation _____

_____

_____

_____

four basic color sensations _____

_____

_____

_____

complementary afterimage _____

_____

_____

_____

trichromatic theory _____

_____

_____

_____

opponent-color theory _____

_____

_____

_____

two-stage color theory _____

_____

_____

spatial resolution _____

_____

_____

pattern filter _____

_____

_____

feature detectors _____

_____

_____

_____

hertz _____

_____

_____

_____

decibel _____

_____

_____

_____

cochlea _____

_____

_____

_____

place theory of pitch _____

_____

_____

_____

pitch of the missing fundamental _____

_____

_____

_____

temporal theories of pitch _____

_____

_____

_____

pheromones _____

_____

_____

gate control theory of pain _____

_____

_____

kinesthesis _____

_____

_____

1. If a subject can detect a difference in temperature of 1°C at 20°C, how small a difference can he or she detect at 60°C, according to Weber's law?
   a. 1°
   b. 2°
   c. 3°
   d. 4°

2. The color solid simultaneously represents _____.
   a. hue, amplitude, and brightness
   b. saturation, intensity, and brightness
   c. purity, amplitude, and intensity
   d. hue, brightness, and saturation

3. When complementary colors are mixed together properly, they yield
   a. a primary color
   b. a psychological primary
   c. white
   d. colors not found in the spectrum

4. The _____ is the minimum physical energy necessary to activate a given sensory system.
   a. difference threshold
   b. absolute threshold
   c. psychometric function
   d. stimulus intensity

5. Sound is a function of pressure changes in the air that can be represented as waves. In such a wave
   a. amplitude refers to the amount of compression and expansion of the air
   b. frequency is measured in the number of vibration cycles per minute
   c. amplitude is measured in Hertz
   d. frequency is shown by the amount by which the wave is displaced above or below the baseline

6. Since the cells identified by Hubel and Wiesel are tuned to specific aspects of a stimulus, they are often referred to as
   a. cell recorders
   b. feature detectors
   c. visual receptors
   d. pattern-recognition factors

7. Three appropriately spaced colors on the color circle may be mixed to produce
   a. white
   b. neutral gray
   c. black
   d. almost any color

8. Which of the following is *not* one of the relationships shown on the color solid?
   a. Hue is represented by points along the radius.
   b. Brightness ranges from white at the top to black at the bottom.
   c. Hue is represented by points around the circumference.
   d. Saturation varies from highly saturated on the outside to gray in the center.

9. Weber's law relates the _____ to the _____ required for a just noticeable difference.
   a. absolute threshold, difference threshold
   b. initial stimulation, incremental stimulation
   c. Fechner scale, absolute threshold
   d. absolute threshold, psychophysical function

10. The _____ represent(s) the final stage in the process by which the ear turns air pressure changes into neutral impulses.
    a. organ of Corti
    b. basilar membrane
    c. hair cells of the organ of Corti
    d. cochlea

11. A complex cell in the visual cortex responds to
    a. a particular shape, such as a square or circle
    b. a line at a particular angle in a particular location in the visual field
    c. a line at any angle in the visual field
    d. a line at a particular angle over a fairly broad area of the visual field

12. The trichromatic theory of color vision is based on the
    a. concept of psychological primaries
    b. discovery of pigment primaries
    c. notion that there are three different kinds of color receptors
    d. concept of complementary primaries

13. The _____ threshold is defined in terms of the minimum difference in stimulation necessary to tell two stimuli apart, i.e., the _____.
    a. absolute, crucial stimulus change
    b. difference, barely detectable change
    c. absolute, minimal stimulus difference
    d. difference, just noticeable difference

14. Our skin provides us with a sensation of "hot" when
    a. specific "hot" nerve-end structures in the skin are stimulated
    b. "warm" and "cold" skin receptors are stimulated simultaneously

c. skin receptors for "warm" are stimulated beyond the intermediate threshold

d. "warm" and "pain" skin receptors are stimulated simultaneously

_____15. The _____ plots the percentage of "yes" responses against a measure of the physical energy of the stimulus source.
a. absolute threshold curve
b. difference threshold curve
c. psychometric function
d. threshold function

_____16. The place theory of pitch perception focuses on the _____ , whereas temporal theories focus on the _____ .
a. nervous impulse; organ of Corti
b. basilar membrane; auditory nerve
c. location of the tone; source of the tone
d. auditory cortex; temporal lobe

_____17. Feedback about the position of our body parts as we walk and climb is provided by the _____ sense.
a. equilibratory
b. vestibular
c. kinesthetic
d. otolithic

_____18. If an image is projected onto the retina in such a way that the same cells continue to be stimulated, the image begins to
a. seem unfamiliar
b. quiver and oscillate in small movements
c. fade and disappear
d. change color

_____19. The colors opposite each other on the color circle will be
a. of the same wavelength or multiples of that wavelength
b. complementary colors
c. additive
d. subtractive

_____20. After a few minutes in a dark room we can see better than when we first entered because the
a. rods have adapted
b. rods and cones have elongated
c. cones have adapted
d. bipolar cells have adapted

KEY TO SELF-QUIZ

20. c	15. c	10. c	5. a
19. b	14. b	9. b	4. b
18. c	13. d	8. a	3. c
17. c	12. c	7. d	2. d
16. b	11. d	6. b	1. c

INDIVIDUAL EXERCISES

SEEING AND NOT SEEING

Introduction

There are several procedures that can help you experience aspects of your visual system not normally noticed. The text describes the eye in detail, but it is sometimes hard to relate that description to your own experience. Exercises such as the following, as well as those in the text, can help you really "see" what is happening.

A. Phosphenes

First note that your eyes are sensitive to more than light. If you apply gentle pressure to them, with the lids closed, you will "see" patterns of color, called "phosphenes." These result when the eye translates pressure into a visual experience.

B. Fundus

Next, consider that light, the usual stimulus for the eyes, has to travel through a series of eye tissues and fluids before it is registered by the rods and cones. Normally you do not see the portions of the eye through which the light must pass, because they remain in a fixed location with respect to the retina. As noted in the discussion of stabilized vision in the text, anything not moving with respect to the retina is not seen. The network of blood vessels in the eye, however, can sometimes be noticed as a pattern of fine flickering movement when an exceptionally strong pulse causes the vessels to expand rhythmically. Light must pass through this network of blood vessels lying on the inside surface of the eye before reaching the photoreceptors (rods and cones).

This network of blood vessels, called the "fundus," can be seen more directly with the aid of a flashlight. Cover the end of the flashlight with a piece of aluminum foil and punch a 1/8" hole in it to provide a small beam of light. Go into a dark room and shine this beam into one eye at an angle, holding the flashlight directly under the eye just above the chin and aiming the beam toward the top of your head; you will probably have to experiment with the angle in order to get the proper result. Look straight ahead and move the flashlight around slightly. What you will see is a pattern of lines on a glowing reddish background, rather like the veining in a leaf; this is the fundus.

C. A Familiar Sight Not Normally Seen

Another portion of your anatomy, also rarely "seen," is much more obvious than the fundus. If you think about it as you read, you will discover that you can see not only this workbook but also a view of each side of your nose. The invisibility of your nose depends on sensory adaptation. You are so used to views of your nose accompanying every scene that you no longer notice them. (If you now have trouble *not* noticing them, don't worry about it; as you turn your attention to other activities, your nose will resume its customary place in the scheme of things.)

D. A Familiar Lack of Sight Not Normally Noticed

Just as you do not normally see your nose, so do you not normally miss what you do not see in the blind spot of each eye. The illustration on page 155 of your text shows you how to locate your blind spots. (For the right eye, you can reverse the description given in the text. Close your left eye and stare at the spot; the cross will disappear.) It's even more instructive to take the example further and show how objects, even people, disappear as well. Try a simple object first. After you have made the dot disappear, as instructed on page 155, hold that position and slide your pencil across the book so that the eraser moves over the dot and thus into the blind spot. The eraser should also disappear. Notice that you do not *perceive* a hole or blank spot; you just do not see the eraser.

With a little practice, you can achieve the same effect in the real world. Remember that the blind spot is a few degrees to the outside of the fovea, that is, your point of gaze; this is a little more than the width of your outstretched hand. With your right eye closed, a small object about a hand's width to the left of your direct gaze is not seen. Thus if you point your gaze about that far to the right of someone's face as you look at them (with your right eye closed, remember), you should be able to decapitate them, so to speak. A person across a table is about the proper distance; at that range you can get clothes, a ring of hair, and nothing in the middle. This exercise is not only useful as a perceptual demonstration; it's a great time killer if you are trapped at a boring lecture.

E. Seeing Color

Surprisingly, people often do not know that they are colorblind. We are not normally aware of how we learn to label colors or of how color constancy works to keep our perception of colors stable. A familiar object appears to be the same color regardless of the light conditions under which we view it. But it is possible to overcome the effects of color constancy. Pick something you know the color of very well—your car, some item of clothing, and so on. Then look at it in various light conditions—from brilliant sun to as dark as you can still see at all. If you try to look at the object as if you and it were completely new to the world, you may be able to overcome the color constancy effect and see how different its color appears under differing conditions. (Note that you will be able to observe these differences much more easily for a friend's object and vice versa, since the constancy will not be as strong for an unfamiliar object.)

You can also experiment with color constancy by wearing tinted glasses. One aspect of looking at the world through rose-colored glasses is that after a while you adapt, and it tends to look like the same old world. Try some of the brilliant lenses available in department stores—green, orange, violet, or even rose—the ones apparently designed more to be looked *at* than to look through. You will find that at first everything seems brighter than usual, and colors appear peculiar. But if you wear the glasses for a while, the world will seem more normal—as if you had been born with this particular kind of vision. You will still be able to name most colors appropriately, although a careful test will show some problems—just as it does with those who are colorblind from birth. One final experience awaits you, however. When you take the glasses off, the world will seem unusually drab for a time; your innate tendency to compensate for changes in visual stimulation will overcompensate when the lenses are first removed. Mercifully, your visual adaptation system will soon have things normal again.

F. The Importance of Vision

Finally, give a moment's thought to the extent to which sight dominates our lives. If you have never had a blind friend, imagine now that you do and think about trying to explain something to him or her. Whether your explanation concerns people, cars, clothes, schoolwork, how to get somewhere, or whatever, you will be surprised to discover the extent to which you rely on vision and think in visual terms.

You may even wish to try the exercise, developed by sensory-awareness groups, of being "blind for a day" and being led about by someone as you concentrate on your other senses. (Remember if you attempt this exercise that you are still thinking in visual terms—something the congenitally blind cannot do.)

As a last way of noting the extent to which sight, when not blocked off, overrides the other senses, think about where the sound comes from in a movie or TV. Obviously, it actually comes from the speaker(s), which are often discriminably separated from the picture. But equally obvious, the sound *seems* to be located in the visually apparent source, for example, the moving mouth on the screen. Similarly, a ventriloquist does not "throw" his or her voice. The ventriloquist simply provides cues, such as different voice and movement of the dummy. *You* "throw" the voice to the dummy.

When some other sense conflicts with vision, it is almost always vision that prevails. The same phenomenon causes airplane pilots many problems because they tend to attempt to align the aircraft visually, even in the face of evidence and training to the contrary.

6
Perceiving

LEARNING OBJECTIVES

6-1. Be able to discuss the theoretical positions of the structuralists, Helmholtz, and the Gestalt psychologists in their respective analyses of perception.

6-2. Understand the distinction between perceptual organization and perceptual integration. Be prepared to give examples of both phenomena.

6-3. Be able to list and to describe various monocular and binocular cues for the perception of distance.

6-4. Know what is meant by stroboscopic motion. Be able to review evidence from both psychophysical and single-cell experiments that supports the idea of motion filters in our sensory system.

6-5. Be able to show, with examples, how each of the five perceptual constancies contributes to our perception of stable wholes. Be familiar with perceptual illusions and two mechanisms that have been proposed to explain them.

6-6. Be familiar with pandemonium theory and the steps it postulates in the recognition of an object. Understand the distinction between parallel and serial processing.

6-7. Be able to discuss, with examples, the effects of context expectations, and motives on perception. Be able to describe the process of selective attention as it influences perception.

6-8. Be familiar with research on the type of eye movements a person makes while reading. Understand the implications of this research for speed reading and skimming.

6-9. Be able to discuss the nativist and empiricist views of perception, presenting relevant evidence from several areas of research.

6-10. Be able to define three types of ESP plus PK. Be familiar with how these are investigated in the laboratory, as well as the reasons why many psychologists are skeptical of the results.

threshold

1. In the last chapter we were concerned with simple tasks such as detecting a flash of light or measuring the difference _____ between two tones. In this chapter we are concerned with more complex tasks such as judging size and distance and identifying objects and events. These tasks involve more complex stimuli which evoke more complex experiences that we call *percepts*.

percept

2. The processes that give rise to a _____ are the focus of this chapter. One such process involves *perceptual organization*. The process by which *elements*, or parts, of a stimulus are organized into a percept is called perceptual

organization

_____ .

ground

figure-ground

3. An example of perceptual organization is the *figure-ground relationship*. If a stimulus contains two or more regions, we usually see part of it as a figure and the rest as _____ . The perceptual organization of figure and ground constitutes the _____ – _____ relationship.

figure

4. When we look at a picture of a woman standing on a beach with the ocean behind her, the woman is the _____ and the ocean is the ground.

elements (*or* parts)

5. The significance of perceptual organization in producing a perceptual experience was recognized by proponents of *Gestalt psychology*, a school of psychology that developed in Germany early in the 20th century. Gestalt is a German word that has no exact English translation, though "form," "configuration," or "pattern" comes close. The word helps to emphasize that the whole affects the way in which the elements, or parts, of a stimulus are perceived; perception acts to draw the _____ together into a holistic pattern, or Gestalt.

percept

6. A principle of perceptual organization proposed by Gestalt psychologists is the *law of simplicity: the percept corresponds to the simplest possible interpretation of the stimulus.* This law asserts that the perceptual processes are organized to generate a _____ that provides the simplest possible explanation for the array of elements that make up the stimulus input.

law

Gestalt

percept

7. The _____ of simplicity is one of several principles of perceptual organization advanced by _____ psychologists. These principles are concerned with explaining how the perceptual system takes a complex stimulus input and transforms it into a particular _____ .

perceptual

three

8. Distance perception is another example of _____ organization. Early perceptual theorists had difficulty explaining distance perception because they tended to think of the percept as corresponding to the retinal image.

The surface of the retina has only two dimensions, yet we perceive in _____ (*number*) dimensions. Gradually it was discovered that a visual stimulus includes *distance cues* that can be used by the perceiver to infer distance.

two	**9.** The stimulus is represented on the retina in _____ (*number*) dimensions, but
distance	it contains _____ cues that can be used to generate a percept
three	with depth and distance. In other words, a percept in _____ (*number*)
	dimensions.
	10. There are a number of distance cues that combine in complex ways to determine
	perceived distance. They can be classified as *monocular* or *binocular* depending
both	on whether they involve one eye or _____ eyes.
	11. Having two eyes adds to the richness of distance perception, but a person with
monocular	only one eye can still use _____ cues to determine the
	distance of an object. For example, if one object cuts off the view of another, we
	infer that the first object is nearer. Since we can make this observation with only
monocular distance cue	one eye, it is a _____ _____ _____ .
	Let us consider a second example of a monocular distance cue.
	12. If an image contains an array of similar but different sized objects, a person will
	interpret the objects as being at different distances, with the smaller images seen
	as being further away. The fact that objects decrease in size with distance is another
distance	cue that a person with only one eye can use to estimate _____ .
	13. Thus we see that there are many cues that can be used to infer the distance
	of an object. Some of these require the use of only one eye; these are called
monocular	_____ distance cues. Others require the use of both eyes;
	these are called binocular cues.
	14. When we judge the distance of an object, we generally depend upon both
monocular, binocular	_____ and _____ cues.
(*either order*)	
	15. When you look at a silver dollar held at eye level, the pattern of stimuli impinging
	on your eyes is quite different from the pattern produced by the same coin lying on
	a table. In both instances, however, you perceive the shape of the coin as round. In
shape	other words, the _____ of the coin is perceived as *constant* regardless
	of the viewing angle.
	16. Similarly, we tend to perceive an object as having a *constant* lightness regardless
	of the degree of illumination on it. A baseball is perceived as just as white whether
	it is lying in the bright sunlight or in the shade of a tree. That is, the baseball is
constant	perceived as having a _____ lightness.
	17. The color of a familiar object does not appear to change with changes in illumi-
	nation. The owner of a blue car sees it as blue whether looking at it in bright sun-
	light, in dim illumination, or under a yellow street light. Its color is perceived as
constant	_____ .
	18. The tendency to perceive objects as the same regardless of changes in the con-
	ditions of perception is called *perceptual constancy*. We recognize a tin can as
	being cylindrical regardless of its position. This is an example of perceptual
constancy	_____ .

19. The fact that we perceive an object as being of a certain lightness or color even
when the illumination is changed is another illustration of _____

perceptual
constancy
_____ .

20. A closed door is rectangular in shape, but as it swings toward you its shape goes
through a series of distortions. When the door is partially open, it is actually a
trapezoid, in terms of the pattern of stimulation on the retina. When it is completely open, we see only a vertical line the thickness of the door. Although we can
easily distinguish these changes, what we perceive is an unchanging door swinging
on its hinges. The fact that you perceive the door as a rectangle regardless of its

perceptual constancy
position is an illustration of _____ _____ .

21. Psychologists distinguish among several kinds of perceptual constancy. For example, the tendency to perceive objects as the same *shape,* regardless of the viewing

shape
angle, is known as _____ constancy.

22. When we see a man close to us, we may recognize that he is about 6 feet tall. If we
perceive this same man at a distance of 100 yards, the image on the retina is much
smaller than it was when he was right next to us. Still we perceive him as being

size
approximately the same *size,* 6 feet tall. This is an example of _____
constancy.

23. We perceive a tin can as being cylindrical, regardless of its position because of

shape
_____ constancy.

24. We perceive a fence post at the end of the block as being as tall as the one next to

size
us because of _____ constancy.

25. The fact that a piece of black velvet looks just as dark whether it is viewed in the

lightness
sun or in the shade is an example of _____ constancy.

26. The fact that an orange is perceived as orange even when the conditions of illumina-

color
tion change is an example of _____ constancy.

constancy
27. Another kind of perceptual _____ is *location* constancy.
Even though the stimuli impinging on our eyes change rapidly as we move about, we
perceive objects as maintaining a fixed location.

28. The tendency to perceive objects as being in a fixed location, regardless of con-

location
tinual changes in stimulation, is known as _____ constancy.

29. When we speak of perceptual constancy, then, we are speaking about the tendency

constant
to perceive objects as _____ regardless of alterations in illumination, viewing angle, distance, or other conditions of perception.

30. The general name given to the tendency to perceive objects as the same regardless

perceptual
of changes in the conditions of perception is _____

constancy
_____ .

31. We have examined five kinds of perceptual constancy: _____ ,

_____ , _____ , _____ , and _____ constancy.

32. The perceptual constancies suggest that our perceptions are organized in some way. In certain situations, that process of organization can lead to false or distorted percepts, called *perceptual illusions*. Geometrical illusions constitute one class of

geometrical

perceptual illusions. You are probably familiar with _____

illusions

_____ like those below.

33. For the figure on the left, the top horizontal line looks longer than the bottom one, although both are actually the same size. The same is true for the figure in the middle; the two horizontal lines are identical in length. For the figure on the right, the line that projects through the two vertical lines is actually straight, though it

illusions

appears staggered. These figures are examples of perceptual _____ .

34. These illusions are based on a false interpretation of certain cues in the image. The illusion on the left is a good example. The two horizontal lines are equal in length, but the slanted lines on each side provide a distance cue that indicates that the upper part of the figure is farther away than the lower part. This distance cue is

larger

integrated with the image size of the upper line to make it appear _____ .

35. In this case, the distance cue leads us to unconsciously lengthen the upper horizon-

percept

tal line, thereby generating a peceptual illusion. A false or distorted _____ is called a perceptual illusion.

36. Most of the time we are bombarded with many stimuli. We are unable to perceive all of them. Some of them intrude on our consciousness no matter what we do, but, within limits we are able to select what we perceive. The process by which we

select

_____ is called *selective attention*.

37. Usually what we select depends on what is important to us at the moment. As you read you are probably unaware of the tightness of your shoes or sounds coming from outside the building. Your unawareness of these stimuli illustrates the process

selective

of _____ attention.

38. Another aspect of selective attention becomes apparent when a person is given time to look at a picture or scene. If we watch the eyes of someone doing this, it is evident that the eyes are not stationary. The eyes are still for a brief period, then jump

jump

to another position, are still for another brief period, then _____ again, and so on. The periods during which the eyes are still are called *fixations* and the quick, almost instantaneous movements between fixations are called *saccades* ("saccade" is French for jump).

saccades

39. Perception occurs only during fixations and not during the jumps, or _____. The points of a picture on which the eyes fixate are not random; rather the

fixations

_____ are on features of the picture that are most informative. The selective nature of these fixations is yet another example of selective attention.

40. As adults, we know that we are capable of certain kinds of visual perception. But disagreements remain over whether our abilities to perceive aspects of our environment are learned or whether we are born with them. Those who support the role of learning are called *empiricists*. Those who maintain that we are born with the ability to perceive the way we do are called *nativists*. If one argues that the perceptual constancies must be learned, he or she is supporting the viewpoint of the

empiricists

_____ .

41. The empiricists feel that we have to learn to perceive the world in the way that we

nativists

do. The _____ , on the other hand, argue that this ability is innate.

42. Most psychologists today agree that practice and experience play a vital role in determining what we perceive. In other words, they emphasize the importance of

empiricists

learning in perception. This is the position of the _____ . The question that remains is whether we are born with some ability to perceive the world or whether it is all learned.

43. When (by the removal of cataracts) vision is given to people who have been blind all their lives, they cannot distinguish a square from a triangle or tell which of two sticks is longer without feeling them. This evidence supports the role of

learning

_____ in perception.

44. On the other hand, as you will see in the text, there is evidence that certain perceptual processes are innate and intact at birth. These innate processes tend to be at

nativist

lower levels in the perceptual system. Thus, the _____ viewpoint is not wrong.

45. Is perception innate or learned? The answer is some of each. The evidence indicates that we are born with considerable perceptual capacity which is shaped and developed by learning. One way to conceptualize this joint role of heredity and learning is that the lowest levels in the perceptual system are intact at birth and the higher

learning

levels develop as a result of _____ .

46. When we discuss perception, we are usually speaking of *sensory perception*, that is,

senses

perception that takes place through the _____ . It has been suggested that there may be perceptions that do not require any sense-organ stimulation. These phenomena have been called *extrasensory perception* (ESP).

47. Research on extrasensory perception has been carried on for a number of years. Although some psychologists believe that the evidence for the existence of certain

extrasensory

forms of _____ perception is indisputable, most remain unconvinced.

49. There are several different phenomena classified as ESP. *Telepathy* means the transference of thought from one person to another. In more familiar terms,

telepathy

_____ is the word for "mind reading."

50. A person who claims to be able to transmit thoughts across a distance to another

telepathy

person is maintaining that _____ exists. Of course, one who claims to be able to receive such thoughts also supports the existence of this phenomenon.

51. One of the most common types of research in ESP is based on experiments in card guessing. The experimenter may ask the subject to guess the symbol on a card that is in a sealed envelope. No one knows what card it is. The ability of the subject to perceive the card is called *clairvoyance*. At times, one may not be sure whether telepathy or clairvoyance is at work. If someone else knows, for instance, what the

clairvoyance

card is, then the subject might be perceiving the card directly (_____)

telepathy

or might be reading the thoughts of the person who knows (_____).

52. Another kind of ESP is *precognition*, or the perception of a future event. For a

precognition

person who bets on horse races, _____ would seem to be the most valuable kind of ESP.

53. The phenomena of ESP are discussed under a number of classifications:

telepathy

a. Thought transference from one person to another, or _____ .

precognition

b. The perception of a future event, or _____ .

c. The perception of an object or event that is not influencing the senses, or

clairvoyance

_____ .

54. A related phenomenon has to do with the influence of a mental operation over a material body or an energy system—for example, the idea that wishing for a given number affects the number that will come up in a throw of dice. This is called *psychokinesis*. If you can move a vase on your desk by merely willing it to move,

psychokinesis

you are demonstrating the operation of _____ .

55. A person who feels that he or she is a better roulette player than others is (unless

psychokinesis

cheating) operating with some belief in _____ .

TERMS AND CONCEPTS

percept _____

_____

_____

_____

structuralists _____

_____

_____

_____

unconscious inference _____

_____

_____

_____

Gestalt psychology _____

_____

_____

_____

perceptual organization _____

_____

_____

_____

perceptual integration _____

_____

_____

figure-ground _____

_____

_____

egocentric distance _____

_____

_____

_____

relative distance _____

_____

_____

_____

binocular parallax _____

_____

_____

_____

binocular disparity _____

_____

_____

_____

stroboscopic motion _____

_____

_____

_____

selective adaptation _____

_____

_____

_____

perceptual constancy _____

_____

_____

_____

lightness constancy _____

_____

_____

color constancy _____

_____

_____

_____

*Indicates term used in Critical Discussion

shape constancy _____

_____

_____

_____

size constancy _____

_____

_____

_____

location constancy _____

_____

_____

_____

geometrical illusion _____

_____

_____

_____

pattern filter _____

_____

_____

_____

size-distance invariance principle* _____

_____

_____

_____

recognition _____

_____

_____

_____

pandemonium theory _____

_____

_____

_____

parallel processing _____

_____

_____

_____

feature list _____

_____

_____

_____

serial processing _____

_____

_____

_____

schema _____

_____

_____

_____

ambiguous stimulus _____

_____

_____

_____

orienting reflex _____

_____

_____

_____

selective attention _____

_____

_____

_____

saccade _____

_____

_____

_____

attentional set _____

_____

_____

_____

preferential looking method _____

_____

_____

_____

*Indicates term used in Critical Discussion

critical period _____

_____

_____

_____

parapsychological phenomena _____

_____

_____

_____

extrasensory perception _____

_____

_____

_____

telepathy _____

_____

_____

_____

clairvoyance _____

_____

_____

_____

precognition _____

_____

_____

_____

psychokinesis _____

_____

_____

_____

SELF-QUIZ

_____ 1. When we judge the color of an object, we do so on the basis of
- a. wavelength of the light being reflected
- b. information about the color of surrounding objects
- c. information about the nature of the illuminating light
- d. all of the above

_____ 2. Apparently, early exposure to a certain amount of light stimulation is important for
- a. learning figure-ground perception
- b. normal neural development
- c. innate visual ability
- d. color discrimination

_____ 3. Lightness constancy
- a. allows us to adjust our muscles when we pick up large light objects
- b. helps us judge the size of the object independent of its retinal image
- c. depends on the relationships among the intensities of light reflected from different objects
- d. requires intense concentration to distinguish it from other constancies

_____ 4. If one could influence the numbers turning up on dice by thinking about them, this would be an example of
- a. clairvoyance
- b. psychokinesis
- c. telepathy
- d. precognition

_____ 5. The ability to focus on stimuli in which we are interested while resisting distracting stimuli is called
- a. concentrated attending
- b. stimulus focusing
- c. structured perceiving
- d. selective attention

_____ 6. The retinal image of an object
- a. increases as the distance between the object and the eye increases
- b. is a compromise between the object's real size and its perceived size
- c. decreases as the object is moved away from the eye
- d. is constant and independent of the object's distance

_____ 7. Monocular cues that an artist may use to give depth to a picture include
- a. placing distant objects higher in the picture
- b. making the "grain," or texture gradient, finer as distance decreases
- c. making nearer objects smaller
- d. all of the above

_____ 8. When subjects read fairly difficult material, monitoring eye movements indicates
- a. that groups of 4 to 5 words are fixated at a time
- b. that almost every word is fixated
- c. that saccade time and fixation time are about equal
- d. that the eyes move smoothly across the line of text

_____ 9. The view that we are born with the ability to perceive the way we do is held by
- a. sensory psychologists
- b. nativists
- c. empiricists
- d. most contemporary psychologists

_____ 10. Gestalt psychologists are interested primarily in the
- a. tendency to perceive holistic patterns
- b. superiority of auditory perception
- c. tendency to perceive detached sensory features
- d. theory that the whole is the same as its parts

_____ 11. A person with vision in only one eye _cannot_ see
- a. spatial relationships
- b. three-dimensional configurations
- c. well in dim light conditions
- d. with stereoscopic vision

_____ 12. Helmholtz proposed that a percept is arrived at by a process of inference of which the perceiver is unaware. Helmholtz referred to this process as
- a. visual extraction
- b. feature detection
- c. retinal sensitization
- d. unconscious inference

_____ 13. The perceptual constancies (for example, size, shape, and location constancy) suggest that perception
- a. is oriented toward constant sensory features

b. is oriented toward things rather than sensory features

c. is based on one constancy per sensory feature

d. provides constant-feature inputs that must be further integrated

_____14. Schema is

a. the singular of schemata

b. another term for a feature list

c. a concept used in pattern recognition models

d. all of the above

_____15. In research investigating the effects of experience on visual development, some kittens were raised with visual exposure only to vertical stripes. Subsequent testing showed that these kittens

a. had deteriorated retinas

b. were essentially blind to horizontal stripes

c. had difficulty discriminating forms

d. had essentially normal vision

_____16. A percept that is erroneous because it differs from the state of affairs described by physical science with the aid of measurements is called a(n)

a. delusion

b. illusion

c. saccade

d. location constant

_____17. What is the law of simplicity?

a. The whole is more than the sum of the parts.

b. The percept corresponds to the simplest possible interpretation of the stimulus.

c. The simplest illusions are based on violations of visual constancy.

d. Simple material can be read faster than complex material.

_____18. A movie of someone climbing a mountain is an example of

a. stroboscopic motion

b. the law of simplicity

c. real motion

d. induced movement

_____19. Saccade refers to

a. the smooth movement of the eyes as they scan a perceptual field

b. a type of body rhythm associated with the sleep cycle

c. the quick, almost instantaneous, movement of the eyes

d. a jump in the EEG associated with selective attention

_____20. Which of the following makes use of the fact that each eye sees a slightly different view?

a. sequentially flashing lights on a theater marquee

b. a stereoscope

c. motion picture film

d. the Necker cube

KEY TO SELF-QUIZ

20. b	15. b	10. a	5. d
19. c	14. d	9. b	4. b
18. a	13. b	8. b	3. c
17. b	12. d	7. a	2. b
16. b	11. d	6. c	1. d

CLASS EXERCISE

EXTRASENSORY PERCEPTION

Introduction

Extrasensory perception is a controversial topic in psychology. Many psychologists doubt that it is possible to transfer thoughts from one person to another without any physical intermediary. Others claim that thought transference—a form of ESP known as telepathy—has been adequately demonstrated in the laboratory. This exercise is similar to some laboratory experiments that have been conducted to demonstrate the existence of telepathy. The procedure has been simplified, however, to avoid the necessity of elaborate statistical analysis.

Equipment Needed

Any familiar coin and a screen to shield the "sender" from view of the class.

Procedure

The instructor will select from the class someone who feels that he or she might be a good "sender of thoughts." The sender will sit behind a screen and toss the coin for ten separate trials, each time concentrating on the side of the coin that faces up (heads or tails) and trying to transfer this image to the class, which will act as subjects. One student will observe the sender and record the results of each toss. It is best if the sender shakes the coin in a glass or cup and then inverts the container to deposit the coin on a flat surface.

The instructor will start each trial by saying the word "now"; the sender will toss the coin and concentrate on the upturned image; the instructor will say "receive," and the students will try to concentrate on the image being sent; when the instructor says "record," students will write by the proper trial number the word "heads" or "tails," depending on the image they feel they have received.

Treatment of Data

On the basis of chance we would expect five heads and five tails from ten coin tosses. And if subjects' guesses were based on chance alone, rather than ESP, we would expect them to be correct on five out of ten guesses—or 50 percent of the time. With only ten trials we would expect considerable chance variation from the 50/50 results. Many more trials would be required before chance effects would become insignificant. But our experiment should give us a rough approximation.

The instructor will read the results of the ten trials so that you can score your guesses. He or she will then determine by a show of hands the number of students obtaining one correct guess, two correct guesses, and so on. How many students had results that were below chance level? How many above chance level? How many exactly at chance level? What do you think the results demonstrate concerning the possibility of ESP?

The instructor will now select the three students with the lowest number of correct guesses and the three with the highest number and repeat the experiment with the same sender and these students.

Questions for Discussion

1. Are the students who were good receivers in the first part of the experiment still scoring above chance for the second ten trials? Are the students who were initially poor receivers still poor?

2. How do these results affect your interpretation of the findings from the first experiment?

3. What additional controls would you want to see enforced to make this a better ESP experiment?

INDIVIDUAL EXERCISES

STROBOSCOPIC MOTION

This drawing illustrates stroboscopic motion. Hold your hand in either position and alternately close your right and left eyes. While actually seen in a stationary position, your index finger appears to move. Thus you get a perception of motion without a moving stimulus.

Why does this occur? Can you think of an industry that depends on this same phenomenon?

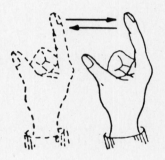

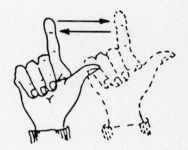

PERCEPTUAL REORGANIZATION

Look at the figure shown on the following page and try to figure out what the next one in the sequence would be like and why. Do not read further until you have done so.

If you decide you do not know, look again at the figures, using this clue: Look only at the right half of each figure. Now you should experience the shock of perceptual reorganization as the figures suddenly make sense.

Now that this perceptual hypothesis has been confirmed and "locked in," notice something else. It is probably not possible for you to now see them as the mysterious, complex figures they were before. They are now irreversibly obvious to you, so much so that if you show them to friends who have not seen them before, you will find it hard to understand why they are not immediately and glaringly obvious. It is this organizing of visual images into perceptions that is both useful to us and inhibitory—useful in quickly sorting the world for us, inhibitory in keeping us from seeing things "with a fresh eye," as in art or problem solving.

AFTEREFFECTS OF MOTION

Cut out the spiral disk on the next page and paste it on a piece of cardboard. Attach it with a thumbtack to the end of a pencil. Spin the disk slowly and stare steadily at it as it moves. Stop the disk and notice what happens. Does it seem to be turning in the opposite direction? If you were turning the disk so that the spiral was expanding, it will seem to contract when stopped, and vice versa. When the spiral is turning steadily, our visual system tends to suppress the perceived motion, apparently by generating some sort of opposing process. When the actual movement stops, the opposing process continues for a while, and you see it as apparent motion in the opposite direction.

Now look at the spiral again as it spins slowly, then turn to look at a blank wall or a picture. The opposing process will make even the wall or picture appear to move in the opposite direction to the direction of the spiral's movement. The process is not limited to spirals but appears to occur for any motion in the visual field.

You may have noticed a similar effect in nature. If you look steadily at a waterfall or a flowing river for a while and then transfer your gaze to the rocks beside the falls or the river bank, whatever you are looking at appears to move in the opposite direction from the flow of water.

7
Learning and Conditioning

LEARNING OBJECTIVES

7-1. Be able to explain what is meant by the term associative learning. Know the distinction between the two forms of associative learning—namely, classical conditioning and operant conditioning.

7-2. Be familiar with Pavlov's experiments. Be able to define, and to differentiate between, the UCR, the CS, and the UCS. Know how these are related during both the acquisition and extinction of a classically conditioned response.

7-3. Know how generalization and discrimination function in classical conditioning. Be able to give examples of each in human learning. Be familiar with the role of temporal contiguity and predictability in establishing a conditioned response.

7-4. Be prepared to discuss the law of effect in relation to operant conditioning. Be familiar with the "Skinner box" and be able to define extinction and discrimination for operant conditioning in this apparatus. Know two measures of operant strength.

7-5. Be familiar with research on the operant conditioning of autonomic responses. Know how behavior can be shaped and why this is an important advantage of operant conditioning over classical conditioning.

7-6. Be able to define partial reinforcement and provide an explanation of the partial-reinforcement effect.

7-7. Be prepared to discuss the nature of reinforcement, including a discussion of conditioned reinforcement and punishment.

7-8. Be familiar with Premack's principle as an explanation of the effect of reinforcement. Be able to cite examples of a reinforcement hierarchy.

7-9. Be familiar with the ethologists' objections to a behavioristic approach to learning, and their notion of behavioral constraints. Know why experiments on taste aversion are critical to an ethological analysis of learning.

7-10. Be familiar with the evidence the cognitivists cite in their challenge to the behavioristic approach to learning. Know what is meant by the term mental representation and the role it plays in a cognitive analysis of learning.

1. One of the most basic forms of learning is called *associative learning*; it involves

association   making a new connection, or as_____ , between events in the environment.

2. Associative _____ involves making a new association between events

learning   in the environment. Psychologists distinguish between two forms of associative learning: *classical conditioning* and *operant conditioning*.

3. In classical _____ the organism learns that two *stimuli* tend

conditioning   to go together. For example, a baby learns that the sight of a nursing bottle (one

stimulus   stimulus) is associated with the taste of milk (another _____).

4. A child learns that the sound of a tinkling bell is associated with the appearance

classical   of the ice cream truck. This is another example of _____ conditioning.

5. In classical conditioning the organism learns that two _____ tend to

stimuli   go together.

6. In operant _____ the organism learns that some *response* it

conditioning   makes leads to a particular *consequence*. For example, a baby learns that raising a bottle to his or her mouth (the response) brings milk (the consequence).

7. A toddler learns that putting a hand in the flame of a candle (the response) brings

conditioning   pain (the consequence). This is an example of operant _____ .

8. Learning an association between two stimuli is called _____ condi-

classical   tioning. Learning an association between a response and its consequences is called

operant, associative   _____ conditioning. Both are forms of _____ learning.

9. The method of classical conditioning, in which a new association is made between

stimuli   two _____ , is illustrated by the diagram on the following page. To understand the diagram, let's discuss the laboratory arrangement used by Pavlov to study classical conditioning. A dog is placed in a harness and a device attached to its cheek to measure salivary flow; meat powder can be delivered to a pan in front of the dog by remote control. A light is turned on, and a few seconds later meat powder is delivered to the pan. The dog eats, and the recording device measures copious salivation. After this procedure has been repeated a number of times, the experimenter turns on the light without delivering meat powder. The dog salivates

food (*or* meat powder)   nevertheless. The animal has learned to associate the light with _____ .

10. The dog will salivate the first time that meat powder is placed on its tongue, even if the animal has never been exposed to meat powder before. Because salivation to meat powder does not depend on learning, or conditioning, it is called an *unconditioned response* (UCR). We call a response that does not depend on learning a(n)

unconditioned   _____ response.

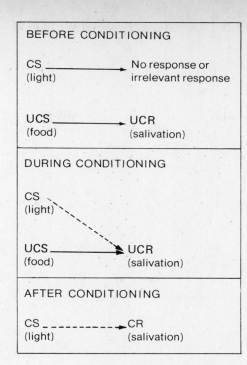

BEFORE CONDITIONING

CS ————————→ No response or
(light)   irrelevant response

UCS ————————→ UCR
(food)   (salivation)

DURING CONDITIONING

CS
(light)
        ⟍
          ⟍
UCS ————————→ UCR
(food)   (salivation)

AFTER CONDITIONING

CS ─ ─ ─ ─ ─ ─ ─ →CR
(light)   (salivation)

CS   Conditioned stimulus
UCS   Unconditioned stimulus
CR   Conditioned response
UCR   Unconditioned response

11. A puff of air aimed at the eye will cause an infant to blink, even though the infant has never experienced an air puff before. Since such eye-blinking does not depend

unconditioned   on learning, it can be called a(n) _____ response.

12. Any response to a stimulus that is unlearned can be called an unconditioned

response   _____ .

13. The stimulus that gives rise to the unconditioned response is called an *unconditioned stimulus* (UCS). In Pavlov's arrangement, the meat powder that elicits saliva-

unconditioned   tion is called a(n) _____ stimulus.

stimulus, response   14. An unconditioned _____ elicits an unconditioned _____ without any prior learning.

15. In Pavlov's arrangement the stimulus that did not originally elicit salivation, but

light   came to do so after repeated pairings with meat powder, was a l_____ . The stimulus that becomes associated with the unconditioned response through the process of classical conditioning is called the *conditioned stimulus* (CS).

conditioned   16. The light is called a(n) _____ stimulus because it acquires

response   its power to elicit salivation (the unconditioned _____) through learning.

17. A conditioned stimulus is a stimulus that would not by itself elicit the desired response but gains the power to do so only by being associated with an

unconditioned   un_____ stimulus.

18. If putting a bottle into the mouth of an infant produces sucking, this illustrates an unconditioned stimulus (bottle in mouth) that elicits an unconditioned response (sucking). If, later on, the child begins to suck at the *sight* of the bottle, then this

conditioned   stimulus (sight of bottle) would be called a(n) _____
                             stimulus.

19. A stimulus that elicits a response the first time the stimulus is offered is called

unconditioned   a(n) _____ stimulus, and the response is called a(n)

unconditioned   _____ response.

20. If we have to associate a stimulus with an unconditioned stimulus in order to evoke

conditioned   a response, the learned stimulus is called a(n) _____
                             stimulus.

21. If the response to an unconditioned stimulus is called an unconditioned response,

conditioned   then the response to a conditioned stimulus will be called a(n) _____
                             response (CR).

conditioned   22. The learned response to a conditioned stimulus is called a _____
                             response.

response   23. The conditioned response resembles the unconditioned _____ but
                             is not always identical; it may differ in some respects.

24. The association between the unconditioned stimulus and the unconditioned re-

unlearned   sponse is (*learned/unlearned*); the association between the conditioned stimulus

learned   and the conditioned response is (*learned/unlearned*).

25. When a new association is formed between a conditioned stimulus and a response, through repeated pairings of the CS with a UCS that normally elicits the response,

classical conditioning   the process is called _____ _____ .

26. The more times we present the conditioned stimulus with the unconditioned stimu-

conditioned   lus, the stronger will be the response to the _____ stimulus.

27. In other words, the more often the conditioned stimulus is associated with the un-conditioned stimulus, the better the animal will learn the association. The pairing of

unconditioned   the conditioned stimulus with the _____ stimulus
                             is called *reinforcement,* because the pairing makes the conditioned response
                             stronger.

CS, UCS   28. If we pair a light (*the CS/UCS*) with meat powder (*the CS/UCS*) twenty times, the salivation to the light will be stronger than if we only pair them ten times. The association between the two stimuli is stronger in the former case because the

reinforced   association has been _____ more often.

29. The paired presentation of the CS and the UCS, which strengthens the conditioned

reinforcement   response, is called _____ .

30.

UCS (*or* unconditioned stimulus)

However, if we condition a dog to salivate to a light (the CS) and then continually turn on the light without giving any meat powder (the _____), eventually the dog will stop salivating to the light.

31.

reinforcement

In other words, if we pair the conditioned and unconditioned stimuli until the dog responds with salivation to the conditioned stimulus and then continually present only the conditioned stimulus, so that there is no _____ , gradually the dog will stop salivating to the stimulus.

32.

conditioned

Repetition of the conditioned stimulus without reinforcement is called *extinction.* The association between the light and the meat powder is weakened by presenting one without the other. In *extinction* we repeatedly present the _____ stimulus without the unconditioned stimulus.

33.

reinforced

When we present the conditioned stimulus without the unconditioned stimulus, the conditioned response is weakened because it is not being _____ .

34.

conditioned

Suppose we condition a dog to respond with salivation to a touch on the back near the hindquarters. To do this, we touch the dog on the back and, a second later, put meat powder on its tongue. Let us call the touch near the hindquarters (which is the _____ stimulus) Stimulus 1 (S_1).

35.

S_1

Once this conditioning has been established, if we touch the dog on another spot on its back (S_2), we find that the dog will make the response of salivation to this stimulus as well, although it has never been reinforced for this stimulus. Therefore S_2 has substituted for _____ .

36.

generalization

Responding to S_2 with the response that was conditioned to S_1, even though S_2 has not been established as a conditioned stimulus, is called *generalization.* The more similar S_2 is to S_1, the stronger will be the tendency to generalize. In _____ , the organism makes the *same* response to a new stimulus that it learned to make to an old stimulus; it does so because the new stimulus is similar in some way to the old stimulus.

37.

same

Generalization consists of the following sequence: (1) a stimulus is conditioned to a response; (2) the organism is presented with a new stimulus that is similar to, but not identical with, the conditioned stimulus; (3) the organism responds to the new stimulus as though it were the _____ as the old one.

38.

generalization

When an organism makes the same response to a new stimulus (S_2) that it has learned to make to a different stimulus (S_1), we note the process of _____ .

39.

respond

Let us suppose that, in the experiment described above, every time we touch the dog near the hindquarters (S_1) we put meat powder on its tongue and we never put meat powder on its tongue after touching the dog on the other spot (S_2). Eventually the dog will no longer respond to S_2, although it will continue to _____ to S_1. The animal has learned to tell the two stimuli apart (to react to them differentially).

same (*or* conditioned)

40. In the situation just described, the dog has learned to *discriminate* between the two stimuli and thus does not make the _____ response to both of them.

41. When the organism learns *not* to make the same response to both of the stimuli—that is, when it distinguishes between them—we call the process *discrimination*. When there are two stimuli, one of which is *always* reinforced and the other *never*

discriminate (*or* distinguish)

reinforced, the organism will in time _____ between them and respond to the former and not to the latter.

42. If we condition a dog to salivate to a tone of 1,000 Hz, reinforcing the tone with food, and then present a 500 Hz (lower pitch) tone, the dog will probably salivate in response to both tones. However, if we never reinforce the 500 Hz tone with food but always reinforce the 1,000 Hz tone, the dog will eventually stop salivating in response to the 500 Hz tone but will continue to salivate to the 1,000 Hz tone.

discrimination

This is an example of the process of _____ .

learning

43. Classical conditioning is one form of associative _____ ; another is operant conditioning.

operant

44. In _____ conditioning the organism learns an association between a response and its consequence.

45. Operant conditioning differs from classical conditioning in several ways. In classical conditioning the conditioned response resembles the normal response to the unconditioned stimulus; for example, salivation is a dog's normal response to

food (*or* meat powder)

_____ .

46. Salivation to food or an eye-blink to an air puff are essentially involuntary

responses

_____ to a particular stimulus.

47. *Operant behavior,* in contrast, is voluntary and spontaneous; it is not an automatic

stimulus

response to a specific _____ .

48. A baby bats at a rattle and kicks the covers; a dog sniffs at a ball and scratches at the rug. Since these responses are voluntary and spontaneous, they are considered

operant

_____ behavior. Operant responses usually "*operate*" on the environment.

49. If we put a hungry rat in a maze that contains food, it will make certain responses to get to the place where the food is; if we cover the food, the rat will learn to turn

operant

over the cover. These are _____ responses.

50. A certain stimulus may make an operant response more likely to occur, but does not automatically elicit it. For example, the doorbell rings and you go to open the door. The ringing bell is a stimulus that tells you someone is at the door, but it does

voluntary

not force you to answer the door. Going to the door is a (*voluntary/involuntary*) response, and hence is considered operant behavior.

51. The ringing bell is a discriminative stimulus that provides the occasion for an operant response, but it does not elicit the response in the same way that a UCS elicits

UCR

a _____ .

52. Operant conditioning differs from classical conditioning in another way. In Pavlov's laboratory arrangement the animal was passive; it did not have to do anything in order to receive the unconditioned stimulus (the reinforcement). In teaching the dog to salivate to the light, the experimenter turned on the light and then delivered

unconditioned

the meat powder (the _____ stimulus) regardless of what the animal did.

operant

53. In _____ conditioning, however, the animal must make some kind of response in order to get the reinforcement.

54. In classical conditioning the animal can be passive and still be reinforced; in

operant

_____ conditioning the animal must be active in order to be reinforced.

55. In operant conditioning we increase the probability of a response by following the

reinforcement

response with _____ .

56. For example, we want Mary to develop the habit of working hard in school. To do this we give her extra spending money for each high grade she receives. If the extra money strengthens the response of working hard in school, it constitutes a

reinforcement

_____ of the response of working hard in school.

57. Jimmy continually comes home late for dinner. His mother wants to strengthen the response of mealtime promptness, so she gives Jimmy a special dessert whenever he

reinforcement

is on time. The dessert constitutes a _____ of the response of promptness.

58. We have been assuming that every time an organism did something we would reinforce it. Thus every time a rat ran to the end of the maze, we would give it food. Suppose, however, we gave the rat reinforcement only every other time it performed the act. This procedure is called *partial reinforcement*. When we

partial
reinforcement

reinforce an organism only part of the time, we are using _____

_____ .

59. Since a child's mother is not always present to reinforce a desired response,

partial

_____ reinforcement is the state of affairs that is most prevalent in children's lives.

60. One of the characteristics of partial reinforcement is that it makes the behavior more resistant to extinction than the behavior that is subject to 100 percent rein-

partially

forcement. Thus when a child is _____ly reinforced for a given behavior, this behavior tends to persist against many nonreinforcements.

61. When Jimmy cleans his room his mother notices his efforts only 40 percent of the time. She rewards him each time that she notices. With this reinforcement schedule,

longer than

Jimmy's behavior of cleaning the room will last (*longer than/not as long as*) it would if 100 percent reinforcement were used.

62. As in classical conditioning, an operant response can be extinguished. If suddenly stop giving Mary extra spending money for making good grades, we run the risk that Mary will eventually stop working hard (if money was her only reason for working). We would be producing *extinction* of the response of working hard by

reinforcement withdrawing _____ .

63. If a rat has learned to press a bar to receive food and the delivery of food no longer follows a bar press, we say that the operant response of bar-pressing is undergoing

extinction _____ .

64. Classical conditioning and operant conditioning are two important but clearly different forms of learning. In classical conditioning, learning depends on the experimenter's pairing of the unconditioned stimulus with the conditioned stimulus; in

passive this sense the learning is (*active/passive*), since the organism cannot determine when the pairing will occur. In operant conditioning, the organism acts on the environment in order to obtain reinforcement. The strength of the organism's response

reinforcement increases whenever the response is followed by _____ .

65. So far we have discussed classical and operant conditioning, two forms of learning

associative that are called _____ learning. More complex forms of learning (such as playing chess, finding your way about a new city, or learning how to program a computer) are difficult to explain in terms of conditioned associations.

66. Learning in these situations involves more than associations between stimuli and

responses r_____ ; it requires perceiving and understanding the relationships among a multitude of events. Perceiving, understanding, and organizing relationships among events involve *cognitive processes*.

67. In learning to play chess, for example, you must perceive the relationships among the chess pieces and understand how these relate to your knowledge of the rules of the game and the moves your opponent is making. Learning the game is not simply a matter of stimulus-response associations but of perception, understanding, and

cognitive organization which involve _____ processes.

68. Simple forms of learning may be governed by the law of classical and operant conditioning. But associative learning alone cannot account for some of the complex forms of learning (such as language learning and problem solving) that we will encounter in later chapters. These involve our ability to perceive and

understand _____ relationships among objects and events in our environment.

69. To explain learning one needs to take into account both associative and

cognitive _____ processes.

70. Even a rat learning how to find its way through a maze illustrates what is meant by a cognitive explanation of learning. A rat running through a complicated maze is not learning a sequence of right and left turns to reach the goal box (reinforce-

maze ment); rather the rat is developing a *cognitive map* of the _____ .

cognitive

71. The term "_____" map implies that the rat is developing a "mental picture" of the layout of the maze. Learning, even for a rat, is not a

responses

"stamping in" of a sequence of left and right _____ , because they are eventually followed by reinforcement. Rather, it is the forming of a mental representation that abstractly represents the rat's knowledge about the

layout *(or synonym)*

_____ of the maze.

72. When tested in the maze, the rat does not respond reflexively, but instead retrieves

cognitive map

its _____ _____ from memory, and uses the map to select an appropriate path through the maze.

73. The concept of a cognitive map is an example of the more general concept of a mental representation. According to a cognitive explanation of learning, the crux of intelligence lies in an organism's ability to represent aspects of the world mentally and

mental representation

then to operate on those _____ _____ rather than on the world itself.

mental representation

74. The notions of a(n) _____ _____

cognitive

is a key ingredient of a(n) _____ explanation of learning.

TERMS AND CONCEPTS

associative learning _____

_____

_____

_____

classical conditioning _____

_____

_____

_____

conditioned response (CR) _____

_____

_____

_____

unconditioned response (UCR) _____

_____

_____

_____

unconditioned stimulus (UCS) _____

_____

_____

_____

conditioned stimulus (CS) _____

_____

_____

_____

acquisition _____

_____

_____

_____

extinction _____

_____

_____

_____

second-order conditioning _____

_____

_____

_____

generalization _____

_____

_____

_____

discrimination _____

_____

_____

_____

temporal contiguity _____

_____

_____

_____

predictability _____

_____

_____

_____

operant conditioning _____

_____

_____

_____

law of effect _____

_____

_____

_____

operant strength _____

_____

_____

_____

shaping _____

_____

_____

_____

autoshaping _____

_____

_____

_____

partial reinforcement _____

_____

_____

_____

partial-reinforcement effect _____

_____

_____

_____

conditioned reinforcer _____

_____

_____

_____

Premack's principle _____

_____

_____

_____

punishment _____

_____

_____

_____

ethologist _____

_____

_____

_____

taste aversion experiment _____

_____

_____

_____

behavioral blueprint _____

_____

_____

_____

mental representation _____

_____

_____

_____

cognitive map _____

_____

_____

_____

_____ 1. In operant conditioning, the reward
   a.   follows the behavior
   b.   comes before the behavior
   c.   occurs at the same time as the behavior
   d.   elicits the behavior

_____ 2. The conditioned stimulus for Pavlov's dog was
   a.   the onset of a light signal
   b.   an electric shock
   c.   a food tube in the mouth
   d.   food powder in the mouth

_____ 3. In operant conditioning, the desired behavior may be reinforced only a fraction of the times it occurs. This is called
   a.   conditioned reinforcement
   b.   operant strength
   c.   partial reinforcement
   d.   discrimination learning

_____ 4. In operant conditioning, the probability of a response is increased as a result of
   a.   discrimination
   b.   extinction
   c.   reinforcement
   d.   stimulus frequency

_____ 5. Generalization and the complementary process of _____ operate to produce specific appropriate behavior, such as a child saying "bow-wow" only in response to dogs.
   a.   conditioning
   b.   reinforcement
   c.   discrimination
   d.   extinction

_____ 6. The phenomenon of autoshaping
   a.   requires an active, observing experimenter who shapes the behavior
   b.   involves both classical and operant-conditioning principles
   c.   occurs in the absence of reinforcing stimuli
   d.   provides a vehicle for the satisfaction of secondary drives

_____ 7. Studies of classical conditioning have shown that
   a.   the predictive relationship between CS and UCS is more important than temporal contiguity for learning
   b.   conditioning can be explained by the frequency of pairing of CR and UCR
   c.   the animals studied anticipate generalization and are able to avoid it
   d.   learning is a passive, mechanistic process in animals

_____ 8. The term _mental representation_
   a.   refers to a cognitive structure stored in memory
   b.   refers to an abstract representation of events and objects in the real world
   c.   is exemplified by the concept of a cognitive map
   d.   all of the above

_____ 9. Which one of the following statements about punishment would your textbook authors _disagree_ with?
   a.   Extreme punishment may elicit aggressive or undesirable behavior.
   b.   Punishment has several significant disadvantages.
   c.   Punishment is effective in controlling some behavior.
   d.   Punishment should never be employed in child-rearing.

_____ 10. In Pavlov's experiment, the dog's salivation, when presented with light that had been associated with food, represented
   a.   a conditioned stimulus
   b.   a conditioned response
   c.   an unconditioned response
   d.   conditioned reinforcement

_____ 11. A dog has been rewarded with a biscuit and a pat on the head each time it rolls over. It continues to do this trick when only the pat on the head is given. The pat on the head has become a _____ reinforcer.
   a.   variable
   b.   partial
   c.   shaped
   d.   conditioned

_____ 12. When a stimulus decreases the probability of a particular response, the process is called
   a.   negative reinforcement
   b.   extinction
   c.   negative conditioning
   d.   punishment

_____ 13. For a given organism, any activity in a reinforcement hierarchy may be reinforced by any activity above it and may itself reinforce any activity below it." This is a statement of

a. the principle of autoshaping
b. Premack's principle
c. the principle of positive reinforcement
d. Skinner's law

_____14. How can we explain the fact that partial reinforcement leads to slower extinction?
a. The organism experiences less difference between extinction and acquisition.
b. Response strength is greatest when reinforcement is continuous.
c. The organism is unable to generalize to the new situation.
d. The differences between the conditions of learning and the conditions of extinction are too great.

_____15. A rat gets sick after eating a novel tasting food. He avoids this food thereafter. Which kind of learning best explains this learned aversion?
a. operant conditioning
b. classical conditioning
c. insight learning
d. stimulus generalization

_____16. One measure of operant strength is the
a. number of trials during acquisition
b. number of responses during extinction
c. complexity of the operant behavior
d. strength of association with food rewards

_____17. Recent studies have verified that
a. classical conditioning must be used in learning that involves visceral responses
b. conditioning techniques are ineffective in regulating autonomic responses
c. autonomic responses can be altered by operant conditioning

d. biofeedback is ineffective in controlling such autonomic responses as heart rate and blood pressure

_____18. In classical conditioning, if the unconditioned stimulus is omitted repeatedly, _____ takes place.
a. acquisition
b. cognition
c. generalization
d. extinction

_____19. If you want to teach Rover to ring the doorbell with his nose, you would
a. need to use operant conditioning
b. try to extinguish responses that do not meet your specifications
c. need to use the shaping technique
d. do all of the above

_____20. In an operant conditioning experiment, the pigeon receives food for pecking a spot only when the light is turned on. The light in this experiment is the
a. discriminative stimulus
b. operant condition
c. primary reinforcer
d. partial reinforcer

KEY TO SELF-QUIZ

20. a	15. b	10. b	5. c
19. d	14. a	9. d	4. c
18. d	13. b	8. d	3. c
17. c	12. d	7. a	2. a
16. b	11. d	6. b	1. a

INDIVIDUAL EXERCISE

MODIFYING ANIMAL BEHAVIOR

The procedure of shaping behavior described in Chapter 7 can be used effectively, even by those who are not professional animal trainers. All it takes is ready access to an animal subject (whether a pet or wild) and a bit of patience.

Pets are the most accessible subjects, of course, and many can be quickly trained. One student, for example, taught her dog to close the front door whenever someone accidentally left it ajar. On verbal command, the dog would stand on its hind paws and push the door shut with its front paws until the door latched. Then it would come for its reward, loving attention backed up sometimes with food treats. You must begin with an existing behavior and selectively reinforce that which comes closest to what you want, gradually sharpening or tightening your criteria for reinforcement as the behavior changes. This dog's polished performance was reasonably easy to shape, beginning with the dog's tendency to prance about when spoken to, but the final result was very impressive for visitors.

To shape the behavior of wild animals, you must be able to get close enough to provide contingent reinforcement. Your first task, then, is to "tame" the animal so that it will approach you without fear. Do this by providing food simultaneously with your presence and then gradually moving the animal closer. Initially, you may have to put out the food before the animal approaches; a peanut thrown toward a wild squirrel or raccoon usually just scares it away. But after the animal has eaten in sight of you for a number of times, you can probably begin to throw the food, tossing each piece a bit closer to you. Always move slowly and speak softly, if at all, until the animal becomes less frightened of you. Always change cues gradually, as wild animals are very sensitive to them; quick movement or sudden noise may badly startle the animal and set back your progress.

If the distance is decreased too rapidly, the animal may exhibit an approach-avoidance conflict: a squirrel, for example, will move toward you but stop short, perhaps only an inch short of its goal, apparently transfixed with the conflict and trembling all over. If this happens, you are trying to push it too far too fast.

Note that what you are doing is not only shaping, in an operant conditioning sense, but also desensitizing the animal's fear of you; this form of behavioral therapy (described on p. 534 of the text) is based on classical conditioning.

Once wild animals have learned to approach you with confidence, it is possible to shape their behavior further.

Birds, squirrels, and raccoons, for example, have been taught to take food from an outstretched hand, a pocket, a shoulder, or the top of a person's head. They have also learned to appear in response to a particular sound (a discriminative stimulus). All of this, of course, takes considerable patience, so you might prefer to start your experiments with a tame pet.

When working with wild animals be very careful; they can bite and may carry rabies. An animal that is too easy to approach may be sick. Getting wild animals reasonably close might be a better goal than attempting to handle them.

INDIVIDUAL OR CLASS EXERCISE

THE PROCESS OF LEARNING

Introduction

Learning so pervades human activity that any curiosity about the nature of people and their behavior sooner or later leads to inquiry about how habits are formed, how skills are acquired, how preferences and tastes develop, how knowledge is obtained and put to use. But what exactly is "learning"? Although there are many varied definitions of this process, it might be defined most simply as the modification of behavior through experience. This exercise will enable you to study the process of learning that goes on in modifying previously acquired behavior.

Equipment Needed

Red pencil, or pen with red ink. A stopwatch or watch with a second hand.

Procedure

Turn to page 110, which you are to use for this experiment. If this is to be a class exercise, your instructor will time you; if not, have a friend tell you to start and then, 20 seconds later, to stop. During this 20-second trial write the letters of the alphabet backward in a vertical column from top to bottom. *Do not sacrifice accuracy for speed.* If you complete the alphabet, start over again. At the end of Trial 1, cover your answers with another sheet of paper. Then use the same procedure for a total of 15 trials.

Treatment of Data

1. At the end of the fifteenth trial, count the number of correct letters on each trial and record these numbers in the space provided at the bottom of page 110.

2. Copy the number of correct letters for each trial under "Score" in the following table.

Trial	Score	Trial	Score	Trial	Score
1		6		11	
2		7		12	
3		8		13	
4		9		14	
5		10		15	

3. If this is to be a class exercise, record on a slip of paper the number of correct letters you had for each trial, so that the average number of correct letters per trial for the class as a whole can be ascertained. When your instructor reads these group averages for each trial aloud, enter them in the space in the following table.

Trial	Group average	Trial	Group average	Trial	Group average
1		6		11	
2		7		12	
3		8		13	
4		9		14	
5		10		15	

4. Now plot your learning curve and, if available, the learning curve of the class as a whole on the graph on page 111. Use a pencil for your curve and a red pencil or red pen for the class curve.

Questions for Discussion

1. Does your progress from trial to trial indicate gradual learning?

2. Are there differences between the shape of your learning curve and that of the class? How do you account for the differences?

3. Were there uncontrolled variables in this particular learning experiment?

4. How would you test for the permanence of learning to write the alphabet backward?

Trials

1	2	3	4	5	6	7	8	9	10	11	12	13	14	15

NUMBER
CORRECT

Trial
number   1   2   3   4   5   6   7   8   9   10   11   12   13   14   15

LEARNING CURVE

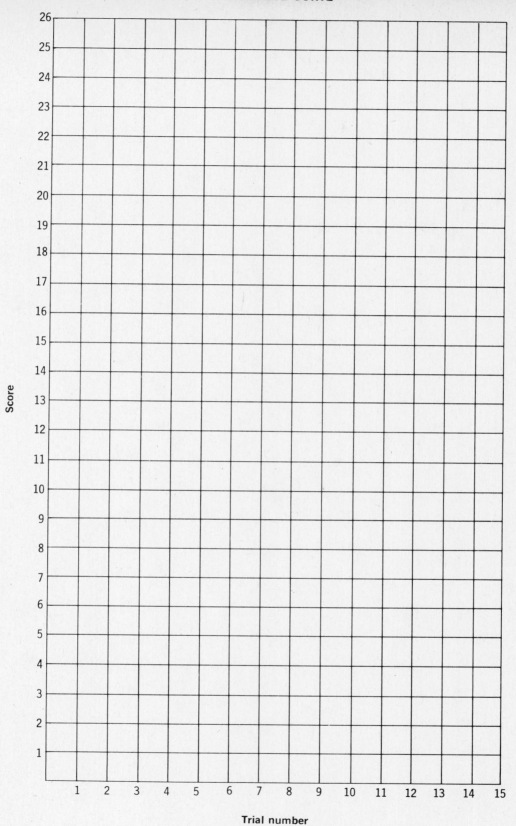

Score

Trial number

8
Memory

LEARNING OBJECTIVES 8-1. Understand the distinctions between the three stages and the two types of memory described in the text.

8-2. Know the difference between acoustic encoding and visual encoding in short-term memory.

8-3. Be able to discuss the limits of short-term storage represented by the number seven plus or minus two (7 ± 2). Explain how this is related to memory span, displacement, and chunking. Be familiar with research on the time required to retrieve information from short-term memory.

8-4. Be able to describe the Atkinson-Shiffrin theory of dual memory and show how free-recall evidence supports it. Be familiar with some of the problems encountered by the theory.

8-5. Understand the concept of encoding for meaning in long-term memory. Give examples of encoding for meaning and encoding using imagery.

8-6. Be able to discuss forgetting in terms of storage versus retrieval failure. Be familiar with the research on retrieval cues, the organizing of storage, and the use of context in recall; be able to show how each aids recovery of long-term memories.

8-7. Be able to illustrate how interference affects memory and how it can be offset. Be familiar with possible emotional factors in forgetting.

8-8. Be able to differentiate between retrograde amnesia and anterograde amnesia. Be familiar with the distinction between fact memory versus skill memory and the evidence for the distinction.

8-9. Know some of the ways to improve memory, via encoding and retrieval. Be able to explain the mnemonic systems called the "method of loci" and the "key-word method." Be familiar with the PQRST method.

8-10. Know what is meant by constructive memory. Be able to show how inferences, stereotypes, and schemata each contribute to constructive memory processes.

1. Memory involves three stages: *encoding, storage,* and *retrieval.* The first stage, en_____ , refers to the *transformation of physical information* into a kind of *code* that can be deposited in memory.

encoding

2. Encoding means to transform physical information into a(n) _____ that can be deposited in memory.

code

3. You look up a telephone number and remember it while dialing. If you remember the number by forming a mental picture of the digits, you are using a *visual* code; if you remember the sound of the names of the digits, you are using an *acoustic* _____ .

code

4. The first stage of memory, _____ , involves transforming physical _____ into a code that can be deposited in _____ . A code may be acoustic or _____ .

encoding

information

memory, visual

5. The second of the _____ (*number*) stages of memory, storage, refers to the retention of encoded information. In order to retain a telephone number long enough to dial it, you must somehow s_____ it in memory.

three

store

6. The first two stages of memory are _____ and _____ . The third stage, retrieval, is the process by which information is recovered from memory when needed.

encoding, storage

7. In order to dial the telephone number you must ret_____ it from memory storage.

retrieve

8. Thus, even the simple act of remembering a telephone number requires three stages: _____ , _____ , and _____ .

encoding, storage, retrieval

9. These _____ (*number*) stages of memory may operate differently in situations that require us to remember material for a few seconds or minutes—*short-term memory*—than in situations that require us to store material for longer intervals—*long-term memory.*

three

10. Thus, in addition to three stages of memory, there are also *two types* of memory. Remembering a new telephone number just long enough to dial it is one type, called _____ - _____ memory.

short-term

11. Remembering your own telephone number for months or years is another type, called _____ - _____ memory.

long-term

12. The three stages of memory— _____ , _____ , and _____ —may operate differently in the two situations.

encoding, storage

retrieval

13. For example, items that are to be remembered only a few seconds—an example of _____ - _____ memory—are often encoded according to the sound

short-term

acoustic

visual

long-term

meaning

short-term, long-term
(either order)

short-term

seven

seven, two

limited

long

encoding, storage
(either order)

7 ± 2

chunk

chunks

meaningful

short-

of the names of the digits. This is called a(n) _____ code. Or they may be encoded in the form of a mental picture of the digits, that is, as a(n) _____ code.

14. Information that is stored for longer intervals—an example of _____-_____ memory—is usually encoded in terms of its *meaning.*

15. If you now try to retrieve the first sentence of this programmed unit, which lists the three stages of memory, you probably do not recall the exact words—either how they looked or how they sounded. You are more likely to remember the _____ of the sentence.

16. Information may be encoded differently, depending on whether it is stored in _____-_____ or _____-_____ memory.

17. Short-term memory has a very *limited* storage capacity. It can store only about *seven* items, plus or minus two (7 ± 2). That is, sometimes a person can store only five items in _____-_____ memory and other times as many as nine. But, on the average the storage capacity of short-term memory is _____ items.

18. If I read a list of 20 names and ask you immediately how many you can remember in order, you are apt to recall _____ names, plus or minus _____ .

19. Short-term memory has a very _____ storage capacity. The storage capacity for long-term memory, in contrast, is virtually *unlimited.*

20. Some people are memory experts, while others have very poor memories. We must conclude that they differ in their (*short/long*)-term memory capacity.

21. So far, we have seen that the two types of memory differ in both their _____ and _____ stages.

22. We have said that short-term memory storage is limited to ____ ± ____ items. But what is an item? Surely, you can remember a sentence you have just heard even though it is longer than seven words.

23. An item is the *largest meaningful unit,* or *chunk,* you can find in the material presented. The string YTDRAES contains seven single-letter items. But if we rearrange the letters to form the word STRAYED, we have only one item, or ch_____ .

24. The sequence YELL A LOUD GAVE THE BOY has five word units. But we can rearrange the words into meaningful phrases, THE BOY GAVE A LOUD YELL, to reduce it to three _____ .

25. Language provides a natural chunking device, since it groups letters and words into larger m_____ units.

26. Even though its storage capacity is limited, we can store more in _____-

term	_____ memory if we regroup sequences of letters or words into mean-
chunks	ingful units, or _____ .

27. We have been discussing the first two stages of memory, _____ and

encoding

storage *(either order)*

retrieval

_____ . The third stage, which involves retrieving information from

memory storage, is called _____ .

28. We can retrieve information from short-term memory fairly quickly because its

storage capacity is (*limited/unlimited*); we don't have far to search. Retrieving

information from long-term memory is often more difficult because its storage

capacity is _____ .

29. One factor that determines the ease with which information can be retrieved from

long-term memory is the manner in which it is transformed for deposit in memory,

or en_____ .

30. We noted earlier that information in long-term memory is usually encoded in terms

of its m_____ . You are more apt to remember a point made in

the textbook if you concentrate on its m_____ rather than the

exact words. And the more you think about and elaborate on the meaning, the

better your memory.

31. Let's review. The three stages of memory, in order, are _____ ,

_____ , and _____ . The two types of memory

are called _____ – _____ and _____ – _____ . Informa-

tion may be transformed for deposit in short-term memory by means of either

a(n) _____ or _____ code.

32. Short-term memory storage is limited to ____ ± ____ items, or _____ .

Long-term memory is un_____ in storage capacity; information

in long-term memory is usually encoded in terms of its _____ .

33. Forgetting often results from difficulty in retrieving information from long-term

memory; the information may be stored—that is, it hasn't been lost from memory—

but we have problems _____ it.

34. In other words, forgetting often reflects (*storage/retrieval*) failure rather than loss

of information from memory.

35. During an exam you struggle unsuccessfully to remember the specific term that an-

swers a question. Five seconds after leaving the room the correct word comes to

you, much to your chagrin. This is an example of _____ failure.

36. You may have experienced a similar situation when a person's name seems on the

tip of your tongue, but you just cannot remember it. You are pretty certain the

name begins with "G," and you start through the alphabet, adding various second

letters to the "G" sound. When you get to "Gr" you suddenly recall the name—

The left margin answer column:

term
chunks
encoding
storage *(either order)*
retrieval
limited
unlimited
encoded
meaning
meaning
encoding
storage, retrieval
short-term, long-term *(either order)*
acoustic, visual *(either order)*
7 ± 2, chunks
unlimited
meaning
retrieving
retrieval
retrieval

"Graham." This tip-of-the-tongue experience indicates that memories often (*are/are not*) lost; they simply require the right kind of *retrieval cue*.

are not

cue

37. A retrieval _____ is anything that can help us retrieve a memory. In the example

retrieval

above, the sound "Gr" is the _____ cue for remembering the name Graham. If I told you that the name you were searching for is the same name

retrieval cue

as a type of cracker, that would be another kind of _____ _____ .

38. People usually do better on recognition tests (for example, "Place a check mark by the words that identify parts of a neuron") than they do on recall tests (for example, "Name the parts of a neuron"), because recognition tests provide better

retrieval

_____ cues.

39. While some memories may be lost from storage, retrieval failures are the major

long-term

cause of forgetting information in _____-_____ memory. Thus, if we want to improve our memory, it will help to know what factors increase the speed and accuracy of retrieval.

40. One important factor is *organization*; the more we organize the material we want to remember, the easier it is to retrieve. Thus, if you want to remember the names of a

organize

large number of people you met at a party, it would help to or_____ the names according to professions—that is, to think of the doctors as one group, the lawyers as another, and so on.

41. After you have read the chapter "Memory" in the text, the best way to remember the material is to go through the chapter again, noting the headings and subheadings. Then put the book aside and make your own outline. This is another example

organization

of using _____ to encode material.

organization

42. One aid to retrieval is _____ ; another is *similarity of context*. It is easier to retrieve a particular bit of information if the context in

context

which you are trying to recall it is similar to the _____ in which the information was encoded.

43. You will probably do better on your psychology exam if it is given in the same room in which you attended lectures, because the context in which you are trying

similar

to retrieve information is _____ to the context in which it was encoded.

44. If you want to recall the name of your high school chemistry teacher, you might try to mentally reconstruct the chemistry classroom—visualize the room, the teacher at the blackboard, and so on. This is another example of using

context

_____ to aid memory.

45. Memory is better when the context during retrieval is similar to that during

encoding

_____ .

organization

46. Two factors that increase the ease of retrieval are _____

similarity, context

and _____ of _____ . A factor that *decreases* retrieval is *interference*.

47. When we learn different things that are similar to one another, trying to retrieve one of them will bring to mind the other similar items. That is, the similar items

interfere   will inter_____ with the one you are trying to recall.

48. Suppose your friend moves across town temporarily and acquires a new telephone number in the process. You finally learn the new number. Your friend returns to the former address, and now you have difficulty remembering the old telephone number that you once knew so well. When you attempt to retrieve the old number,

interferes   the new one comes to mind and _____ with the old one. This is an example of *interference*: the learning of new materials interferes with the retrieval of old ones.

49. Another set of variables that can influence memory involves *emotions.* We tend to remember exciting events (pleasant or unpleasant) more readily than we remember

emotion   neutral ones; in this case, em _____ improves memory. On the other hand, if we become extremely anxious during an exam, we may forget much of

hinder   what we had studied. In this case our emotions (*help/hinder*) retrieval.

50. Sometimes an emotional experience may be so traumatic that we block it from conscious awareness, or *repress* it. When a person cannot consciously recall certain events that are associated with extreme anxiety, the memories are said to be

repressed   re_____.

51. The fact that the person may become aware of these anxiety-producing memories during psychotherapy or while under hypnosis indicates that such memories (*are/*

are not, repressed   *are not*) lost from long-term memory. They are simply _____ .

emotional   **52.** Thus, we see that _____ factors can influence memory in a variety of ways.

53. Several methods for improving memory are discussed in the textbook. One of spe-

PQRST   cial interest to college students, is called the PQRST method. The _____ method is used when reading a textbook chapter and takes its name from the first letter of its five stages: Preview, Question, Read, Self-recite, and Test.

54. In the first stage the student previews the entire chapter by skimming through to

preview   get an idea of its major topics and sections. This p_____ of the chapter probably starts the student organizing the material. As we know, organizing material aids our ability to remember it.

Question, Read   **55.** The second and third stages, _____ and _____ , form a package and apply to each section of the chapter as it is encountered. In the Question stage, the student makes up several questions about the section by looking at the headings and briefly scanning the material.

Read   **56.** With these questions in mind, the student reads the section (the _____ stage) with an eye to answering the questions.

Self-recitation   **57.** After reading a section, the fourth or _____ - _____ stage occurs. The student recites the contents of the section. Recitation offers practice in retrieval, and by improving retrieval we facilitate memory. Thus as each

PQRST   section of the chapter is read, the QRS of the _____ method is applied.

58. Finally, the last stage, the _____ stage occurs after the entire chapter has been read. Students try to recall the main facts, the organization of the material, further elaborate on the ideas presented, and pose additional test questions for themselves.

59. Thus the first and last stages of the PQRST method involve dealing with the chapter

as a whole unit, whereas the middle three stages apply to each _____

of the chapter as it is encountered. The middle three stages are _____ ,

_____ , and _____ - _____ . The first and last stages are Preview and Test.

60. A conscientious application of the _____ method will facilitate your understanding and recall of the material. Most study methods proposed by educators or other experts are variations of this basic method.

61. Memory usually involves more than simply recalling names or numbers or dates. We remember complex materials such as sentences, stories, and scenes. Memory for these more complex materials involves a *constructive process.* For example, we often take sentences as incomplete descriptions of events, and we use our general

knowledge of the world to con_____ a more complete description.

62. When we say that our total memory goes beyond the information given, we mean

that memory is a(n)_____ process.

63. One way we construct memories is by *drawing inferences* from the information given. For example, if I tell you that ''Mark was injured while riding to work,'' you may later recall that Mark was involved in an automobile accident. Since the word

''automobile'' was not mentioned, your memory includes an in_____ . Mark could have been riding on a bicycle or subway train.

64. One way we construct memories is by drawing _____ . Another is by using *social stereotypes.* For example, if you learn that the man you just met is a basketball player, you may later remember him as tall. He is actually

only average height, but you used a social _____ to reconstruct your memory of him.

65. Two ways we construct memories are by drawing_____ and using _____ _____ . A third method, closely related to the notion of stereotypes, is to use a *schema* (plural *schemata*). A schema is a packet of general knowledge about some situation that occurs frequently.

66. A packet of general knowledge about some situation that occurs frequently is called

a(n) _____ . For example, you undoubtedly have a schema for how to drive a car—sit behind the wheel, insert the ignition key, turn the key while pressing the gas pedal, and so on. People often try to fit their experience to a schema and end up with a memory that is partly constructed from it.

67. The text describes more fully the notion of schemata and the way we use them,

inferences, social   along with in_____ and _____ stereotypes, to construct memories. In our memories we preserve information about what has happened in the past, but we also add some new material of our own devising. This is

constructive   what we mean when we say that memory is a(n) _____ process.

TERMS AND CONCEPTS

encoding _____

_____

_____

_____

storage _____

_____

_____

_____

retrieval _____

_____

_____

_____

short-term memory _____

_____

_____

_____

long-term memory _____

_____

_____

_____

acoustic coding _____

_____

_____

visual coding _____

_____

_____

eidetic image _____

_____

_____

7 ± 2 _____

_____

_____

_____

memory span _____

_____

_____

_____

displacement _____

_____

_____

_____

decision time _____

_____

_____

_____

chunks _____

_____

_____

_____

dual-memory theory _____

_____

_____

_____

free-recall experiment _____

_____

_____

_____

recency effect _____

_____

_____

_____

elaboration _____

_____

_____

_____

retrieval cue _____

_____

_____

_____

interference _____

_____

_____

_____

hippocampus _____

_____

_____

_____

state-dependent learning _____

_____

_____

_____

repression hypothesis _____

_____

_____

_____

amnesia _____

_____

_____

_____

anterograde amnesia _____

_____

_____

_____

retrograde amnesia _____

_____

_____

_____

childhood amnesia* _____

_____

_____

_____

fact memory _____

_____

_____

_____

skill memory _____

_____

_____

_____

mnemonics _____

_____

_____

method of loci _____

_____

_____

key-word method _____

_____

_____

PQRST method _____

_____

_____

constructive memory _____

_____

_____

stereotype _____

_____

_____

schema _____

_____

_____

*Indicates term used in Critical Discussion

_____ 1. Individuals suffering from anterograde amnesia
   a. probably cannot remember their name
   b. have deficiencies in short-term memory
   c. will be unable to remember their new address if they move
   d. are unlikely to be able to remember previously learned skills

_____ 2. The mnemonic system of taking an imaginary walk and locating images of objects to be remembered along the route is called the
   a. mental-walk system
   b. method of imagery
   c. image-organization technique
   d. method of loci

_____ 3. A dual-memory theory says that long-term recall may fail because
   a. information was never transferred from short-term memory to long-term memory
   b. not enough cues may be available at the time of attempted recall to locate information in short-term memory
   c. the capacity of long-term memory is limited
   d. all of the above

_____ 4. The kind of forgetting in which memories become inaccessible because of the way in which they relate to our childhood emotional experiences is
   a. retroactive interference
   b. proactive interference
   c. repression
   d. context interference

_____ 5. Psychologists divide memory into three stages:
   a. organization, storage, and retrieval
   b. encoding, processing, and organization
   c. storage, retrieval, and processing
   d. encoding, storage, and retrieval

_____ 6. In the mnemonic system that used imagery in teaching Spanish words, the key word for "caballo" was
   a. caballo
   b. horse
   c. cob-eye-yo
   d. eye

_____ 7. Because better retrieval cues are provided, we usually do better on tests of
   a. state-dependent learning
   b. recognition
   c. state-independent learning
   d. recall

_____ 8. Studies of the encoding techniques used in short-term memory show that
   a. the favored code is an acoustic one
   b. errors in remembered letters tend to be those that look like the target letter
   c. the favored code is a visual one
   d. both visual and acoustic codes are used, with the acoustic fading quickly and the visual retained longer

_____ 9. Which of the following is _not_ an example of constructive memory?
   a. relying on schemata
   b. using mnemonic systems
   c. drawing inferences
   d. using social stereotypes

_____ 10. A subject is shown a short list, then, after a few seconds, asked if a probe item was on the list. The plot of decision time versus number of items on the list is a straight line, indicating that
   a. more retrieval cues are needed for longer lists
   b. short-term memory is hierarchically organized
   c. each additional item in short-term memory adds a fixed amount of time to the search process
   d. all of the above

_____ 11. In free-recall experiments, when subjects are asked to do 30 seconds of mental arithmetic between seeing the list of words and trying to recall them, their recall of _____ items is decreased.
   a. the first
   b. the last
   c. the middle
   d. all

_____ 12. The number seven plus or minus two refers to
   a. the best number of items to combine into a chunk for long-term storage
   b. the maximum number of items that can be encoded into long-term memory without a mnemonic system _____
   c. the number of items that can be encoded by a visual code

d. the limited number of chunks that short-term memory can hold

13. Which of these experiences suggests that poor memory reflects failure in retrieval?
    a. Your teacher's name is on the tip of your tongue but you cannot remember it.
    b. You forget the phone number you looked up a few seconds ago.
    c. You do not remember even reading about an item that appears on an exam.
    d. You make incorrect inferences about a person you met long ago.

14. The notion of *state-dependent learning* suggests that
    a. memory is best when subjects are asked to state the problem in their own words
    b. memory improves when the internal state during retrieval matches that during encoding
    c. memory is best when subjects recall during altered states of consciousness
    d. memory improves when subjects concentrate on the context in which they are learning

15. When we try to remember complex sentences,
    a. we store the schemata but recall the stereotype
    b. we make inferences and store the inferences with the sentence
    c. memories are distorted in short-term memory unless they are rehearsed
    d. we encode the meaning of the words but recall the acoustic code

16. People suffering from retrograde amnesia typically cannot remember
    a. who and where they are
    b. events just prior to a head injury
    c. particularly traumatic events of childhood
    d. what has happened to them following brain surgery

17. When we say that a memory is lost because of displacement, we refer to
    a. exceeding the capacity of short-term memory
    b. the effect of retroactive interference
    c. blocking from consciousness an emotionally disturbing memory
    d. the effect of proactive interference

18. Subjects asked how fast cars were going when they smashed into each other later reported broken glass that they had not, in fact, seen. This illustrates the functioning of _____ in constructing memories.
    a. inferences
    b. schemata
    c. visual encoding
    d. social stereotypes

19. _____ is useful for retrieval of information from long-term storage memory.
    a. Repeating the context in which the original learning occurred
    b. Organizing material as it is stored
    c. Retaking any drug that was present at the time material was originally learned
    d. all of the above

20. Which of these is an example of a schema?
    a. how to spell "cat"
    b. a set of unrelated words in short-term memory
    c. steps to follow when changing a flat tire
    d. a belief that fraternity members drink beer

KEY TO SELF-QUIZ

1. c	6. d	11. b	16. b
2. d	7. b	12. d	17. a
3. a	8. a	13. a	18. a
4. c	9. b	14. b	19. d
5. d	10. c	15. b	20. c

INDIVIDUAL OR CLASS EXERCISES

DIGIT SPAN

Introduction

As discussed in the text, short-term memory seems to be limited to 7 ± 2 items. Psychologists arrived at this figure via a test of memory span; they also noted that the number of single items could be increased by combining, or "chunking," them. The following experiment deals with one type of memory-span test, called digit span. It allows you to demonstrate both the magic number seven and the effects of chunking.

Procedure

Read the following sets of numbers to your listeners in a regularly paced monotone, approximately one per second. (If this is to be a class exercise, the instructor will read them for the class; if not, you may do so with any size group, or have a friend read them to you.) For each set of numbers, the listeners should wait until the reader has read all numbers and only then try to write down the entire set in the order presented. After all sets have been presented (from length 4 to 10), all numbers should be reread so the listeners can check the correctness of what they have written.

DIGIT-SPAN TEST NUMBERS

Length of set	Numbers
4	4–2–8–6
5	6–8–0–9–1
6	2–1–4–7–2–9
7	1–5–7–1–8–6–1
8	9–0–3–6–8–3–0–2
9	7–0–2–1–9–8–1–3–6
10	5–7–1–9–4–1–6–7–5–2

As the sets reach and exceed seven digits the task becomes noticeably harder, then virtually impossible. Those attempting it can *feel* their short-term memory losing the first numbers as the last ones are read; audible gasps and laughter usually mark the class reaction to the longer sets.

If this is a class exercise, the instructor may wish to tabulate the results so as to demonstrate both the generality of the phenomenon and the individual differences. The instructor can note how many students had four correct, five

correct, and so on. The resulting numbers will drop from virtually 100 percent to near zero as the set length increases from five through nine, though some individuals may retain ten or more.

Next try the second set of numbers below. Read each chunk rapidly, then allow a pause similar to the one used between single digits. If desired, the results may be tabulated as before. Whether formally tabulated or not, it will be recognized by all that the chunking allows substantially more digits to be remembered. It is not accidental that telephone numbers are chunked; otherwise, seven-digit numbers would be near the limits of short-term memory, while telephone numbers plus area codes would be virtually impossible!

DIGIT-SPAN TEST NUMBERS IN CHUNKED FORM

Length of set		
Digits	Chunks	Number
6	2	507–413
7	3	439–106–8
8	3	692–630–52
9	3	726–859–613
10	4	318–402–179–6
11	4	015–972–605–52
12	4	591–807–924–613

IMAGERY VERSUS REHEARSAL IN MEMORIZING

Introduction

The purpose of this exercise is to determine the effectiveness of two different techniques for memorizing a list of word pairs (called paired associates). One technique is simply to repeat the two words several times; this is the sort of rehearsal procedure one might use in memorizing the vocabulary of a foreign language. The other technique involves associating the two words by means of some kind of mental image.

Equipment Needed

Stopwatch or watch with a second hand.

Procedure

The experimenter, whether you or the instructor, should find a willing subject and read him or her the following instructions.

The purpose of this experiment is to investigate two different techniques for memorizing word pairs. I will read a list of 20 paired nouns, one at a time. Your task is to learn the pairs so that later, when I give you the first word of a pair, you will be able to tell me the word that goes with it. There are two memory techniques I want you to use. For some pairs you are to repeat the two words aloud four times. For other pairs you are to remain silent while forming a mental image or picture in which the words are associated or interacting in some way—the more vivid or unusual the image the better. For example, if I give you the word pair "dog-bicycle," you might picture a dog dressed in a clown suit riding on a bicycle. Just before I give you each word pair, I will tell you which method of memorizing to use by saying either "repeat" or "image." For the pairs you are to rehearse aloud four times, try to avoid forming any mental images.

After you have been given all 20 pairs, I will say "count," and you are to count backward from 99 until I tell you to stop. I will then test your memory by saying the first word in each pair, and you are to tell me the word that goes with it.

Do you have any questions?

Answer any questions by repeating the appropriate part of the instructions. Start with the first paired associate in the study list on p. 127, give the appropriate instruction, and then say the pair aloud. Continue in the same way until the list is completed. Time the presentation, allowing approximately ten seconds for the study of each pair. You should practice the procedure at least once before trying it out on your subject.

After all 20 paired associates have been presented, ask your subject to count backward from 99 for approximately 30 seconds. This task will prevent him or her from rehearsing the last few paired associates. Now test your subject's memory by reading aloud the words in the first column of the test list (S_1) on p. 127 and recording his or her responses in the second column (S_2). After you have completed the list, check your subject's responses for errors and tabulate the number of correct responses for repetition pairs and the number correct for imagery pairs. Record these numbers in the appropriate space. If this is to be a class exercise, bring your results to class so that your instructor can tabulate the results for the entire class.

Questions for Discussion

1. Which learning technique was most effective for your subject?

2. If done as a class exercise, how did your subject's results compare with those from the entire class?

3. If done as a class exercise, were there individual differences in the total number of words recalled? In the effectiveness of the two memory techniques?

4. Why does the test present the paired associates in a different order from the study list?

5. Why does the study list present the repetition and imagery pairs in a random order rather than some fixed order, such as alternating repetition and imagery pairs?

6. How might the results of this study be applied to memorization tasks you encounter?

7. A properly controlled study would include one group of subjects who learn the list as given and a second group for whom the repetition and imagery paired associates are switched; that is, word pairs the first group memorized by repetition would be learned by the second group through imagery, and vice versa. What variables that might have influenced the present exercise would be controlled by this procedure?

PAIRED-ASSOCIATE STUDY LIST

Instruction	Paired associates
repeat	1. rabbit – house
repeat	2. boy – rope
image	3. shoe – mountain
repeat	4. table – skull
image	5. doctor – flag
image	6. book – fish
repeat	7. slave – party
image	8. lamp – bird
image	9. heart – water
repeat	10. ladder – baby
repeat	11. teacher – pudding
image	12. mule – dress
repeat	13. kettle – fox
image	14. snake – fire
image	15. tree – queen
repeat	16. flower – money
image	17. harp – elephant
repeat	18. bear – candle
repeat	19. clock – moon
image	20. horse – potato

PAIRED-ASSOCIATE TEST LIST

S_1	S_2
1. clock	_____
2. table	_____
3. snake*	_____
4. shoe*	_____
5. flower	_____
6. lamp*	_____
7. boy	_____
8. horse*	_____
9. book*	_____
10. rabbit	_____
11. harp*	_____
12. slave	_____
13. mule*	_____
14. heart*	_____
15. bear	_____
16. ladder	_____
17. doctor*	_____
18. kettle	_____
19. teacher	_____
20. tree*	_____

Total correct (repetition) _____

Total correct (imagery) _____

*Imagery pair

9
Thought and Language

LEARNING OBJECTIVES

9-1. Understand the distinction between the prototype and the core of a concept, including the role these properties play in classical and fuzzy concepts and the way we use them to acquire concepts.

9-2. Explain what a proposition is and how concepts can be combined into propositions. Illustrate how some concepts take the role of subject in the proposition, while others take the role of predicate.

9-3. Be able to distinguish between deductive and inductive reasoning; know the rules we use in evaluating both types of arguments and the biases that influence our judgments.

9-4. Be able to describe the three levels of language in both production and comprehension, including the units (phonemes, morphemes, and sentences) involved at each level. Explain the differences between comprehension and production.

9-5. Be familiar with children's development of language at all three levels.

9-6. Explain why imitation and conditioning are not likely to be the principle means by which children learn to produce and understand sentences. Describe the operating principles children use in forming hypotheses about language.

9-7. Be familiar with the evidence bearing on the question of whether human language learning is innate.

9-8. Be able to explain what is meant by visual thinking, how it has been studied experimentally, and how it may be involved in creative thought.

9-9. Describe three problem-solving strategies that can be used to decompose a goal into subgoals.

9-10. Describe three basic ways in which expert problem solvers differ from novices.

thought

1. Our usual mode of thought, the stream of sentences we "hear in our mind" while thinking, is called *propositional thought*. Sometimes we think in visual images (imaginal thought), but propositional _____ is more common.

proposition

2. A *proposition* is a statement that makes a factual claim. "Birds are animals" makes a factual claim; therefore, it is a _____ .
A proposition consists of *concepts* (such as bird or animal) combined by a particular relation.

properties

3. A concept is a class of objects or events with *common properties*. To have a concept of "bird," for example, means to know the _____ common to all or most birds.

common

concept

4. A concept is a class of objects or events with _____ properties. Since the word "fruit" refers to a class of objects that are edible and usually sweet, we can say that fruit is a _____ .

infer

5. Concepts enable us to *infer properties* that are not directly observed. For example, if someone hands you a strange object and tells you it is a fruit, you assume that it is edible. The concept "fruit" allows you to _____ properties not observed.

infer

6. If you are told that the woman you just met is a doctor, you immediately know certain things about her (for example, that she has a medical degree). The concept enables you to _____ properties that are common to all doctors.

prototype

7. Every concept includes a *prototype* and a *core*. The prototype contains the properties that describe the *best examples* of the concept; the core contains the properties that are *essential* for being a member of the concept. Since most birds fly, the property "able to fly" would be part of the proto_____ of the concept "bird."

is not

8. However, not all birds fly (for example, penguins and ostriches); hence "able to fly" (*is/is not*) a core property of birds.

prototype

core

9. The best examples of a concept are included in its _____ ; the essential properties are specified by its _____ .

typical

10. The more prototype properties an instance of a concept has, the more *typical* people consider that instance to be. Since robins can fly but penguins cannot, most people rate robin as a more _____ bird than penguin.

prototype

11. Typical members of a concept have more (*prototype/core*) properties of their concept than do less typical ones. We tend to categorize typical instances more quickly and remember them more readily than less typical ones.

core

12. Children usually encounter typical members of a concept before they encounter less typical ones. (They are more apt to meet a robin than a penguin.) Consequently, they tend to acquire the prototype of a concept before they learn the _____ .

proposition

13. We can combine concepts to make a statement, or _____ , which incluces a person or object, called the *subject,* and descriptor, called the *predicate.*

predicate

14. Every proposition contains a subject and a _____ . In the proposition "John likes music" the predicate, *likes music,* asserts something about

John

the subject, _____ .

15. "The girl laughed at the joke" is another proposition. *The girl* constitutes the

subject

_____ ; and the assertion about her (laughed at the joke) is the

predicate

_____ .

subject, predicate
(either order)

16. A proposition consists of a _____ and a _____ .

17. A simple sentence like "The baby smiled" contains only one proposition. The sen-

propositions

tence "The baby smiled and mother laughed" contains two _____ .

baby, mother (either order)

There are two subjects, _____ and _____ , and two predicates.

propositions

18. All sentences, no matter how complex, can be broken down into _____ containing subjects and predicates.

19. The sentence "The baby laughed when the cat spilled the milk, but mother got

three

mad" contains _____ (*number*) propositions.

thought

20. The language we use for communicating propositional _____ is structured at three levels. At the lowest level are the *elementary speech sounds,* or *phonemes.*

elementary

21. The English language is composed of about 40 phonemes, or _____ speech sounds, which correspond roughly to the different ways we pronounce the vowels and consonants of our alphabet. The number of phonemes varies from one language to the next.

Phonemes

22. _____ are the elementary sounds of a language, and they may vary in number from one language to the next.

phonemes

23. Each language has *rules* that specify how the elementary sounds, or _____ , may be combined or sequenced to form a word. For example, in English we have words that start with "stri" or "spl" but none beginning with "zb" or "vg," as is common in some Slavic languages.

rules

24. Not all phonemes can be used in all combinations. Each language has _____ that specify how phonemes may be sequenced.

lowest

25. Phonemes are at the (*lowest/highest*) level of language structure. Next are *morphemes,* which are the smallest *meaningful* units in the structure of a language.

phoneme

26. Do not confuse the word "morpheme" with _____ , which refers to elementary sounds of a language.

meaningful

27. Morphemes are the smallest _____ units in the structure of a language. Morphemes may be root words, prefixes, or suffixes, and may consist of from two to six phonemes.

meaningful

28. The words "banana," "god," and "sweet" are single morphemes. That is, they are among the smallest _____ units in the English language.

morphemes

29. Some words consist of two or more morphemes. The word "sweetness" consists of two _____ , "sweet" and "ness," since both parts have meanings of their own (the suffix "ness" implies "being" or "having the quality of").

two

30. The word "sincere" consists of a single morpheme. However, if we add the prefix "in," which means "without," to form "insincere," we have _____ (*number*) morpheme(s).

morphemes

31. The smallest meaningful units in the structure of a language are called _____ . One word, however, may combine several morphemes and have several units of sound, or phonemes.

phonemes

morphemes

32. Words can be analyzed in terms of elementary sounds, or _____ , and meaningful units, or _____ . At the highest level of language structure are *sentence units*, which include sentences and phrases.

proposition

morphemes

phonemes

33. When we produce a sentence we start with a thought, or _____ . We translate this thought into words, which consist of one or more meaningful units called _____ . Finally, we translate the words into speech sounds, or _____ .

phonemes

morphemes

proposition

34. To understand a sentence, however, we proceed in the opposite direction. What we hear are ph_____ . We use these to construct the meaningful units of the sentence—phrases, words, and _____ — to arrive at the thought, or _____ , intended by the speaker.

phonemes

concepts

35. In learning to talk, children must learn to combine the elementary speech sounds or _____ , into words. And they must discover the proper words to apply to various con_____ .

concepts

36. By the time they are about a year old, children begin to utter single words (such as "doggie," "dada," and "foot") that refer to simple _____ . At around a year and a half they begin to combine single words into two-word utterances ("there doggie," "see baby," "go car") that have a *telegraphic* quality.

37. These two-word utterances contain words that carry the most important meaning, while leaving out articles ("the," "a"), auxiliary verbs ("is," "are"), and prepositions ("on," "in"). Because they convey meaning with a minimum of words, such

telegraphic

utterances have been called tele_____ .

38. Children utter single words at about 12 months of age and progress to two-word utterances at around 18 months. They rapidly proceed to more complex sentences by expanding the *verb phrase*. "Daddy hat" becomes "Daddy wear hat" and finally "Daddy is wearing a hat."

verb

39. In forming more complex sentences children first expand the _____ phrase and then *use conjunctions* (like "and" and "so") to form compound sentences.

telegraphic

verb phrase

conjunctions

40. Children progress from tele_____ two-word utterances to more complex sentences by expanding the _____ _____ and using _____ . At the same time, they learn to use certain morphemes that are essential for making sentences *grammatical*.

morphemes

41. We noted earlier that suffixes and prefixes are (*phonemes/morphemes*). The suffix "ing" is a morpheme because it carries meaning when added to a verb to form the progressive ("kick"—"kicking").

grammatical

42. Other morphemes that are essential for making a sentence gr_____ include "ed" to form the past tense of regular verbs ("kick"—"kicked") and "s" added to nouns to form the plural ("boy"—"boys") or to verbs in the present tense for the third person singular ("The boy kicks").

43. Children progress from simple two-word utterances to more complex sentences by

verb phrase, conjunctions

expanding the _____ _____ , using _____ to form compound sentences, and learning the morphemes that make a sentence

grammatical

_____ . And this sequence of language development is remarkably the *same for all children*.

44. Children learn to use the suffix "ing" before "ed" and to use the plural "s" before the third person "s." This illustrates the fact that the sequence of language develop-

same

ment is the _____ for all children.

language

45. The fact that the sequence of _____ development is the same for all children has led some experts to believe that some of our language-learning abilities are *innate*; we are genetically programmed to learn a language.

46. How do children learn all of the complexities involved in speaking a language? One important process appears to be *hypothesis testing*: forming a guess, or

hypothesis

_____ , about some aspect of language, testing it out, and keeping it as a rule if it works.

47. Studies indicate that there are a small number of *operating principles* that children

hypotheses

everywhere use as a guide to forming _____ about language.

principle

For example, one operating _____ is to pay attention to the *ends of words*.

operating

48. Paying attention to the ends of words is one _____

principle

_____ that children use as a guide to forming hypotheses about language; another is to look for prefixes and suffixes that indicate a *change in meaning*.

49. The past tense of regular verbs is formed by adding the morpheme "ed" (for example, "look—looked"). By observing that "ed" at the end of verbs changes the

meaning

m_____ of the verb, children arrive at the hypothesis that "ed" at the end of verbs signals the past tense.

50. We make this assumption by noting what happens to some verbs that have an irregular past tense and do not follow the "ed" rule (for example, "run—ran" and "go—went"). These are common verbs that children learn early, and initially they use the correct past tense; they say "went" and "ran." After learning the "ed" past tense of some regular verbs, children often begin saying "goed" and "runned," which they have never heard or said before. This change suggests that they are

hypothesis

testing a new _____ in their use of language. Eventually, children learn that some verbs are irregular, and they stop overgeneralizing their use of "ed."

51. Some language learning may occur through imitation of adult speech or through conditioning—being rewarded for grammatically correct sentences and reprimanded for mistakes. But more important is the process of learning general rules about

hypothesis testing

language through _____ _____ .

52. In generating hypotheses, children appear to be guided by a small number of

operating

_____ principles.

TERMS AND CONCEPTS

propositional thought _____

_____

_____

_____

imaginal thought _____

_____

_____

_____

motoric thought _____

_____

_____

_____

proposition _____

_____

_____

_____

prototype of a concept _____

_____

_____

_____

core of a concept _____

_____

_____

_____

classical concept _____

_____

_____

_____

fuzzy concept _____

_____

_____

_____

exemplar strategy _____

_____

_____

_____

hypothesis testing _____

_____

_____

_____

linguistic relativity hypothesis* _____

_____

_____

_____

deductive reasoning _____

_____

_____

_____

inductive reasoning _____

_____

_____

_____

heuristic _____

_____

_____

_____

similarity heuristic _____

_____

_____

_____

causality heuristic _____

_____

_____

_____

*Indicates term used in Critical Discussion

base-rate rule _____

_____

_____

_____

conjunction rule _____

_____

_____

_____

phoneme _____

_____

_____

_____

morpheme _____

_____

_____

_____

noun phrase _____

_____

_____

_____

verb phrase _____

_____

_____

_____

Broca's aphasia* _____

_____

_____

_____

Wernicke's aphasia* _____

_____

_____

_____

difference reduction _____

_____

_____

_____

means-ends analysis _____

_____

_____

_____

computer simulation _____

_____

_____

_____

*Indicates term used in Critical Discussion

_____ 1. All languages are made up of _____ such as _____ .
   a. phonemes, "strange"
   b. phonemes, /S/
   c. morphemes, "strangeness"
   d. phonemes, "ness"

_____ 2. How many propositions are contained in the sentence, "Old John caught a big fish"?
   a. 1
   b. 2
   c. 3
   d. 6

_____ 3. The spontaneous speech of a two-year-old has been termed _____ because of such sentences as "Jimmy bike" and "car go."
   a. truncated
   b. telegraphic
   c. abbreviated
   d. primitive

_____ 4. Subjects asked questions about a mental image, for example, of a car,
   a. are typically unable to answer in any detail
   b. can answer questions about any aspect of the image equally quickly, as if they could see all of it at once
   c. seem to scan the image in the same way as they might a real object
   d. find that the details of their image keep changing as they attempt to answer questions about it

_____ 5. To a psychologist, a "concept" refers to
   a. a set of objects that share common properties
   b. an abstract idea, such as _justice_
   c. a state of humans, such as _being old_
   d. all of the above

_____ 6. Children's sentences such as "Annie goed home" and "Harry taked the book" provide evidence supporting the _____ view of language development.
   a. hypothesis testing
   b. innate pattern
   c. conditioning
   d. imitation

_____ 7. To produce a sentence, we go through three levels of language in the following order:
   a. phrases, phonemes, morphemes
   b. sentences, phonemes, propositions
   c. propositions, phonemes, morphemes
   d. phrases, morphemes, phonemes

_____ 8. Researchers working with language use by chimpanzees have _not_ been able to teach them to
   a. speak words
   b. combine or generalize signs in ASL
   c. type out messages
   d. any of the above

_____ 9. In analyzing the components of speech we note that a simple thought is often expressed as a _____ with two major components, the _____ and the _____
   a. predicate, subject, proposition
   b. proposition, predicate, subject
   c. proposition, predicate, verb phrase
   d. predicate, noun phrase, verb phrase

_____10. How does the use of language by apes differ from the use of language by humans?
   a. There are no fundamental differences between the two usages.
   b. Signs used by apes are not equivalent to human words.
   c. Apes seem to combine signs differently than humans combine words.
   d. Human utterances are more repetitious than ape utterances.

_____11. Computer simulation programs are designed for the purpose of
   a. demonstrating that human problem solving works via the same steps that a computer takes
   b. demonstrating that a computer can solve problems faster than humans can
   c. trying to understand how humans solve problems
   d. trying to find a better way to program computers

_____12. Which of the following can be arranged in a hierarchy of concepts so that each is included in the next?
   a. plants, pine trees, flowers

b.   bears, polar bears, white animals

c.   football players, needlepointers, athletes

d.   sports cars, vehicles, automobiles

_____13. When we break up the sentence "My friend Lorri is a doctor," we note that

a.   "My friend Lorri" is a noun phrase

b.   "friend" is the subject

c.   "My friend Lorri" is the predicate

d.   "is a doctor" is a noun phrase

_____14. Our speed in judging whether a particular example is a member of a concept depends on the typicality of the concept. Which of the following is likely to take the longest decision time?

a.   a dog as an animal

b.   a chair as furniture

c.   an ostrich as a bird

d.   a house as a building

_____15. A *bachelor* is an adult, unmarried male. These characteristics form the _____ of the concept bachelor.

a.   exemplar

b.   prototype

c.   hierarchy

d.   core

_____16. When children learn concepts by the exemplar strategy

a.   fuzzy concepts will be acquired more quickly than classical concepts

b.   the learning of classical concepts will be hindered

c.   atypical instances will be included in the concept

d.   typical instances of a concept will be classified correctly

_____17. When making inductive judgments we are likely to violate the rule

a.   similarity

b.   causality

c.   base-rate

d.   all of the above

_____18. Certain word endings used to mark verb tense and plurals (for example, "ing," "ed," "s") are called

a.   grammatical morphemes

b.   semantic phonemes

c.   grammatical phonemes

d.   telegraphic morphemes

_____19. To test the hypothesis "If a card has a consonant on one side, it has an odd number on the other," which of the following cards should you turn over: E, K, 2, 5?

a.   E and 5

b.   E and K

c.   2 and 5

d.   K and 2

_____20. Given an upside-down letter "R" and asked if it is normal or backward, subjects

a.   were often incorrect

b.   mentally rotated the image to find out

c.   used a verbal code to help decide

d.   all of the above

KEY TO SELF-QUIZ

20. b	15. d	10. c	5. d
19. d	14. c	9. b	4. c
18. a	13. a	8. a	3. b
17. c	12. d	7. d	2. c
16. d	11. c	6. a	1. b

INDIVIDUAL EXERCISES

CONFLICT IN CODING

Introduction

We normally encode events in a manner appropriate to them. Our memory of material we have read is verbal, while our recollection of a sunset may be pictorial. This exercise, based on the Stroop Test, intentionally sets two forms of coding into conflict. It demonstrates not only how disconcerting such conflict can be, but also how difficult it is to override firmly established verbal responses.

Equipment Needed

Display cards in color, to be created from white paper and colored marker pens as described on the next page.

Procedure

1. Make up three display sheets as follows. If you want to do the test for a group, make them as large as necessary for clear viewing by the group. (The experiment makes an interesting party game.) For individual usage, sheets of standard size typewriter paper are large enough. You should use plain white opaque paper or cardboard that will take ink well and bright felt-tip markers that will produce distinctly different colors.

2. On the first sheet, the experimental one, print the names of colors in large, thick block letters: YELLOW, GREEN, etc. But print them in *different* colors from the color names. The first word thus could be YELLOW but printed in thick block *green* letters. Make at least four or five lines, with about five words per line, a total of perhaps 25 words; each word will be repeated several times in the display, but the same word should not be used twice in succession. Use only basic color names and easily discriminable colors: perhaps red, yellow, blue, green, orange, and brown. Vary the color used to print a particular color name; that is, don't print YELLOW in green ink every time it appears.

3. Make up two control sheets, one with patches of color that are not words, the other with the color names printed all in black. Make the color patches similar in size and color density to the words on the first sheet, and make the black-ink names similar in size to the colored ones on the first sheet. (It is not necessary to have the colors and words in the same order as on the experimental sheet.)

4. Present the sheets to your subject (yourself, if no one else is handy) in any order. The tasks for the control sheets are to name the colors on one and to read the color names on the other. Use a stopwatch to time each performance as precisely as possible. Subjects will of course find these tasks so easy as to be trivial. The experimental task, however, using the third sheet, is to correctly name the *ink* colors used as fast as possible; that is, to name the color that a word is printed in and not the word itself. (If the word YELLOW is printed in green ink, the subject should say "green" when he or she comes to it.) A subject who makes a mistake must correct it before continuing. This is not nearly as easy as it sounds; a reasonably quick, errorless run through 25 names is a surprisingly difficult task.

5. Compare the time needed for the experimental task to that of the control tasks; it will undoubtedly be substantially longer.

Questions for Discussion

1. Why is this task so difficult? Would it be more or less difficult for a five-year-old child? For a nonnative speaker of English?

2. Can you figure out any way to become more proficient at the task? What do you want to do? (Hint: try turning the page upside down. Can you think of ways of achieving similar results without turning the page upside down?)

CONFLICT IN PROBLEM SOLVING

Introduction

As noted in the text, some problems are easier to solve visually, while others require a logical and sequential approach. Although there are problems that can be solved by either approach, some problems may respond to only one; use of the other approach may inhibit or prevent a solution. This exercise is designed to let you experience some of the conflict in strategies that often accompanies problem solving.

Procedure

Try to solve the following problem before reading further. As you do, pay attention to the strategies you use.

Which line does the "Z" go on and why?

```
A    EF HI KLMN      T VWXY
BCD  G  J      QPQRS U
```

Most people seek to solve such a problem by logic. It looks like a sequence, and you might try to solve it as you would when asked to complete a series of letters—such as CDCD . . ., or the more difficult RSCDSTDE. . . . The use of logic tends to bias you toward the logical process of the left hemisphere. But this is actually more of a right-hemisphere task, one calling for visual thought and analysis. Try it again from this perspective before going on.

If you still do not get it, consider a final clue: the property you are seeking is letter *shape*. The solution should now be obvious. Is it?

The answer is that the "Z" goes on the top line, with all the other letters made of straight lines. Any attention paid to the numbers of letters on each line, to words beginning with the letter, and so on, simply interferes with finding such a solution. Note that the effect here is similar to that of the color-naming task in the preceding exercise: previously learned associations to visual patterns interfere with the task. But here the associations are less specific; rather than a simple interference of word name, complex patterns of logical problem solving intrude.

Questions for Discussion

1. What strategies did you use? Did they include visual as well as logical ones before you were told to do so? Were you able to use visual strategies when directed to do so? Are these as easy to describe or explain as the logical-verbal ones?

2. How might you manipulate conditions so that someone else would find the problem easier or harder to solve?

LANGUAGE USE AS PROBLEM SOLVING

While you use language in problem solving, your understanding of language itself often has elements of problem solving. The examples in this section focus on some of these problem-solving elements.

Many of these problems involve reading. Making sense of a written message can be considered akin to decoding or to problem solving. First the basic elements, the letters, must be recognized. Before you write this off as trivial, consider the following sentence.

TAE CAT SAT TAERE

You probably had no difficulty reading it, but look again. Is the open-topped figure an "H" or an "A"? Obviously it can be either for you, depending on context. A similar example is the figure shown in the middle of the box above; it is seen as a letter in one context and a number in another.

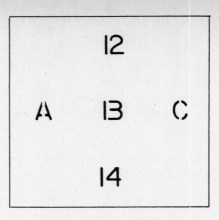

Once you have decoded the letters and/or numbers, you must deal with the meaning of individual words. Here again you find that context often specifies them. English uses words like "fly," for example, as either a verb or a noun, with the context specifying which. Thus the answer to

WHAT HAS SIX WHEELS AND FLIES?

can be either two Cessnas or a large garbage truck.

Sometimes punctuation is used to help you. Try to punctuate the following so that it makes sense.

TIME FLIES YOU CANNOT THEY FLY TOO FAST

Part of the difficulty is that the first words are well known in one context, that is, where "flies" is a verb and "time" a noun. But you can only punctuate this if you reverse the grammatical relationship. If you consider the first two words above to be a question about using a stopwatch on flying insects, the rest of the punctuation follows.

Minor punctuation marks such as commas can be important, even necessary, clues. Consider the meanings of the following sentence, depending on whether or not it has two commas in it.

THE REPUBLICANS SAY THE DEMOCRATS ARE LIARS.
THE REPUBLICANS, SAY THE DEMOCRATS, ARE LIARS.

But even brief and unpunctuated sentences can offer several meanings if such multipurpose words as "time" and "fly" are used. Consider the following.

TIME FLIES LIKE AN ARROW.

Because of the common usage of "time flies," you probably read this sentence to mean that the passage of time is swift. But a Harvard computer simulation program designed to interpret English came up with four interpretations for the same sentence.* Can you supply the other three? The answers are given at the bottom of the right column. (Remember that they do not have to make a great deal of sense; they only need to be possible English constructions.)

In some cases where we have difficulty interpreting sentences, the problem is sequence. While most sentences are unambiguous, extracting the intended proposition(s) from more complex, or nested, ones can become difficult. Consider the following. What does it say?

THE LEATHER RACING SADDLES ARE MADE OF IS VERY SMOOTH.

The jolt and retracking you probably experienced in reading this results from the use of a sequence that seems to be of one form but turns out to be another. Consider how it would read if "of is very smooth" were replaced with "by hand." Of course one could help the reader by inserting "that" before "racing," but it is not required by the rules of English.

Other legitimate sentences remain ambiguous even when reread. For example, in the sentence "They are eating apples," "they" may refer to people or to apples. The need for brevity in newspaper headlines often yields similar examples, as in this one from a recent story.

OFF-DUTY POLICEMAN KILLS MAN WITH A CLUB
(Who had the club?)

While problems of ambiguity arise more frequently with written language, they may also occur in interpreting speech, despite the fact that speech is usually less complex and offers more contextual cues. Some of the possible ambiguous interpretations of phonemes and morphemes, for example, have entered folklore as children's games or adult jokes. "I scream for ice cream" delights children who are just discovering such possible ambiguities, but adults are not immune to the charms of such word play. Remember knock-knock jokes?

*Raphael, B., *The thinking computer: Mind inside matter* (San Francisco: Freeman, 1976) p. 186.

KNOCK KNOCK
WHO'S THERE?
SAM AND JANET
SAM AND JANET WHO?
SAM AND JANET EVENING

Some "trick" problems make use of verbal constructions deliberately designed to mislead you through your own normal interpretation process. Consider the following:

> I have in my hand two U. S. coins totaling 55 cents and one of them is not a nickel. What are they?

Obviously the coins must be a half dollar and a nickel. How? Well, one of them is *not* a nickel; the *other one* is. If you recognized the deception, it may be because the problem is easier when it is in front of you where it can be reexamined. This trick works best as a verbal problem because once the words have been turned into meaning, the original form is lost. When you try to review the problem, you tend to remember not the exact original statement but instead your interpretation that "Neither one is a nickel."

Part of learning any language is learning the rules for recognizing and interpreting its sounds, words, and sentences. Yet, as we have seen, problems and ambiguities remain. Remember, when you consider how much of your thought process is verbally based, that your thoughts are also subject to such problems. Those who teach creative problem solving often focus on the need to carefully analyze one's verbal processes both in the interpretation of the problem and in search patterns for solutions.

Answers for the first problem on this page.

1. Time moves in the same manner that an arrow moves.
2. Measure the speed of flies in the same way that you measure the speed of an arrow.
3. Measure the speed of the flies that resemble an arrow.
4. A particular variety of flies called "time-flies" are fond of an arrow.

10
Basic Motives

LEARNING OBJECTIVES

10-1. Be familiar with the distinction between survival motives, social motives, and curiosity motives.

10-2. Be able to define homeostasis in terms of a sensor, ideal value, and comparator. Understand the distinction between need and drive.

10-3. Be prepared to discuss body temperature regulation and thirst from the perspective of a homeostatic system.

10-4. Be familiar with variables that affect hunger. Be able to describe the LH syndrome and the VMH syndrome.

10-5. Be familiar with research on obesity, including restrained versus unrestrained eaters, emotional arousal, and responsiveness to external cues.

10-6. Understand the relationship between exercise and metabolic rate; be able to discuss various approaches to weight control.

10-7. Be familiar with the major male and female sex hormones and their role in sexual differentiation and sexual behavior.

10-8. Be familiar with research on the role of early experience and cultural factors in shaping sexual behavior.

10-9. Be able to discuss the motives implicit in maternal behavior and curiosity.

10-10. Understand how the concept of arousal level may overcome some of the problems of drive-reduction theory in formulating an integrated concept of motivation.

1. By a motive we mean something that *energizes* the organism (that is, incites the organism to action). Hunger can energize an organism to action: therefore hunger

   motive   can act as a _____ .

2. When an organism is quiescent, we say that it is not motivated; when it is energized,

   motivated   we say that it is _____ .

3. Motivated behavior is also characterized by *direction.* When an organism is incited to action by hunger, it does not simply act at random; its actions are in the

   direction   _____ of food.

4. Motivation, then, is concerned with factors that give behavior direction and that

   direct   energize it. A hungry organism will _____ its behavior toward food and a thirsty organism towards drink. Both will engage in activity more

   energetically   _____ than an unmotivated organism.

5. In this chapter we deal with *basic motives*; namely, unlearned motives that humans share with other animals. Hunger and thirst are motives that we share with other

   basic   animals, and are examples of _____ motives.

   motives   6. Basic _____ are of several types. One corresponds to *survival motives* of the organism, such as hunger and thirst. A second deals with *social motives*, such as sex and maternal behavior. And a third deals with *curiosity motives*, which are not directly related to the welfare of the organism.

   motives   7. Many survival _____ operate according to the principle of *homeostasis*, which is the body's tendency to maintain a constant internal environment.

8. Body temperature, for example is maintained within a few degrees in a healthy individual. When you get hot you perspire, and perspiration evaporating from the body surface has a cooling effect. Perspiring is thus one of the automatic mechanisms

   homeostasis   that maintain _____ by keeping body temperature within normal range.

   constant   9. Homeostasis refers to the body's attempt to maintain a _____ internal environment.

10. When the concentration of sugar in the blood drops below a certain ideal value, the liver releases stored sugar (in the form of glycogen) to restore the proper blood-

    homeostasis   sugar level. This is another example of _____ .

    internal   11. Homeostasis refers to the body's attempt to maintain a constant _____ environment. There are many internal states that must be maintained within narrow limits; there are sensors in the body that detect changes from the ideal value and activate certain mechanisms that correct the imbalance and restore

    homeostasis   _____ .

12. When the amount of water in the body cells becomes low, you feel thirsty and are motivated to drink water to restore the balance of fluid in the cells. This is another

homeostasis

example of _____ .

13. We can use the homeostatic framework to distinguish between the concepts of *need* and *drive*. A need is any physiological departure from the ideal value. Its psychological counterpart is a drive, an aroused state or urge that results from need. Drive,

need

then, refers to the psychological consequences of a _____ .

need

14. A lack of food creates a bodily deficit; we call this lack a _____ .

15. Any bodily deficit, or state of deprivation (such as lack of oxygen, food, or water),

need

can be defined as a _____ .

16. The need for food is physiological, not psychological, but a state of physiological need has *psychological consequences*. The psychological consequences of a need

drive

are called a *drive*. The need for food leads to the hunger _____ .

17. While need and drive are related, they are not the same. For example, drive does not necessarily get stronger as need gets stronger. People who have fasted for a long time report that their feelings of hunger come and go, although their need for food persists. The need persists but the psychological consequences of the need, the

hunger drive

_____ _____ , fluctuate.

18. In the text, the control of body temperature and the regulation of water intake are cited as excellent examples of homeostatic systems. Research on these topics have

homeostasis

identified the mechanisms employed by the body to maintain _____ .

19. Hunger can also be analyzed as a homeostatic system, but it is much more complicated and readily influenced by psychological and social factors. Clearly not every person is able to maintain homeostasis; just walk down a street and we see examples

overeating

of extreme _____ (*obesity*) and extreme undereating (*anorexia*).

crucial (*or synonym*)

20. Because regulation of food intake is _____ to the survival of the organism, nature has provided several homeostatic controls. These control systems are integrated in a region of the brain called the *hypothalamus*.

21. One area of the hypothalamus, the *lateral hypothalamus (LH)*, initiates eating.

hypothalamus

Another area of the _____ , the *ventromedial hypothalamus (VMH)*, inhibits eating.

22. If the lateral hypothalamus is stimulated with a mild electric current, an animal that has just completed a large meal will begin to eat again. This is evidence that

initiation

the lateral hypothalamus plays a role in the _____ of eating.

23. If the ventromedial hypothalamus is stimulated electrically, a hungry animal will stop eating in the midst of a meal. This is evidence that the hypothalamus plays a

inhibition

role in the _____ of eating.

24. Knowing this much, you would guess that if a large part of the ventromedial hypothalamus is removed or destroyed, the animal will eat too _____ .

much

25. And this is exactly what happens. When tissue in the ventromedial hypothalamus is destroyed, the animal _____ until it becomes obese.

overeats

26. You might guess that in the opposite case, when tissue in the lateral hypothalamus is destroyed, an animal will eat too _____ .

little

27. What actually happens when the lateral hypothalamus is destroyed is that the animal refuses to eat at all and will die unless fed artificially.

opposite

28. These two regions of the hypothalamus thus appear to act in _____ ways to regulate food intake.

29. Moreover, there appear to be two kinds of control systems in the hypothalamus: a *short-term control system* that responds to the organism's immediate nutritive needs and tells it when to start and stop a meal, and a *long-term control system* that attempts to maintain a stable body weight over a long period of time, regardless of how much the organism eats in any one meal. The fact that most people maintain the same body weight from year to year (give or take a few pounds) suggests

long

that the body must have some kind of _____ -term control system for regulation of food intake.

control

30. The hypothalamus appears to have both short-term and long-term _____ systems for regulating eating.

31. Experiments have pinpointed several variables that are related to our immediate feeling of hunger: *blood-sugar level, stomach fullness,* and *body temperature.* These are variables to which the hypothalamus responds in controlling when we start and

short

stop eating a given meal; they are thus important to the _____-term control system.

32. When our blood-sugar level is low we feel weak and hungry; studies indicate that certain cells in the hypothalamus are sensitive to the level of sugar in the

blood

_____ .

33. But we usually stop eating before the food we have consumed can raise the blood-

fullness

sugar level significantly. A more immediate result of eating, stomach _____ apparently signals the brain that food is on the way.

34. Certain cells in the hypothalamus appear to respond to a full stomach to inhibit

ventromedial

further eating. As you would expect, these cells are in the _____ region of the hypothalamus.

35. When the stomach is empty we have periodic contractions of the stomach walls called hunger pangs. This increased activity of the stomach walls signals cells in

lateral

the _____ hypothalamus to start the organism eating.

36. Two variables that affect the short-term control of eating are blood-sugar level and stomach fullness. A third short-term control variable is temperature: decreased brain temperature initiates eating; increased brain temperature inhibits eating. This

less

is probably one reason why you have _____ of an appetite in hot weather.

37. The variables that affect the long-term control system so as to keep our body weight about the same from year to year are not fully known. But experimental

lateral

evidence suggests that the _____ and ventromedial hypothalamus, interact reciprocally to maintain an individual's weight at a set point.

38. Obesity is a major health problem. A popular view is that obesity stems from unresolved emotional problems. Although such explanations may be appropriate in some cases, research has failed to isolate a specific personality type that character-

obese

izes _____ people.

39. Rather, research suggests that obesity results from a complicated interplay of *metabolic, psychological*, and *social factors*. The importance of each of these factors varies from individual to individual. In some people obesity may result primarily from a metabolic condition, in others from a psychological problem, and

social

yet in others from a _____ cause.

40. Despite the complexity of the problem, weight control is possible in most cases. One approach to weight control involves a program called *behavior modification*.

modification

The goal of behavior _____ is to make the overweight individual aware of the factors that lead to overeating and to help him or her establish a new set of eating and exercise habits.

41. Individuals are taught to keep a daily record of their eating habits, to become

aware

_____ of the situations that prompted them to overeat, to avoid stimuli associated with their overeating, to reward themselves for appropriate eating behavior, and to develop a suitable exercise program.

behavior

42. Research on methods for treating obesity has compared _____ modification with various other treatments including drug therapy (which involves using an appetite suppressant drug to control food intake). Both treatments proved to be effective in controlling eating and reducing weight.

43. However, once treatment was discontinued the drug therapy group had a significantly greater tendency to regain weight than did the behavior modification group. An increased sense of self-control on the part of individuals in the

behavior modification

_____ _____ group may have been the reason.

44. Individuals who received the behavior modification treatment could attribute their

self-control

weight loss to their own efforts at _____ – _____ , thereby strengthening their resolve to continue controlling their weight after the treatment was over. Individuals who received an appetite suppressant drug, on the other hand, probably attributed their weight loss to the drug and did not develop a strong sense of self-control. When the drug was withdrawn, releasing biological pressures to regain weight, their sense of self-control was not strong enough to prevent them from returning to their old eating habits.

45. This and other research suggests that short-term weight loss can be accomplished in a variety of ways. But the ability to keep weight off permanently depends on establishing _____ - _____ over eating habits and therefore over the total number of calories consumed.

self-control

46. An important social motive is sex. Sex is not vital to the survival of the organism, as is _____, but it is essential to the survival of the species.

food

47. Sexual behavior depends on internal factors (primarily *hormones*) and *stimuli in the environment*. If a female rat is injected with a male hormone, it will try to mount other females when placed in a cage with them. This illustrates the influence of _____ on sexual behavior.

hormones

48. If the same rat is placed in a cage with male rats, it will revert to the female sexual pattern when confronted with a sexually aggressive male. This illustrates the influence of _____ stimuli on sexual behavior.

environment (*or* external)

49. As we go from lower to higher mammals, experience and learning play an increasingly important role in sexual behavior. If a rat is raised in isolation with no contact with other rats, it will usually show the proper sexual response when first confronted with a receptive mate. Thus _____ behavior in the rat appears to be largely innate.

sexual

50. A monkey raised in isolation, on the other hand, seems to have no clear idea of the appropriate sexual behavior when confronted with a receptive member of the opposite sex. In monkeys, sexual behavior is primarily influenced by _____.

learning (*or* experience)

51. Harry Harlow, a psychologist who has done extensive research on the importance of early experience in monkeys, has suggested that normal heterosexual behavior in primates depends on three factors: (a) the influence of *hormones*; (b) the development of the *appropriate sexual responses* in early play with other monkeys; and (c) an *affectional bond* between members of the opposite sex.

52. Monkeys reared in isolation do not lack the appropriate sex hormones; but because they have never had the chance to play with the other young monkeys, they have not learned the appropriate _____ responses. And because they have never interacted with either a mother or other monkeys, they have not learned the trust necessary to form an affectional bond.

sexual

53. Although we cannot automatically extend these findings with monkeys to sexual development in humans, observations indicate that the same three factors may be important to the development of normal heterosexual behavior: hormones, the development of appropriate sexual responses, and an _____ bond between members of the opposite sex.

affectional

54. Among humans an additional influence on sexual behavior is provided by the *culture* in which a person is raised. All cultures place some restrictions on sexual behavior, and what the culture says is right or wrong will have a significant influence on the sexual _____ of its members.

behavior

55. Some cultures are very *permissive*, encouraging sex play among the children and placing few restrictions on adult sexual relationships. Some cultures are very *restrictive*, frowning on any indication of sexuality in childhood and restricting adult sexual behavior to narrowly prescribed forms. Most societies would fall some-

restrictive

where between the very permissive and the very _____ .

56. Until recently, how would you have classified American society in terms of its attitudes toward sexual behavior? Fairly restrictive or fairly permissive? If you said "restrictive," you are closer to the opinions of most authorities in evaluating the attitude of the average American up until the 1960s.

57. There are indications, however, that the United States, along with most other West-

permissive

ern nations, has become more _____ in its attitudes toward sexual behavior. (The text discusses the reasons and evidence for this change.)

motives

58. The two basic _____ we have discussed so far are hunger and sex. Other basic motives covered in the text are body temperature, thirst and maternal behavior.

59. All of these motives have some basis in the physiological condition of the organism. But there is another determiner of action, important to both animals and humans, whose physiological correlates are unknown—the need for *sensory stimulation*. Both animals and people enjoy exploring new places and manipulating objects.

sensory

They appear to need a certain amount of _____ stimulation.

60. Both people and animals are motivated to seek stimulation—to explore actively their environment, even when the activity satisfies no identified bodily need. Thus

survival

there appears to be a class of basic motives, in addition to _____

social

motives and _____ motives, which are called *curiosity motives.*

61. When people participate in experiments where the normal amount of stimulation is greatly reduced, their functioning is impaired and they cannot tolerate the situation

stimulation

for very long. A certain amount of sensory _____ is necessary for the well-being of the organism.

62. The need for sensory stimulation can be understood in terms of the concept of *arousal level*. The organism's arousal level can range from sleep and lethargy to

arousal

alertness and intense excitement. Theoretically, there is an optimal _____ level in terms of internal and external stimuli. Conditions that depart too severely

level

from this optimal _____ in either direction incite the organism to act to restore the equilibrium.

63. Arousal level can be affected by such internal stimuli as hunger and sex or by such

optimal

external stimuli as the loud clanging of a bell. The concept of an _____ arousal level provides a framework in which to view the results of experiments on sensory deprivation.

64. Too little stimulation can motivate the organism just as much as too intense or dramatic a change in stimulation can. We seek novelty and complexity in our environment, but situations that are too strange or too complex arouse anxiety. We will

optimal

say more about an _____ level of arousal when we consider emotion in the next chapter.

TERMS AND CONCEPTS

survival motives _____

_____

_____

_____

social motives _____

_____

_____

_____

curiosity motives _____

_____

_____

_____

homeostasis _____

_____

_____

_____

sensor _____

_____

_____

_____

ideal value _____

_____

_____

_____

comparator _____

_____

_____

_____

need _____

_____

_____

_____

drive _____

_____

_____

_____

hypothalamic thermostat _____

_____

_____

_____

osmoreceptors _____

_____

_____

_____

obesity _____

_____

_____

_____

anorexia _____

_____

_____

_____

satiety detectors _____

_____

_____

_____

LH syndrome _____

_____

_____

_____

VMH syndrome _____

_____

_____

_____

set point _____

_____

_____

_____

metabolic rate _____

_____

_____

_____

fat cells* _____

_____

_____

_____

set-point hypothesis* _____

_____

_____

_____

estrogen _____

_____

_____

_____

progesterone _____

_____

_____

_____

androgens _____

_____

_____

_____

hermaphrodite _____

_____

_____

_____

transsexual _____

_____

_____

_____

instinct* _____

_____

_____

_____

imprinting* _____

_____

_____

_____

sensory deprivation studies _____

_____

_____

_____

drive-reduction principle _____

_____

_____

_____

optimal arousal level _____

_____

_____

_____

*Indicates term used in Critical Discussion

_____ 1. Psychologists usually narrow the broad concept of motivation to those particular factors that _____ and _____ behavior
   a. organize, control
   b. energize, direct
   c. activate, modify
   d. determine, control

_____ 2. In the study of restrained and unrestrained eaters, after the restrained eaters had overeaten through preloading
   a. they continued to overeat at the same rate
   b. they were more willing to diet
   c. they were reluctant to eat more
   d. their control broke down

_____ 3. Rats that are obese because of hypothalamic damage
   a. eat slightly more than normal, to maintain the obesity
   b. eat less if force-fed to "super obesity"
   c. overeat substantially if starved briefly
   d. all of the above

_____ 4. _____ typically think of themselves as members of the opposite sex.
   a. Male homosexuals
   b. Lesbians
   c. Transsexuals
   d. all of the above

_____ 5. Cultures differ with regard to their sexual taboos; _____ is prohibited by most cultures while _____ are viewed with varying degrees of tolerance.
   a. homosexuality, masturbation and incest
   b. sexual activity among children, incest and premarital sex
   c. incest, masturbation and homosexuality
   d. masturbation, premarital sex and homosexuality

_____ 6. According to Harlow, monkeys who are deprived of contact with other monkeys when they are young have unusual sexual responses at maturity because
   a. their hormonal development does not proceed normally
   b. they fail to develop specific sexual responses, such as pelvic thrusting
   c. they do not experience normal sexual arousal

   d. they fail to develop trusting, affectionate relationships with other monkeys

_____ 7. Storm's theory of homosexuality proposes that sexual preference in adulthood depends on
   a. sexual arousal before the age of 8
   b. psychological readiness at puberty
   c. the social environment that is present when the individual's sex drive comes into full force during adolescence
   d. heterosexual availability in adulthood

_____ 8. The term _____ refers to physiological state of deprivation; the term _____ refers to the psychological consequences of that state.
   a. drive; need
   b. need; incentive
   c. need; drive
   d. drive; incentive

_____ 9. An experiment comparing methods for treating obesity found that
   a. drug therapy was more effective than behavior modification in the short-term
   b. behavior modification produced a greater weight loss than drug therapy on a one-year follow-up
   c. both methods produced both a short-term and long-term weight loss
   d. all of the above

_____10. When obese rats with lesions in the ventromedial hypothalamus are force-fed until they become "super obese," they
   a. eat enough to maintain their weight at this "super obese" level
   b. reduce their food intake until they return to their normal (nonobese) weight
   c. continue to overeat and become increasingly obese
   d. reduce their food intake until they return to their "normal obese" level

_____11. If one marital partner has a very high SSS score and the other has a very low score, the likelihood of marital disharmony
   a. increases
   b. decreases
   c. decreases only if the male has the high score
   d. decreases only if the female has the high score

12. Surveys of college students' sex-related problems suggest that
    a. females list more problems and complaints than males do
    b. males list more problems and complaints than females do
    c. females are more likely to express fears and insecurities; males are more likely to complain about women
    d. males are more likely to express insecurities; females are more likely to complain about men

13. The concept of _____ can be compared to a thermostat, which turns the heat on when the temperature falls below a certain level and off when the temperature rises.
    a. homeostasis
    b. need
    c. drive
    d. incentive

14. Destruction of cells in the ventromedial hypothalamus causes an animal to
    a. eat more slowly
    b. not eat at all
    c. overeat
    d. respond to long-term but not to immediate nutritive needs

15. If the lateral hypothalamus cells of a rat are stimulated electrically with a weak current, the rat will
    a. eat even if it is satiated
    b. eat if it is hungry
    c. eat more slowly
    d. stop eating altogether

16. The concept of arousal level involves the assumption that
    a. minimum arousal leads to motivated behavior
    b. maximum arousal is necessary for motivated behavior to occur
    c. the organism is constantly attempting to increase its arousal level
    d. there is an optimal level of arousal for the organism

17. Subjects who experienced experimental sensory deprivation over an extended period
    a. became bored, restless, irritable, and upset
    b. found it created a soothingly altered state of consciousness akin to meditation
    c. were often better able to concentrate on problems in the absence of distractions
    d. experienced subjective time distortions, but gave no evidence of this in the pattern of their response to the experimenters

18. If a monkey is fed each time it takes a puzzle apart, the monkey will
    a. play with the puzzle more than it did before the food reward was introduced
    b. lose interest in manipulation and view the puzzle as a means of acquiring food
    c. play with the puzzle the same amount of time as it did before the food reward was introduced
    d. stop playing with the puzzle entirely

19. Study of neural mechanisms for the control of sexual behavior have shown us the complexity of such control. For example, it has been found that
    a. men with severed spinal cords can have erections and ejaculate
    b. male rats stimulated electrically in the hypothalamus will indiscriminately mount any available partner
    c. male monkeys can be switched from eating to sexual behavior by switching electrodes in the posterior hypothalamus
    d. all of the above

20. It is true that
    a. most transsexuals are homosexuals
    b. most transsexuals are males
    c. most homosexuals are transsexuals
    d. most transsexuals are bisexual

KEY TO SELF-QUIZ

20. b	15. a	10. d	5. c
19. a	14. c	9. d	4. c
18. b	13. a	8. c	3. d
17. a	12. c	7. c	2. d
16. d	11. a	6. d	1. b

INDIVIDUAL EXERCISE

CUES FOR EATING

Introduction

Human beings share aspects of such basic motives as hunger with other species, but they also eat for a variety of other reasons: the odor or sight of food acting as an incentive, social customs, personal habits, and so forth. As the text notes, overweight individuals seem to eat more in response to external cues and less to internal cues than normal-weight subjects. Whether you consider yourself to be overweight or simply desire to maintain a well-balanced diet, it is instructive to pay some attention to what, when, and why you eat. One way to do this is to keep a journal or diary of food intake.

Procedure

The easiest way to keep such records is to first develop a one-page form that you can use for each day's food intake. The top of the page should include the date and any other data you might wish to analyze later, for example, day of the week, weather (including temperature), amount of sleep the night before, amount of exercise, and so forth. The main part of the form should have column headings for the primary data—time, food eaten, and hunger pangs or other cues relevant to eating. It might also be useful to include a few additional headings, for example, your location, your activity, other people around, and your mood. If you are serious about some form of diet—to lose or gain weight, or for other reasons—it is probably best also to include spaces for calories eaten as well as any other food components you wish to control, for example, fats or carbohydrates.

Try the first version of your form for a day or two to see if it meets your needs. When you have arrived at an appropriate form, duplicate a supply of them; arrange to fill it in every day, without fail. Add up whatever data you wish to analyze (for example, number of meals and total calories) daily and in a weekly summary. Also try to summarize in a few words the cues for each eating episode and categorize them as internal or external.

Initially, you may not find any obvious pattern, but keep at it for a while. Most people quickly discover patterns in their eating behavior that they were not previously aware of. Even if you do not wish to change the eating habits you discover, you will be learning more about yourself.

As you monitor yourself in this way, you are actually taking the first step of a self-modification program; such programs play an important role in behavior therapy (see Chapter 16 of the text). The next steps involve choosing some aspect(s) of your eating behavior that you wish to change and setting up a personal reward system to shape the desired behavior. If you are interested in such a program, an excellent reference is *Human Behavior: Analysis and Application*, from which the sample record form and self-management contracts on the following pages are taken. Other references on self-modification of behavior are also noted below.

References

1. Mahoney, M. J., & Mahoney, K. (1985) *Permanent weight control*. New York: Norton.

2. Reese, E. P., Howard, J., & Reese, T. W. (1978) *Human behavior: Analysis and application* (2nd ed.). Dubuque, Iowa: Brown.

3. Thoresen, C. E., & Mahoney, M. J. (1974) *Behavioral self-control*. New York: Holt, Rinehart & Winston.

4. Watson, D. L., & Tharp, R. G. (1985) *Self-directed behavior: Self-modification for personal adjustment* (4th ed.). Belmont, Calif.: Wadsworth.

EXAMPLE OF DAILY RECORD USED IN SELF-MANAGEMENT OF WEIGHT

Day _Th_   Date _10/11_   WEIGHT _138_   GOAL _118_   CALORIES, eaten _3828_

Baseline _X_   Program _____   Maintenance _____   Calories, exercise _100_

Amt. sleep last night _6 h._   Weather _cold_   Total meals _7_

Time	Place	Activity	People	Mood	Amount	FOOD	Calories	Sum
7:30	Dorm	Breakfast	People?	bitchy	1 1 1 2	o.j. h.b. egg revolting coffee c. & s. toast, butter	120 78 40 210	} 448
10:30	College Inn	break	Debbie, Neal Dinny, Barb	BORED	1 1	Danish coffee	125 40	165
Noon	Dorm	lunch	Jill, Pearl, Eva, Stephanie	OK	1 1 2	milk spaghetti cake ☹	160 couldn't eat 500	} 660
4:30	Snack bar	after lab	Ed, David, Jerrilynn	Ravenous	1 1	cheeseburger Fr. fries (make up for lunch)	470 250	720
6:30	Dorm	dinner	Jerri, Betsy Denise, Chip, Cathy	good	2 1 2 1	meat (lamb?) peas sm. potatoes choc. ice cream	470 115 120 100	} 805
10:30	Snack bar	a well-deserved break	Tim & Marci Cindy, Richard Skye & Talley TOM	tired	2 1	beer sm. potato chips	300 230	530
11-12	Room	studying	Rhea for a while; Esther & Madeleine came by	zonked	½ box (maybe 10?) 	choc. chip cookies	500?	500

448
765
1360
1835
3828

Total meals _7_ Total Cal. _3828_

EXERCISE

Moderate (200/hr; 33/10 min)		Vigorous (300/hr; 50/10 min)		Strenuous (400/hr; 70/10 min)	
Walking (slow)	_15_	Walking (3 mph)	_10_	Stren. sports	_____
Bicycling	_____	Horseback riding	_____	Dancing (fast)	_____
House work	_____	Bowling	_____	Jogging	_____
	_____	Swimming	_____		_____

Total time _15_ Cal. _50_   Time _10_ Cal. _50_   Time _____ Cal. _____

COMMENTS: _This was not a good day_

Name: _____ General Goal: _20 lb. weight loss_____

Duration of Contract (dates) _Oct 4___ to _Oct 11.___ Program _✔___ Maintenance _____

<u>Data</u>

    Keep daily _✔_ or _____ records of:

      _weight_____   _extra exercise (time)_____

      _calories_____   _____

      _#between meal snacks___   _____

    Data will be analysed and plotted: _every night_____

<u>Program</u>
    <u>Behavior</u>   <u>Consequences</u>

        Keep records at 5 pts each; 10 pt graph   30 pts
        1600 cal. weekdays; 1800 weekends (2 days)   50
        Only 2 snacks a day: Total 300 cal. (500 weekend)   10
        Eat at least 2 balanced meals a day   10
        Exercise 15 min/day (during week)   10

    <u>Stimulus control</u>
        No food in room   10
        Eat only <u>with</u> someone, in regular place   10

    <u>Alternative behavior</u> (if applicable)
        when feel urge to eat, remember <u>Richard</u> can
        wear my jeans and I can't Resist urge —
        think "gorgeous me"
    <u>Covert</u> (behavior, consequences)

                        If points, possible daily total _130_

    Bonus?
        50 points each pound lost
        200 "free" calories if stay within limit whole week

<u>Exchange</u>
           <u>Reinforcers</u>   (Aversive Consequences?)
    movies, TV, reading etc - 10 pts/hr   Point cost: 1 pt each 10 cal.
    shower — 10 pts   over limit
    weekend away — 100 pts   <u>Also</u>: if 200 cal. over,
    gas for car -   10 pts   tell Richard I blew it
    clothes - 100 pts per $10.00 worth   if 300 cal. over, all calls
                                   from pay phone for a
                                  <u>week</u>

Signature _____ Date _____

11
Emotion

1. The basic feelings we experience include not only motives such as hunger and sex but also emotions such as joy and anger. Emotions and motives are closely related.

motives

Emotions can energize and direct behavior in the same way that _____ do. Despite their similarities, motives and emotions need to be distinguished. One basis for distinguishing between them is that emotions are triggered from the outside, whereas motives are activated from within.

2. Emotions are usually aroused by external events; motives are usually aroused by

internal

_____ events (for example, a homeostatic imbalance). Another distinction between emotions and motives is that emotions invariably activate the *autonomic nervous system*, whereas motives may not.

3. These distinctions are not absolute. Nevertheless, emotions and motives are sufficiently different in their source of activation and their involvement of the

autonomic

_____ nervous system to merit separate treatment.

4. When we experience an intense emotion, such as fear or anger, a number of bodily

bodily

changes occur. These _____ changes may include rapid heart rate and breathing, dryness of the throat and mouth, increased muscle tension, trembling of the extremities, and a "sinking feeling" in the stomach.

5. Most of the bodily changes that occur during emotional arousal result from activa-

nervous

tion of the *sympathetic division* of the autonomic _____ system as it prepares the body for emergency action.

sympathetic

6. The _____ system gears the body for energy output. As the emotion subsides, the *parasympathetic system* (the energy conserving system) takes over and returns the body to its normal state.

7. The actions of the sympathetic system clearly contribute to the intensity of emotional experience. The greater the psysiological arousal generated by the

sympathetic

_____ system, the greater the intesnity of the emotion.

8. But can we distinguish between emotions in terms of the particular pattern of

arousal

physiological arousal? Is there one pattern of physiological _____ for joy, another pattern for fear, another for anger, and so on?

9. The question is not easily answered. Many of the early experiments in this area

physiological arousal

failed to find distinct patterns of _____ _____ for different emotions. In fact, just a few years ago most psychology textbooks reported that the pattern of autonomic arousal does not differ significantly from one emotion to another.

10. However, recent research, using more sophisticated procedures, has established that

emotion

the pattern of autonomic arousal does vary in some ways from one _____ to another. For example, heart rate is faster for the emotions of anger and fear than for the emotions of happiness and disgust; and the former two can be distinguished by the fact that skin temperature is higher in anger than in fear.

pattern

11. Thus research indicates that we can distinguish between some emotions in terms of the _____ of autonomic arousal.

12. One of the earliest theories of emotion was the *James-Lange theory*, which proposed that what we feel as emotional is the *feedback* from the autonomic arousal.

Lange

According to the James-_____ theory, we see a bear, start to run, and then experience the emotion we call fear.

13. The notion that the feeling of sorrow results from the tears that flow when a person

James

hears tragic news is a statement of the _____-Lange theory of emotion.

James-Lange

14. The _____ – _____ theory maintains that emotion is defined by the bodily changes that are perceived and labeled after they occur. The experience of emotion is *feedback* from the bodily changes.

15. An alternative explanation of emotion proposes that the bodily changes and the experience of emotion occur at the same time. "Butterflies" in the stomach and the felt emotion of fear occur together; the brain and the sympathetic nervous system

simultaneously (*or synonym*)

are aroused _____ by an emotion-producing situation.

16. Because an emotional experience is not a momentary event but takes place over time, it is difficult to determine whether the autonomic arousal precedes or accompanies the emotion. When you are suddenly confronted with possible danger (for example, a loud sound that might be an explosion, a narrowly avoided accident), your pounding heart and feeling of weakness in the knees may precede full aware-

is not

ness of the danger. In this instance the James-Lange theory of emotion (*is/is not*) correct.

17. More often, however, autonomic arousal follows the appraisal of a situation as dangerous. You realize that the gray shape behind the door is not a shadow but a man with a gun; the emotional experience of fear precedes the autonomic activity.

is

This observation (*is/is not*) in accord with the James-Lange theory.

18. Regardless of what point in the emotional sequence physiological arousal has its effect, it influences the *intensity* with which we experience emotion. People whose spinal cords have been injured so that they receive no sensations from the internal organs report that their experience of emotion is less intense than it was before their

intensity

injury. Feedback from internal bodily changes is important to the _____ of the emotional experience.

19. When we experience an event, we interpret the situation with respect to our personal goals and well-being. This interpretation is known as *cognitive appraisal*. Cog-

appraisal

nitive _____ has two distinct parts: the appraisal process itself and the resulting belief.

cognitive

20. Our _____ appraisal of a situation contributes to our emotional experience. If someone tells us he cannot stand the sight of us, we may feel very angry or hurt if that person is a friend, but feel barely perturbed if the person is a mental patient we have never met before.

cognitive appraisal

21. In this example, our _____ _____ of the situation determines the intensity of our emotional experience.

appraisal

22. Cognitive _____ is also heavily responsible for differentiating emotions. Unlike autonomic arousal, the beliefs resulting from cognitive appraisal are rich enough to distinguish among many different emotions, and the appraisal process itself is fast enough to account for the speed with which some emotions occur.

appraisal

23. Thus our emotional experience depends on the autonomic feedback that we receive and on the _____ _____ of the emotion producing situation. Research indicates, however, that cognitive appraisal by itself can be sufficient to determine which of several emotions is experienced.

cognitive appraisal

24. Under certain experimental conditions, the same autonomic feedback an be given to a subject over a range of different situations. Under these conditions cognitive appraisal of each situation causes the subject to experience a range of different _____ :

emotions

25. These experiments indicate that both autonomic arousal and cognitive appraisal contribute to the intensity of the emotion, and that sometimes cognitive appraisal alone can determine the specific _____ we experience.

emotion

26. While research indicates that autonomic arousal may aid in differentiating emotions, it seems to play less of a role than does _____ _____ .

cognitive
appraisal

27. The *facial expression* that accompanies an emotion serves to communicate that emotion to other people. Different facial expressions are associated with different emotions, and most observers have little difficulty in identifying the _____ that each facial expression conveys.

emotion

28. These facial expressions have a universal meaning, regardless of the culture in which the individual is raised. Whether an individual is from the United States, Japan, or a remote preliterate tribe in New Guinea, the _____ _____ associated with different emotions are the same.

facial

expressions

29. The universality of certain emotional expressions suggest that they are innate responses. We do not have to learn the facial expression that goes with a given emotion; rather, it is _____ .

innate

30. Research indicates that facial expressions, in addition to their communicative function, also contribute to our experience of emotion. Just as we receive feedback about our autonomic arousal, so we receive feedback about our _____ expression.

facial

31. These two sources of feedback combine with the _____ _____ of the situation to produce an emotional experience.

cognitive

appraisal

32. Thus the specific emotion experienced and the intensity of that emotion depend on the nature of the autonomic arousal, the feedback from the _____

facial

expression

_____ , and the individual's cognitive appraisal of the situation.

33. Among our various emotional reactions, psychologists have singled out one in particular for extensive study, namely, *aggression*. This special treatment is partly

aggression

due to the social significance of _____ .

34. Another reason why psychologists are so interested in aggression is that different theories of social interactions explain the phenomenon in quite different ways. Thus Freud's *psychoanalytic theory* views aggression as a drive, whereas *social-*

aggression

learning theory views _____ as a learned response.

drive

35. These two views—aggression as a _____ versus aggression as a

learned

_____ response—have dominated much of the research on aggression.

psychoanalytic

36. According to Freud's early _____ theory, many of our actions are determined by instincts, particularly sexual instincts. When expression of these instincts is blocked or frustrated, an aggressive drive is induced.

37. Later psychoanalytic theorists generalized this *frustration-aggression hypothesis*. They proposed that whenever a person's efforts to reach *any* goal is blocked, an

drive

aggressive _____ is induced. The drive motivates behavior to injure the obstacle (person or object) causing the frustration.

frustration-
aggression

38. There are two critical aspects to the _____-_____ hypothesis. One is that the cause of aggression is frustration. The other is that frustration has the properties of a basic drive, namely, that it energizes and directs behavior.

39. Thus the frustration-aggression hypothesis expands on Freud's ideas and is not limited to frustration of sexual instincts. Rather it argues that frustration of any

drive

sort (sexual or otherwise) sets up an aggressive _____, which is satisfied only when the frustrating object has been removed.

40. Social-learning theory takes a quite different approach to aggression. It focuses on

learn

the behaviors people _____ in response to environmental contingencies.

41. Some behaviors may be rewarded while others may produce unfavorable results.

rewards

Through the process of differential _____, people learn the more successful behavior patterns.

social-
learning

42. With this emphasis on learning, it is no surprise that _____-_____ theory rejects the concept of aggression as a frustration-produced drive. The theory proposes instead that aggression is similar to

learned

any other _____ response.

frustrated

43. A person who is _____ by a blocked goal or disturbed by some stressful event experiences an unpleasant emotion. How the individual responds to this emotion depends on the kind of responses he or she has found successful in the past for coping with stress.

44. According to social-learning theory, those responses that have been rewarded in the past will be repeated again. The frustrated individual will aggress, withdraw, try harder to surmount the obstacle, or resort to alcohol depending on which behavior

rewarded · was _____ in the past.

45. Frustration provokes aggression in people who have learned from past experience

learning · to respond to adverse situations with aggressive behavior. Social-_____ theory assumes that (1) frustration is just one of several causes of aggression and (2) aggression is a response with no drivelike properties.

46. A survey of the research literature indicates that both theories have some evidence in their favor. Research findings with lower animals provides considerable support for the idea of an innate aggressive drive. But research with humans tends to favor

learned · the idea that aggression is a _____ response.

47. From an evolutionary perspective, the relative importance of drive versus learning

aggressive · in explaining _____ behavior appears to change as we go from lower to higher species. Learning plays an increasingly important role as we go up the evolutionary scale.

drive

learned response

48. Studies with humans that try to distinguish between aggression as a _____ and as a _____ _____ often focus on *catharsis*. Catharsis refers to purging an emotion by experiencing it intensely.

49. If aggression is a drive, then releasing pent-up aggressive feelings should be cathartic; expressing aggression should decrease the person's need to aggress. You might

psychoanalytic · expect this view to be proposed by (*psychoanalytic/social learning*) theorists.

cathartic · **50.** If the expression of aggression is c_____ , then hitting a per-

decrease · son who has angered you should (*increase/decrease*) your feelings of anger.

51. Studies of children indicate, however, that behaving aggressively does not reduce aggressive behavior, and may even increase it. These findings (*do/do not*) support

do not · the idea that expressing aggression is cathartic.

52. When college students are given the opportunity to shock a subject in a laboratory experiment, they give progressively stronger shocks as the trials progress. Acting aggressively appears to increase subsequent aggression. This fails to support the view

cathartic · that expressing aggression is _____ .

53. Some officials of the television industry defend violent television programs on the grounds that expressing aggression vicariously (by observing violence) is beneficial; viewers discharge their aggressive impulses through viewing and thus become less likely to perform aggressive acts. In light of what we have said about catharsis, such

false · a claim is probably (*true/false*).

54. Several lines of research indicate that there is a positive relationship between the

television · amount of exposure children have to violence on _____ and the extent to which they act aggressively. The text discusses ways in which exposure to filmed violence may elicit aggressive behavior.

55. In summary, the majority of research studies point to the conclusion that viewing violence leads to aggressive behavior, particularly in young children. This argues

cathartic · against aggression as _____ , and against the view that aggression is a drive.

TERMS AND CONCEPTS

autonomic nervous system _____

_____

_____

_____

sympathetic division _____

_____

_____

_____

parasympathetic division _____

_____

_____

_____

James-Lange theory _____

_____

_____

_____

polygraph* _____

_____

_____

_____

voice-stress analyzer* _____

_____

_____

_____

cognitive appraisal _____

_____

_____

_____

epinephrine _____

_____

_____

_____

prosopagnosic _____

_____

_____

_____

facial feedback hypothesis _____

_____

_____

_____

opponent-process theory* _____

_____

_____

_____

psychoanalytic theory of aggression _____

_____

_____

_____

social-learning theory of aggression _____

_____

_____

_____

frustration-aggression hypothesis _____

_____

_____

_____

death instinct* _____

_____

_____

_____

vicarious learning _____

_____

_____

_____

models _____

_____

_____

_____

catharsis _____

_____

_____

_____

*Indicates term used in Critical Discussion

_____ 1. Which statement *best* describes the relationship between physiological arousal and emotional states?
   a. Patterns of physiological arousal are related to specific emotions.
   b. Arousal accompanies emotion, but specific physiological patterns do not differ from one emotion to another.
   c. Arousal and emotion are independent of each other.
   d. Only "fight-or-flight" situations produce both arousal and emotion.

_____ 2. Observations of people during crises such as fires and floods indicate that
   a. the performance of most individuals is not greatly affected by crisis
   b. only about 15 percent show organized, effective behavior
   c. most individuals are temporarily stunned or frozen with panic
   d. prior mood state determines the individual's degree of impairment under stress

_____ 3. The fact that aggressive behaviors can be elicited in laboratory-bred rats by stimulation of the hypothalamus supports
   a. a biologically based aggressive drive
   b. the frustration-aggression hypothesis
   c. behavioral theories of aggression
   d. the theory of instrumental aggression

_____ 4. In addition to taking a more generally cognitive position than strict behaviorists, social learning theorists stress the importance of _____ learning, that is, learning by _____ .
   a. operant, reinforcement
   b. vicarious, observation
   c. latent, nonreinforced trials
   d. self-discovery, doing

_____ 5. According to Darwin, facial expressions of emotions
   a. are learned through conditioning
   b. are found only in humans
   c. are primarily dependent on cultural influences
   d. result from inherited patterns that originally had some survival value

_____ 6. The frustration-aggression hypothesis
   a. assumes that aggression is a basic instinct
   b. claims that frustration and aggression are both instinctive patterns
   c. assumes that frustration produces aggression
   d. was developed by social learning theorists

_____ 7. From a psychologist's viewpoint, much of the controversy over whether aggressive behavior should be displayed on television centers on the question of whether it is
   a. cathartic as opposed to stimulating aggressive acts
   b. frightening to children
   c. excessively violent
   d. justified by the circumstances

_____ 8. The James-Lange theory of emotion says that
   a. the thalamus has the central role in arousal
   b. we are afraid because we run
   c. perception of the emotion leads to physiological changes
   d. all of the above

_____ 9. Social learning theory proposes that aggression
   a. is instinctive
   b. results from an aggressive drive
   c. results from frustration
   d. is no different from any other learned response

_____10. Researchers studying the influence of television aggression on children found that watching violent television programs increased aggressive behavior in boys but not necessarily in girls. This difference may be related to the fact that
   a. girls in our society are seldom reinforced for aggression
   b. most of the aggressive television models are male
   c. in general, girls in our society imitate aggression less than boys
   d. all of the above

_____11. The most common basis for differentiating between motivation and emotion assumes that the former is aroused by _____ and that the latter is aroused by _____ .
   a. drives; instincts
   b. instincts; drives
   c. internal stimuli; external stimuli
   d. external stimuli; internal stimuli

_____12. The ability to recognize facial expressions of emotion seems to be located in the

a. hypothalamus
b. left cerebral hemisphere
c. right cerebral hemisphere
d. sympathetic nervous system

_____13. When photographs of emotional expressions are shown to people of different cultures, basic emotions are
a. recognized across all cultures
b. recognized only across industrialized cultures
c. recognized only across preliterate cultures
d. poorly recognized across cultures

_____14. Which of the following is *not* a true statement regarding emotional arousal level and performance?
a. The optimum level of arousal differs for different tasks.
b. Individuals are very similar in the extent to which their behavior is disrupted by arousal.
c. Intense arousal can seriously impair the performance of organized behavior.
d. Performance is optimal at moderate levels of arousal.

_____15. Most of the physiological changes that occur during intense emotion result from activation of the
a. sympathetic system
b. parasympathetic system
c. thalamic system
d. thalamus

_____16. In the Schachter and Singer experiment, subjects were injected with epinephrine and given different information about the drug's effects. This experiment was designed to
a. distinguish among emotions on a physiological basis
b. examine physiological responses to the drug
c. produce artificial euphoria through purely chemical means
d. identify the factors that determine how an emotion is labeled

_____17. A *prosopagnosic* is an individual who
a. cannot recognize facial expressions of emotions
b. has a brain lesion in the hypothalamus
c. has an imbalance in the autonomic nervous system
d. has great difficulty recognizing familiar faces

_____18. Ordinary-seeming individuals who commit hideously brutal crimes often
a. have been meek and conforming in the past
b. have a previous history of aggressive behavior
c. are unaware of the seriousness of the crime
d. are unusually passive in their behavior

_____19. When veterans with spinal-cord injuries were interviewed about their emotions, it was found that the _____ the lesion, the more emotionality _____ following injury.
a. lower, increased
b. lower, decreased
c. higher, decreased
d. higher, increased

_____20. A Chinese novel might describe a happy person by saying "He scratched his ears and cheeks." This description suggests that
a. all expressions of emotion are determined by maturation
b. cultures teach some unique forms of emotional expression
c. facial expressions are significant in conveying meaning
d. humans experience a wide range of emotions

KEY TO SELF-QUIZ

20. b	15. a	10. d	5. d
19. c	14. b	9. d	4. b
18. b	13. a	8. b	3. a
17. d	12. c	7. a	2. b
16. d	11. c	6. c	1. a

INDIVIDUAL EXERCISES

MEASURING MOTIVATION

Introduction

Psychologists study motivation in many ways. In laboratory studies, precise instruments that measure physiological responses in motivated behavior can be used. However, for classroom purposes it is difficult to make the necessary arrangements to measure physiological changes. For that reason the sentence-completion test that follows has been chosen. Many psychologists feel that it has clinical value in the study of personal adjustment.

Procedure

Below are 50 incomplete sentences. Take about 30 minutes to complete all the sentences. Try not to omit any item. Be sure to express your real feelings. The results will be more valuable if you write down thoughts that occur to you spontaneously, as soon as you see the first word or words of each item. You will be the only person to score the test and to see the results. Therefore, try to be frank and honest by writing the first thought that comes to mind.

After completing the test, score your sentences according to the directions given on p. 287 of the Appendix.

1. College _____

_____

_____

2. I need _____

_____

3. My nerves _____

_____

_____

4. Women _____

_____

_____

5. Secretly, I _____

_____

_____

6. My father _____

_____

_____

7. I wish _____

_____

_____

8. I'm afraid _____

_____

9. People _____

_____

10. The future _____

_____

_____

11. I worry about _____

_____

_____

12. Men _____

_____

_____

13. I know _____

_____

_____

14. At night _____

_____

15. Marriage _____

_____

16. My mother _____

_____

17. If I could _____

_____

_____

18. My studies _____

_____

_____

19. My friends _____

_____

_____

20. I get annoyed _____

_____

21. I daydream about _____

_____

22. There are times when _____

_____

23. My feelings _____

_____

_____

24. My goal _____

_____

_____

25. I find it difficult _____

_____

_____

26. Most of my friends _____

_____

27. I know it is silly but _____

_____

28. When I was a youngster _____

_____

_____

29. When I marry _____

_____

_____

_____

30. My father thinks my mother _____

_____

_____

31. My family _____

_____

_____

32. I would do anything to forget _____

_____

_____

33. A real friend _____

_____

_____

34. Most of my friends don't know _____

_____

35. I think a mother _____

_____

_____

36. I could be happy if _____

_____

_____

37. Ten years from now _____

_____

_____

38. Most of all, I _____

_____

_____

39. Sex _____

_____

_____

40. Compared with others, I _____

_____

_____

41. I can't understand _____

_____

_____

_____

42. My father and I _____

_____

_____

43. Dating _____

_____

_____

44. My mother thinks my father _____

_____

_____

45. What I want most _____

_____

_____

46. My mother and I _____

_____

_____

47. My biggest fault _____

_____

_____

48. Sometimes I _____

_____

_____

49. My dreams _____

_____

_____

50. My appearance _____

_____

_____

Questions for Discussion

1. Does your score place you above or below the median? What does this mean?

2. Which items were most difficult for you to complete? Why?

3. Does your score correspond to your own evaluation of your adjustment?

4. Does the test reveal some of your current difficulties? Why or why not?

5. How might a clinical psychologist find your responses helpful in diagnosing your difficulties?

6. What are some of the cautions that should be observed in interpreting the results?

THE COIN-FLIP DECISION MAKER

Equipment Needed

A coin

Procedure

1. This procedure allows you to "focus" on your emotional responses when you are conflicted or confused about a decision. You have weighed the pros and cons but cannot decide on the evidence alone; you wonder just how you would really *feel* after deciding one way or the other. Next time you have this problem, try the coin technique, as follows.

2. Take out your coin and tell yourself that you will let a flip of the coin determine the decision. Put one choice on heads, the other on tails, and flip the coin.

3. The instant the coin lands and you realize what the outcome is, pay special attention to your own reaction. Do you hear a sigh of relief? Or a still small voice asking, "Two out of three?"

4. Frivolous as it may seem, such a technique may be useful. It appears to provide an instant role-playing situation, in which you sense how you would really feel if the decision had been made for you, rather than trying to predict your feelings through logic alone.

12
Mental Abilities and Their Measurement

LEARNING OBJECTIVES

12-1.   Be familiar with the range of tests that measure ability and understand the two dimensions (aptitude–achievement, general–specific) that describe such tests.

12-2.   Be able to specify the difference between reliability and validity and why each is necessary for a test to be trustworthy.

12-3.   Be familiar with the development of tests of intellectual ability and the general format of the Stanford-Binet and Wechsler Intelligence Scales. Know how items are selected and how IQ scores are interpreted.

12-4.   Be able to discuss the relationship between ability test scores and academic performance, including the problems of selection and group differences in test scores.

12-5.   Be able to describe how factor-analytic techniques were used by Spearman and Thurstone to separate the different abilities that contribute to intelligence.

12-6.   Be familiar with the componential approach to analyzing performance on intelligence test items.

12-7.   Understand the distinction some psychologists make between "academic intelligence" and "practical intelligence," and the significance of the distinction in evaluating current tests of intelligence.

12-8.   Be familiar with the evidence for genetic contributions to intelligence. Understand what a heritability estimate does and does not tell you.

12-9.   Be able to discuss environmental influences on intelligence, including the concept of reaction range and evidence from Head Start programs.

12-10.   Know what the public concerns about psychological testing are and what psychologists think about these concerns.

1. Ability tests are designed to provide an objective measure of a person's knowledge, skills, and special talents. The written test you take to obtain a driver's license measures your knowledge of motor vehicle laws; it is thus one type of

ability

_____ test.

2. The final examination you take at the end of this course measures your

knowledge

kn_____ of the various concepts and facts covered in

ability test

the lectures and in the textbook. It is also an _____ _____ .

3. In attempting to appraise an individual's abilities, psychologists often distinguish between what a person can do now and what the person might do if trained. Ability tests that identify what you can do now, measuring knowledge or skills already attained, are called *achievement tests.* Ben has had two years of typing instruction in high school. If we were interested in how fast and how accurately he can type

achievement

now, we would administer an _____ test.

4. Since course examinations and driver's license tests measure attained knowledge

achievement

and skills, they would also be considered _____ tests.

5. Tests designed to measure *capacity to learn*—that is, to predict what you can accomplish with *training*—are known as *aptitude tests.* Tests designed to measure skills already attained, or what a person can do now, are called

achievement

_____ tests.

6. Suppose a company has fifty unskilled applicants for a job as machinist and intends to train only ten of the fifty applicants to become machinists. An industrial psychologist employed by this company would probably administer an

aptitude

_____ test to determine which of the fifty applicants have the greatest capacity to learn to become machinists.

7. Tests designed to measure capacity to learn—that is, to predict what one can

aptitude

accomplish with training—are known as _____ tests.

capacity

8. Aptitude tests are designed to measure _____ to learn, that is,

training

to predict what one can accomplish with _____ .

9. Before lawyers are admitted to the bar, they must pass a test of knowledge and

achievement

understanding of legal precepts. The test they take is an (*achievement/aptitude*) test.

10. If a law school can admit only forty out of several hundred applicants, an

aptitude

_____ test might be administered to determine which applicants have the greatest capacity to learn to become skilled lawyers.

11. However, as the text points out, the distinction between aptitude and achievement tests is not clear-cut; it is more useful to think of them as falling along a continuum

with tests designed to predict what one can accomplish with training

aptitude

(_____ tests) at one end and tests that measure accom-

achievement

plished skills (_____ tests) at the other.

12. The distinction between tests at the two ends of the aptitude-achievement

continuum

_____ is based both on the *purpose* of the test and on the *specificity of relevant prior experience.*

13. For example, the Law School Scholastic Aptitude Test (LSAT), used to select applicants to law school, includes a test of reading comprehension, because this is a skill one must have to be an effective lawyer. Since a reading comprehension test

achievement

measures how well one has learned to read, it is actually an (*aptitude/achievement*) test. But in this case it is used as part of an aptitude test.

14. Since the purpose of the LSAT is to select those applicants who will do well in law

aptitude

school, it is considered an _____ test, although it also measures achievement.

15. Tests can be distinguished along the aptitude-achievement continuum in terms of

purpose

their p_____ as well as the specificity of relevant

prior

_____ experience required.

16. A test designed to predict the degree to which a student will benefit from music lessons prior to any instruction would be at the aptitude end of the aptitude-achievement continuum both because of its purpose and because it does not require

experience

specific prior _____ .

17. Your final examination in this course would fall at the achievement end of the continuum because its purpose is to measure attained knowledge and because the

is

experience required to do well on the test (*is/is not*) very specific.

18. Aptitude and achievement tests are distinguished from each other primarily in

purpose

terms of their _____ and the specificity of relevant

prior experience

_____ _____ required.

19. If test scores are to be used for scientific purposes, they must be *trustworthy*. In scientific terms this means that they must meet two requirements: *reliability* and

trustworthy

validity. Test scores that are not _____ are not likely to be regarded as useful by scientists.

20. If they are to be regarded as trustworthy, all test scores used for scientific purposes must meet two requirements. These two requirements are *reliability* and

validity

_____ .

21. By *reliability* we mean that the scores are dependable and reproducible, that they measure *consistently* whatever it is they measure. To be regarded as

reliability

trustworthy, test scores must have both _____ and

validity (*either order*)

_____ .

22. Test scores that measure consistently are said to have the characteristic of

reliability

_____ , since the scores are dependable and reproducible.

23. Few of us would want to use a ruler made of rubber, because the measurements could vary considerably from one measurement to the next and would not give consistent and reproducible results. Such measurements would lack

reliability

_____ .

24. A steel ruler, however, should give us consistent, dependable, and reproducible results from one measurement to the next and would therefore have the charac-

reliability

teristic of _____ .

25. Psychologist X has developed a new intelligence test, which she had administered to a large group of students. She administered the same test twice to the same group of students and found that the pattern of scores on the second test compared quite closely to the pattern on the first test. Because her test gave consistent results, which are dependable and reproducible, her test presumably has

reliability

_____ .

26. By reliability we mean that the scores are dependable and reproducible, that they

consistently

measure _____ whatever it is they measure.

27. By *validity* we mean that the test scores measure what the tester *intended* to measure. For instance, if your instructor desires to measure what you have learned in this course and the test does measure your actual achievement, the test has the

validity

characteristic of _____ .

28. If your instructor desires to measure knowledge achieved in the course, but the test measures your intelligence rather than your achievement, the test is not measuring

validity

what it is intended to measure and it therefore would lack _____ .

29. By validity we mean that the test scores measure what the tester

intended

_____ to measure.

reliability **30.** By _____ we mean that the scores measure consistently

validity

whatever it is they measure; by _____ we mean that the scores measure what the tester intended to measure.

31. A test may be reliable but invalid. That is, a test may measure consistently yet not

intended

measure what the tester _____ to measure.

32. Suppose that a psychologist designed a new test intended to measure intelligence. The same test was administered to the same subjects on two occasions and the scores for all subjects on both occasions were quite consistent; however, the test results correlated poorly with those of well-established intelligence tests. The new

validity

test has reliability but probably lacks _____ .

33. The psychologist, in attempting to learn how reliable the new test is, administered it twice to the same group of students. To compare the first and second sets of scores, we need to know the *degree of relationship* between the two sets of scores. This relationship is provided by the *correlation coefficient* (commonly abbreviated as *r*), a term already familiar to you as a measure of the degree of correspondence

coefficient

between two sets of scores. In this case, the correlation _____ between the two sets of scores is a *reliability coefficient.*

34. To estimate the degree of relationship between two sets of scores in order to find

reliability

out how reliable a test is, we need a(n) _____ coefficient.

35. Well-constructed psychological tests of ability commonly have reliability coefficients above *r* = .90. The psychologist who designed a new intelligence test should

.90

find an *r* of _____ or above for the test if it is to be considered as reliable as other well-constructed ability tests.

36. To measure *validity* we must also have two scores for each person taking the test, one being the test score and the other a score on a *criterion* of some sort. For instance, if we designed a test of ability to sell life insurance and obtained scores

criterion

for a number of persons, we would also need a(n) _____ of some sort, which in this case might be the total value of insurance policies sold by those taking the test.

37. A criterion might be a standard selected as the goal to be achieved in a task, or a set of scores or other records against which the success of a predictive test is verified. For instance, if effective life insurance salesmen sell at least $100,000 of insurance

criterion

in a year, this figure might serve as a standard, or _____ .

38. If we want to measure a test's validity, we need not only each person's score on the

criterion

test, but also his or her score on a(n) _____ of some sort.

39. To measure validity we need to derive the *degree of relationship* between test scores and a criterion measure. This correlation coefficient is known as a *validity coefficient.* The correlation coefficient that tells us how well the test measures

validity

what it is supposed to measure is a (*validity/reliability*) coefficient.

40. When we derive the degree of relationship between test scores and a criterion

validity

measure, we obtain a(n) _____ coefficient.

41. Tests that are designed to measure a person's general capacity for learning are called intelligence tests. Since the purpose of an intelligence test is to predict what the

aptitude

individual can learn if given appropriate schooling, it is considered an (*aptitude/ achievement*) test. However, as the textbook points out, an individual's score on an intelligence test does depend to some extent on prior experience.

42. The first tests to approximate contemporary intelligence tests were developed by the French psychologist Alfred Binet. Binet devised a scale of *mental age*; average mental age (MA) corresponds to chronological age (CA), which is the age determined from date of birth. Thus, a child of normal intelligence with a chronological

mental

age of 10 years should have a(n) _____ age of 10.

43. A child with a chronological age of 13 who has normal intelligence would also have

13

a mental age of _____ .

correspond

44. A child of normal intelligence has a mental age that will _____
to his or her chronological age.

Chronological

45. _____ age refers to the age determined from
the date of birth.

46. A bright child's mental age is above his or her chronological age; one would expect,

below

then, that a dull child's mental age would be _____ his or her chronological
age.

mental

47. A retarded child has a(n) _____ age below his or her chronological age.

48. The *intelligence quotient* (IQ) is a convenient index of brightness. It expresses
intelligence as a ratio of the mental age to chronological age:

$$IQ = \frac{\text{Mental age (MA)}}{\text{Chronological age (CA)}} \times 100$$

The 100 is used as a multiplier to remove the decimal point and to make the
average IQ have a value of 100. If a child with a chronological age of 9 has a mental

100

age of 9, the IQ, or intelligence quotient, is _____ .

80

49. What is Tim's IQ if his mental age is 8 and his chronological age is 10? _____

50. A child with an IQ *below 70* is considered *mentally retarded*. A child with an IQ
above 139 is considered to have *very superior* intelligence. If Jill has a mental age

140

of 14 and a chronological age of 10, her IQ would be _____ .

51. The most widely used intelligence tests are the *Stanford-Binet,* which is a revision

Binet

of the earlier test devised by Alfred _____ , and the Wechsler scales—the
Wechsler Adult Intelligence Scale (*WAIS*) and the *Wechsler Intelligence Scale for
Children* (*WISC*).

Stanford

52. Both the _____-Binet and the Wechsler scales group their test
items according to the type of intellectual ability the item is intended to measure.

Intelligence

53. The Wechsler Adult _____ Scale, for example, obtains separate
scores on 12 *subtests.*

54. Six of the subtests are *verbal,* testing such abilities as mathematical reasoning,

subtests

vocabulary, and recall of series of digits; the other six sub_____ are
nonverbal, or *performance,* tests that involve assembling picture puzzles, manipulating blocks to form specific designs, or recognizing the missing detail in a picture.

Adult

55. The final IQ score on either the Wechsler _____ Intelligence Scale or the

Intelligence

Wechsler _____ Scale for Children is obtained

subtest

by averaging all the sub_____ scores. Separate IQ scores can be obtained
for the sum of the verbal tests and the sum of the performance tests.

56. Since the Wechsler scales provide more information about a person's abilities than just a single mental-_____ score, or IQ score, they are frequently used for diagnostic purposes. By analyzing the scores on both the _____ subtests and the _____ subtests, it is possible to determine a person's special abilities and weaknesses.

age

performance

verbal (*either order*)

57. What are the abilities that underlie intelligence? One method used to identify clusters of abilities that combine to make up the IQ scores obtained on tests such as the _____ - _____ and the Wechsler scales is called *factor analysis.*

Stanford-Binet

58. Factor _____ is a statistical procedure used to determine the *common factors* that contribute to a body of data. The same people are given a large number of tests, each individual test composed of similar items. The scores on all the tests are then intercorrelated. If two tests correlate highly with each other, they have a lot in *common* with each other. Tests that show high intercorrelations have much in _____ with each other.

analysis

common

59. Tests that have low intercorrelations would have (*little/much*) in common with each other.

little

60. This is the basic method of _____ analysis. It is a statistical procedure that provides a systematic way of finding a small number of *common factors* that can account for a large array of intercorrelations.

factor

61. Factor _____ attempts to discover the underlying abilities that produce intelligence test results. In one study by Thurstone an analysis of more than sixty different tests yielded seven *primary abilities.* These primary abilities were the _____ factors that emerged from the application of _____ analysis.

analysis

common

factor

62. Thurstone concluded that these _____ abilities were the basic abilities that comprise intelligence.

primary

63. Other investigators, however, using factor _____ with different kinds of test items, have found many more abilities underlying intelligence than the primary abilities discovered by Th_____ . The number of abilities discovered depends partly on the kinds of test items used.

analysis

Thurstone

64. A more recent approach to understanding intelligence attempts to analyze the *component processes* that underlie the factors identified by the method of _____ analysis. This componental approach is described in the text.

factor

65. A question frequently debated is "How much of our intelligence is *inherited* and how much is *acquired* through experience?" One way to find evidence on this question is to compare the IQs of people who are *related genetically.* If people who are related _____ are no more alike in IQ than total strangers, then we would assume that intelligence is entirely (*inherited/acquired*).

genetically

acquired

66. Studies of this type generally have found that the closer the genetic relationship, the more similar the IQ. Thus, the average correlation between the IQs of identical twins is about .90, while the average correlation between the IQs of siblings who are not twins is about .55. Since identical twins are closer genetically than ordinary siblings (having developed from the same ovum), these results indicate that there (*is/is not*) a genetic component to intelligence.

is

67. But if identical twins are reared from birth in different homes, the correlation between their IQs is not as high as if they were raised together. This finding points to the importance of (*heredity/environment*) in the development of intelligence.

environment

68. Experts differ in the importance they attribute to genetic and to environmental factors in the determination of intelligence. But it is clear that an individual's tested IQ depends on both _____ and

heredity

_____ .

environment

TERMS AND CONCEPTS

aptitude test _____

_____

_____

achievement test _____

_____

_____

intelligence test _____

_____

_____

reliability _____

_____

_____

validity _____

_____

_____

reliability coefficient _____

_____

_____

criterion of validity _____

_____

_____

validity coefficient _____

_____

_____

mental age _____

_____

_____

chronological age _____

_____

_____

Stanford-Binet test _____

_____

_____

intelligence quotient (IQ) _____

_____

_____

verbal scale _____

_____

_____

performance scale _____

_____

_____

individual ability tests _____

_____

_____

group ability tests _____

_____

_____

culture-fair tests* _____

_____

_____

_____

factor analysis _____

_____

_____

_____

general intelligence factor (*g*) _____

_____

_____

special factors (*s*'s) _____

_____

_____

primary mental abilities _____

_____

_____

component model _____

_____

_____

_____

heritability _____

_____

_____

reaction range _____

_____

_____

Head Start programs _____

_____

_____

*Indicates term used in Critical Discussion

_____ 1. _____ developed the first tests designed to measure intelligence.
   a. Alfred Binet
   b. Lewis Terman
   c. Sir Francis Galton
   d. Louis Thurstone

_____ 2. A good test must be trustworthy, that is, it must be both reliable and valid. In considering these qualities we note that
   a. a test cannot be reliable without being valid
   b. valid scores are those that are reproducible
   c. reliability is tested by use of criterion scores
   d. scores are reliable if scores on half the test correlate highly with the other half

_____ 3. Psychologists who use the technique of factor analysis see intelligence as
   a. a general capacity for comprehension and reasoning
   b. a generally invalid concept
   c. an array of relatively independent special abilities
   d. all of the above

_____ 4. According to the intelligence quotient index suggested by Stern and adopted by Terman, IQ is computed as
   a. $\dfrac{\text{Mental Age}}{\text{Chronological Age}} \times 100$
   b. $\dfrac{\text{Chronological Age}}{\text{Basal Mental Age}} \times 100$
   c. $\dfrac{\text{Basal Mental Age}}{\text{Chronological Age}} \times 100$
   d. $\dfrac{\text{Mental Age}}{\text{Basal Mental Age}} \times 100$

_____ 5. Achievement tests are designed to
   a. predict what a person can accomplish with training
   b. measure accomplished skills and indicate what a person can do at present
   c. measure continuous behavior under standard conditions
   d. assess the impact of broad, general experiences

_____ 6. To assure uniformity of testing procedures and to protect the reliability and validity of a test, examiners must do all of the following except:

   a. Carefully follow the instructions for administering the test.
   b. Carefully follow the instructions for scoring the test.
   c. Try to reduce the effects of extraneous variables.
   d. Allow each examinee ample time to complete the test.

_____ 7. Aptitude tests measure
   a. creativity
   b. an accomplished skill
   c. results of specific training programs
   d. a capacity to learn

_____ 8. Ability tests can be classified along two dimensions or continuums. Which one of the following tests would fall closest to the *specific* end of the general-specific continuum?
   a. a test designed to predict success in real estate sales
   b. an individual IQ test
   c. the Law School Admissions Test
   d. a Spanish vocabulary test

_____ 9. Thurstone objected to Spearman's conclusions but used his methodology, factor analysis. With it he identified
   a. the general intelligence factor (*g*) involved in intelligence
   b. seven primary mental abilities
   c. 120 unique intellectual factors
   d. over 30 special factors important in intelligence

_____ 10. It is important to note that heritability estimates for intelligence
   a. are always above .65
   b. apply to populations but not to individuals
   c. imply that environmental conditions are not important
   d. all of the above

_____ 11. The distribution of IQ scores in the population
   a. approximates a normal curve
   b. places most children in the middle ranges of the scale
   c. places few children at the extremes of the distribution
   d. all of the above

_____12. Aptitude tests differ from achievement tests primarily in the
a. way the tests are used
b. type of items
c. length of the test
d. reliability of test scores

_____13. The Scholastic Aptitude Test
a. is an achievement test, since it measures the effectiveness of prior schooling
b. is an aptitude test, since it predicts success in college quite well
c. illustrates the blurring of the distinction between aptitude and achievement tests
d. all of the above

_____14. Aptitude and achievement tests are alike in that they
a. both measure current status
b. may include similar questions
c. yield results that are often highly correlated
d. all of the above

_____15. With increased schooling the average correlation between IQ scores and academic achievement
a. increases
b. decreases
c. remains the same
d. is unpredictable because of selection factors

_____16. In considering public concerns about testing, it is worth noting that
a. ability tests are objective and may prevent discrimination in hiring
b. intelligence tests are excellent predictors of success in life
c. an individual's IQ score is unaffected by environmental conditions
d. all of the above

_____17. The assumptions of an intelligence test
a. include the expectation that it predicts other important performances
b. can never be strictly met
c. include the subject's familiarity with the standard language of the test
d. all of the above

_____18. The proportion of a trait's variation within a specified population that can be attributed to genetic differences is called the
a. inheritance
b. genetic determinant
c. heritability
d. variability ratio

_____19. If a validity coefficient is computed between students' college entrance examination scores and first-term college grades, the grades are the
a. equivalent form
b. aptitude test
c. repeated measure
d. criterion measure

_____20. When people generally achieve the same scores on Form A of a test that they achieve on Form B, you can conclude that the test is
a. valid
b. reliable
c. both A and B
d. neither A nor B

KEY TO SELF-QUIZ

20. b	15. b	10. b	5. b
19. d	14. d	9. b	4. a
18. c	13. d	8. d	3. c
17. d	12. a	7. d	2. d
16. a	11. d	6. d	1. c

CLASS EXERCISE

INDIVIDUAL DIFFERENCES

Introduction

Despite the fact that humans resemble one another in some fundamental ways, they also differ from one another in many important characteristics, such as skills, attitudes, intelligence, aptitudes, interests, and personality. In many practical situations, as in the selection of employees, the measurement of these individual differences is important, especially if one wishes to select the best performers and eliminate the poor performers at a given task. This exercise is intended to show that individual differences exist even on relatively simple tasks.

Procedure

When your instructor gives you instructions to begin, immediately rearrange the following scrambled sentences to make meaningful sentences. Write your meaningful sentence in the space provided below each scrambled sentence. You will be permitted ten minutes for this task. You may not be able to finish in the time allowed, but do the best you can.

1. MEN THEM LIVES GOOD DO AFTER THE THAT

   _____

   _____

2. EYES YOU THEIR UNTIL SHOOT OF WHITES DON'T SEE THE

   _____

   _____

3. THE HUMAN WORLD IS THING MOST FREE VALUABLE THE MIND THE IN

   _____

   _____

4. TELL YOUR DEVIL GO THE TO STYLE YARN YOUR AND LET

   _____

   _____

5. IT MOMENTS WE THAT RARE LIVE ONLY IS AT

   _____

   _____

6. DO MUCH TOO KNOWING ANSWERS NOT BLAME ME FOR THE ALL NOT

   _____

   _____

7. THE FAULTS CONSCIOUS IS OF TO NONE OF GREATEST BE

   _____

   _____

8. MISUNDERSTAND BETTER IS UNDERSTAND LOT A THAN TO LITTLE A IT TO

   _____

   _____

9. THE BOASTING IT OF THAT MADE OF CAN SUCCESS BE USE WORST IS

   _____

   _____

10. BETTER FOOLISH FOOL THAN WIT A WITTY A

    _____

    _____

11. FIRST CURIOSITY OF LOT ONLY LOVE IS FOOLISHNESS AND A LITTLE A

    _____

    _____

12. THE LAUGHTER OF ASTONISHING IS POWER

    _____

    _____

13. MONEY UNHAPPINESS CURE CANNOT

    _____

    _____

14. FAILURE GROWS WITH REPUTATION YOUR EVERY

    _____

    _____

15. HOURS FOR MAN HIMSELF AND WILL HE ABOUT A LISTEN TO TALK

    _____

    _____

16. THE NOBODY BELIEVE WILL ONE IS THE THING TRUTH

    _____

    _____

17. MY TRUTH THE TO TELL OF JOKING IS WAY

_____

_____

18. LIVING IS MAKES WORTH THAT LIFE PLEAS-URE NOT IT

_____

_____

19. RIGHT BE RATHER PRESIDENT I HAD THAN

_____

_____

20. VERY MINDS COMPLEX OF IDEAS SIMPLE WITHIN LIE REACH THE ONLY

_____

_____

Total number unscrambled _____

Treatment of Data

1. The unscrambled sentences are given on p. 288 of the Appendix; if your sentence is meaningful, it need not have precisely the same word order as that given in the Appendix. Count the number of meaningful sentences you wrote from the scrambled sentences. Enter your score where it reads "Total number unscrambled _____."

2. Your instructor will ask you to submit your score on a small slip of paper so that the data for the class as a whole can be plotted on the graph that appears on p. 183.

Questions for Discussion

1. Is the curve symmetrical or skewed (see p. 642 of the text)?

2. Is there a clustering around the central tendency?

3. Which of the scrambled sentences took the longest time to unscramble? Why?

4. What conclusions can you draw regarding individual differences in performing a simple task such as this?

5. What would you conjecture about the particular abilities of those students who unscrambled the most sentences in the time allotted?

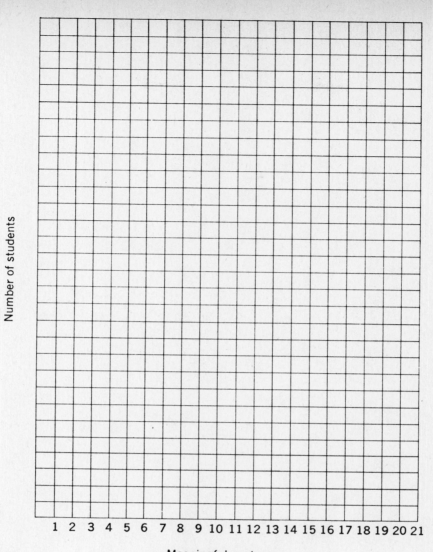

Number of students

1 2 3 4 5 6 7 8 9 10 11 12 13 14 15 16 17 18 19 20 21

Meaningful sentences

13
Personality and Its Assessment

LEARNING OBJECTIVES   13-1.   Be able to show, with examples, how inherited characteristics, common experiences, and unique experiences contribute to personality.

Be familiar with the following theoretical approaches to personality; be able to discuss the key concepts of each and to evaluate its contributions.

13-2.   Trait theory

13-3.   Social-learning theory

13-4.   Psychoanalytic theory

13-5.   Phenomenological theories

Be familiar with the techniques, advantages, and disadvantages of each of the following methods of assessing personality.

13-6.   Observational methods

13-7.   Personality inventories

13-8.   Projective techniques

13-9.   Be familiar with the research on personality consistency over time and what longitudinal studies tell us about the stability of personality.

13-10.   Be able to discuss the research on personality consistency across situations, including the reasons why studies have typically shown low cross-situational correlations. Explain what is meant by interactionism.

1. *Personality* is a difficult concept to define, but we will begin by referring to personality as the *characteristic patterns of behavior, thought and emotion* that determine an individual's adjustment to the environment. According to this definition, every person (*has/does not have*) personality.

has

2. The characteristic patterns of behavior, thought, and emotion that determine an individual's adjustment to the environment may be said to make up his or her

personality

_____ .

3. When we speak of Margaret's personality, we are referring to the characteristic pat

behavior, emotion

terns of _____ , thought, and _____ that determine her adjustment to her environment.

4. Some of the characteristics that influence personality are *innate*, that is, present at birth. Robert, a large, sturdy baby, lies placidly in his crib and is not easily upset.

innate

These in_____ characteristics, physical size and emotional reactivity, may well influence his personality in later life.

5. Susan at three weeks of age is a small, frail infant who is fussy and continually

innate, personality

active. These _____ characteristics may well contribute to her _____ as an adult.

6. The characteristics that are present at birth constitute the individual's *potential*—a potential that develops through maturation and learning as the person grows up. The experiences encountered in growing up shape or modify the innate

potential

po_____ . Some of these experiences are *common experiences,* shared by most individuals growing up in a certain *culture.*

7. If a particular culture emphasizes the value of cleanliness and early toilet training,

common

then most individuals growing up in this culture will share _____ experiences in these areas.

8. If a culture expects females to be docile and submissive, then most of the girls

experiences

growing up in this culture will share some common _____ that

tend to develop these qualities. These experiences will *modify* the girls'

innate

_____ potential. A girl who is active and vigorous as an infant may be

culture

come more placid as her personality is shaped or modified by the _____ .

modify

9. Some of the experiences that shape or _____ the person's innate potential

culture

are common to most individuals in a certain _____ . Other experiences are *unique* or *individual*; they cannot be predicted from knowledge of the culture in which the person was raised.

10. John grew up with a drunken father who badly mistreated him. This would be an

unique

example of an individual or _____ experience for John—one that is not

common

_____ to most children in his culture.

innate	**11.** Thus the _____ potential of the individual is shaped or modified by
common	_____ experiences (those shared by most members of the culture) as well
unique, personality	as by _____ or individual experiences to form the _____ we see in the adult.
	12. Many theories attempt to explain and describe personality, but most can be grouped into one of *four* types or classes: *trait, social-learning, psychoanalytic,* and
four	*phenomenological.* We will look at each of these _____ (*number*) types of theories in turn.
	13. Trait theories assume that people can be distinguished from one another on the basis of certain *measurable* and *persisting* characteristics called *traits.* A trait is a
measured	persisting characteristic that can be m _____ .
	14. Thus, one may think of intelligence as a trait, since it is a measurable and relatively
persisting (*or synonym*)	_____ characteristic.
trait	**15.** Aggressiveness may also be considered a(n) _____ to the extent that it is a measurable and persisting personality characteristic.
	16. When we attempt to describe a person in terms of certain persisting characteristics
trait	that can be measured, we are using a(n) _____ theory.
	17. Trait theorists study personality by means of questionnaires or rating scales that are
traits	designed to measure persisting characteristics, or _____ . If a psychologist asked your best friend to rate you on a scale describing degrees of such characteristics as friendliness, honesty, aggressiveness, conscientiousness, and so forth, he or
trait	she would be studying personality with the _____ approach.
	18. A second theoretical approach to the study of personality is *social-learning theory.*
learning	Social- _____ theory assumes that personality is shaped by the *conditions of learning* a person encounters in the course of growing up.
	19. Thus, differences in personality from one person to the next can be explained in
learning	terms of differences in their l_____ experiences.
measurable	**20.** Trait theories assume that personality traits are consistent and m_____ characteristics of an individual. Social-learning theorists maintain that many personality traits are not consistent but depend instead on the *specific situation* in which the behavior occurs.
	21. Harriet considers herself to be an "honest" person. She is careful to give the correct change when she works part time as a store clerk, she is scrupulous about filling out her income tax return, and she has never cheated on an examination. However, when she finds a wallet full of money on the sidewalk, she fails to return it, even though the owner's address is clearly indicated. This example points to the fact that
honesty	there is no unitary trait called h_____ . Whether a person behaves in an
specific	"honest manner" depends on the _____ situation.

situation

22. Social-learning theorists assume that many personality traits are not consistent but depend on the specific _____ in which behavior occurs.

social

23. According to _____ -learning theory, people behave in ways that are likely to produce *reinforcement.*

24. Ted's parents praise him whenever he acts aggressively toward his classmates and wins a fistfight, but they punish him whenever he shows any aggression toward them. Social-learning theory would predict that Ted will display aggression only in

reinforcement

those situations where he has received r_____ . He will not show aggression in all situations.

is not

25. Thus, according to social-learning theory, aggression (*is/is not*) a trait; it is a learned response to a specific situation.

26. So far we have discussed two approaches to personality. One, which describes

trait

people by measuring their persisting characteristics, is called _____ theory. The

social-
learning

other, which emphasizes learned responses to specific situations, is called _____-

_____ theory. A third, and quite different, approach to personality is provided by *psychoanalytic theory,* as formulated by Sigmund Freud.

27. Freud conceived of personality as composed of three major systems: the *id*, the *ego,* and the *superego.* The id represents the innate instinctual drives (including sex and aggression). The id seeks immediate gratification of impulses without regard for the consequences. A person who acts impulsively, without concern for more remote

id

consequences, is likely to be expressing the _____ portion of his or her personality.

28. In psychoanalytic theory, the pleasure-seeking, impulsive portion of personality is

id

called the _____ . It is manifested in early childhood but is never completely out-grown, so that behavior stemming from this part of the personality can be found in the most sober of adults.

29. It is obvious that if the id were given full rein we could never have a civilization. We need a part of the personality that will exert control in such a way as to make our behavior conform to reality and social constraint. This is called the *ego.* The aspect of personality that takes into account the real consequences of our search for

ego

pleasure is, then, the _____ .

ego

30. The id is the pleasure-seeking aspect of personality that ignores reality; the _____ is the more rational portion that tries to take reality into account.

id

31. Because it seeks immediate pleasure, the _____ is said to be controlled by

ego

the *pleasure principle*; because it conforms to environmental realities, the _____ is said to be controlled by the *reality principle.*

32. The third part of the personality, according to psychoanalytic theory, is the *super-ego,* an aspect that develops out of the ego's experiences with social reality and parental prohibitions. Parental commands become part of the individual, who then feels guilt if he or she violates this internalized code. The common word for the

ego, superego

superego is *conscience.* If the ego proposes a course of action that is in violation of one's conscience, the _____ will be opposed by the s_____ .

33. Let us set up a hypothetical situation involving a young boy, in which his thoughts may be attributed to these three aspects of personality. The boy is angry at one of his classmates and thinks, "I'd sure like to beat him to a pulp!" This statement

id   would be an expression of the _____. Next the boy thinks, "But he's bigger than I

ego   and might beat *me* up." This is the _____ at work. Finally the boy thinks, "Well,

superego fighting is wrong anyhow." This would be the judgment of the _____ .
A person's approach to such problem situations reflects the way in which that individual has learned to cope with the conflicting demands of the three parts of his or her personality. (The text also discusses the developmental aspects of the psychoanalytic theory of personality, which are concerned with the form the id impulses take during the various stages of psychosexual development and some of the personality characteristics that develop if a person becomes fixated at any of these stages.)

trait   34. So far we have discussed three approaches to the study of personality: _____ ,

social-learning _____-_____ , and _____ the-

psychoanalytic ories. A fourth approach emphasizes the individual's *subjective experience.* This approach is called *phenomenological* because it is concerned with the individual's own *perception* and *interpretation of events,* or *phenomena.*

subjective 35. Phenomenological theories emphasize _____ experience—the

interpretation individual's own perception and _____ of events.

36. Ruth is playing a game with some of her nursery school classmates. Suddenly she hits out in anger, knocking another child to the floor. A social-learning theorist might analyze the situation in terms of the aggression-provoking actions of the

reinforcement other child and Ruth's past history of r_____ for aggressive behavior. A psychologist taking the phenomenological approach would ask Ruth

interprets how she perceives and _____ the situation—what it means to her.

37. The individual's subjective experience, rather than the objective situation, is the

phenomenological focus of _____logical theories of personality.

phenomenological 38. The phenomeno_____ approach to personality includes some theories that have also been called *humanistic* because they emphasize those characteristics of people that are uniquely *human,* not shared by lower animals.

humanistic 39. Some phenomenological theories are called h_____ because, in

subjective addition to their focus on _____ experience, they emphasize people's uniquely human characteristics. One of the most important of these is *self-actualization*—an innate tendency toward growth and fulfillment (actualization) of all of one's potentials.

40. According to humanistic theories, self-actualization, the innate tendency toward

growth, potentials g_____ and the fulfillment of one's p_____ , is the basic force motivating behavior.

41. The basic force motivating behavior, according to humanistic theories, is self-

actualization

_____ .

42. The phenomenological approach to personality emphasizes _____

subjective

perception, interpretation

experience, the individual's own _____ and _____

humanistic

of events; it includes some theories that are also called _____ be-

self-

cause of their focus on such uniquely human characteristics as _____ -

actualization

_____ .

43. One of the most influential of the psychologists whose approach to personality is both phenomenological and humanistic is Carl Rogers. His theory of personality

Rogers

centers on the *concept of the self.* The self, according to Carl _____ , consists of all the *ideas, perceptions,* and *values* that characterize "I" or "me."

values

44. Your self-concept includes all of the ideas, perceptions, and _____ that

concept

characterize you. Your self-_____ influences both your perception of the world and your behavior. If you do something that is not consistent with your

self-concept

s _____ - _____ , you feel uncomfortable and may even distort or deny your actions to preserve your self-concept.

45. Rogers proposes that we all have an *ideal self* in addition to our self-concept. An ideal self is the kind of person we would like to be. The closer our self-concept is to

ideal

our i_____ self, the more fulfilled and happy we will be.

ideal self

46. The person we would like to be is the _____ _____ . If we are close to our ideal self and have fulfilled most of our potential, then we have come close to self-actualization. (The text describes some more recent theorizing about the self that focuses on (1) the self-concept as a memory structure (or self-schemata) that guides the processing of information and (2) the way a person's self-concept shapes and is shaped by social interactions.)

47. Each of the theoretical approaches we have discussed looks at personality from a slightly different viewpoint. Can you identify each of these approaches from their main emphasis?

psychoanalytic

a. A three-component personality: _____ theories

social-learning

b. Reward and punishment: _____ -_____ theories

phenomenological

humanistic (*either order*)

c. Subjective experience: _____ and _____ theories

trait

d. Consistent and enduring personality characteristics: _____ theories

48. Regardless of one's theoretical approach, in order to study personality we need methods of *assessing* personality. The many methods used to assess

personality

_____ can be classified under three headings: *observational methods, personality inventories,* and *projective tests.*

49. If you watch a child in a classroom, making notes on behavior as he or she studies

observational

and interacts with teacher and classmates, you are using an ob_____ method of assessing personality.

50. If you interview an individual for a job, noting responses to questions and the person's manner of interacting with you, you are also using an observational method of _____ personality.

assessing

51. The impressions gained from an interview or from observing behavior in a natural setting, such as a classroom, can be put into *standardized form* by means of *rating scales.* A rating _____ is a device for recording impressions about a personality trait.

scale

52. A rating scale records your impressions about a personality trait in a s_____ form. A sample item from a rating scale is given below.

standardized

Place a check at the point that describes the individual's poise.

| Nervous and ill at ease | Somewhat tense; easily upset | Average poise and security | Self-confident | Very composed; adapts well to crises |

53. In this example you would record your impression of the individual's poise by placing a check at the appropriate point on the s_____ .

scale

54. In rating personality traits it is important to avoid the *"halo effect."* The halo _____ refers to the tendency to rate someone high on all traits because of a good impression on one or two traits, or to rate the person low throughout because of a poor impression on one or two _____ .

effect

traits

55. Jim has a very friendly and pleasant manner. His employer rates him high on his ability to get along well with others; she also rates Jim high on honesty and efficiency although she has little information on which to base her judgment of the latter two traits. This example shows how the _____ _____ interferes with objectivity in rating others.

halo effect

56. The halo effect is a possible source of error in the use of _____ _____ . Another possible source of error is the tendency of raters to be influenced by *social stereotypes.*

rating

scales

57. Unless the raters know the persons being rated fairly well, they may base their judgments as much on social _____ , how they *believe* a "housewife" or a "high school athlete" or a "long-haired college student" acts and thinks, as on observations of actual behaviors.

stereotypes

58. Two possible sources of error in the use of rating scales are the _____ _____ and _____ stereotypes.

halo
effect, social

59. Rating _____ are most often used when one person assesses the traits of another, but they can also be used for self-ratings. If you were asked "How well do you control your emotions?" and were requested to rate yourself by placing a check mark at the appropriate place on a line that runs from "tend to be unrespon-

scales

rating

scale

sive" to "tend to be overemotional," you would be using a(n)_____

_____ to evaluate your own personality traits.

60. Another method of personality assessment, which relies on an individual's *self-*

inventory

observations, is the *personality inventory*. A personality in _____ is essentially a questionnaire in which the person reports reactions, feelings, and attitudes.

personality

61. The questions on a p_____ inventory are designed to measure certain *traits*. The same questions are asked of each person and the answers are given in a form that can be easily scored. An individual's scores can be compared

traits

with the scores of other people to see how he or she compares on certain _____ .

62. A method of personality assessment in which people respond to a number of ques-

personality inventory

tions about themselves is a(n)_____ _____ .

63. One of the most widely used personality inventories, the Minnesota Multiphasic Personality Inventory (abbreviated MMPI), was designed at the University of Minnesota to measure various phases of personality—thus the word "*multiphasic*."

MMPI

The Minnesota Multiphasic Personality Inventory (abbreviated _____) measures

traits

a number of different personality characteristics or _____ .

64. One method of assessing personality is to record impressions about a person on a(n)

rating scale

_____ _____ . Another method uses a personality inventory such as

Multiphasic

the Minnesota _____ Personality Inventory.

rating

65. The two methods of personality assessment we have discussed so far,_____

scales, personality inventories

(*either order*)

_____ and _____ _____ , are fairly *structured*; they ask specific questions or require judgments about specific traits. A third method, *projective tests*, is much less structured and allows the individual to express him or herself more freely.

less

66. Projective tests are (*more/less*) structured than rating scales or personality inventories. They present an *ambiguous stimulus* to which the person may respond as he

ambiguous

or she wishes. Because the stimulus is am_____ and does not require a specific response, the individual is said to *project* his or her personality onto the stimulus.

ambiguous stimulus

67. A projective test presents a(n)_____ _____ to which the individual responds with an imaginative production rather than a specific

project

answer. The person is said to p_____ his or her personality onto the stimulus.

68. For example, in the *Rorschach Test* a person is shown a series of irregularly shaped

ambiguous

inkblots and asked to tell what they suggest. Since the inkblots are _____

projective

stimuli, the Rorschach Test is a(n) _____ test.

69. Tests composed of relatively unstructured and ambiguous stimuli that elicit projec-

projective

tions of the personality are called _____ tests.

Rorschach 70. One example of a projective test is the R_____ Inkblot Test. Another projective test, the Thematic Apperception Test, consists of a series of pictures about which the person tells stories. In so doing the subject may say things about the characters in the stories that apply to him or herself. The Rorschach Test

inkblots utilizes _____ as stimuli, whereas the Thematic Apperception Test utilizes a series of pictures.

Thematic 71. The _____ Apperception Test utilizes a series of pictures to which the subject responds with stories. Certain themes that recur in the person's imaginative productions are analyzed by the psychologist to arrive at basic motives and conflicts.

72. The Thematic Apperception Test is so called because certain "themes" recur in the imaginative productions of a person. "Apperception" means a readiness to perceive in certain ways, based on prior experience. Hence, the person interprets an ambigu-

picture ous stimulus, in this case a(n)_____ , according to his or her apperceptions and elaborates the stories in terms of preferred themes that reflect personality characteristics.

Rorschach 73. Both the _____ Test, which utilizes inkblots, and the

Thematic Apperception _____ _____ Test, which utilizes pictures,

projective are _____ tests of personality.

trait, psychoanalytic 74. Let's have a final review. We have discussed four theoretical approaches to person-
(*either order*), social- ality: _____ , _____ , _____-
learning, phenomenological _____ , and _____ or _____
humanistic theories. We have also mentioned three general methods for assessing personality:

observational _____ methods, which may involve the use of

rating scales _____ _____ for recording impressions of personality character-

personality inventories istics; _____ _____ , which are essen-

projective tests tially questionnaires; and _____ _____ , which allow more freedom of expression than either of the other methods. The text discusses how assessment methods are used to investigate the *consistency* of personality characteristics across different situations and over the span of a lifetime.

TERMS AND CONCEPTS

personality _____

_____

_____

_____

trait _____

_____

_____

_____

factor analysis _____

_____

_____

_____

vicarious learning _____

_____

_____

_____

person variables _____

_____

_____

_____

id _____

_____

_____

_____

ego _____

_____

_____

_____

superego _____

_____

_____

_____

psychosexual stages _____

_____

_____

_____

oral stage _____

_____

_____

_____

anal stage _____

_____

_____

_____

phallic stage _____

_____

_____

_____

genital stage _____

_____

_____

_____

ego analyst _____

_____

_____

_____

self-concept _____

_____

_____

_____

ideal self _____

_____

_____

_____

self-actualization _____

_____

_____

_____

self-schemata _____

_____

_____

_____

private self-consciousness _____

_____

_____

_____

public self-consciousness _____

_____

_____

_____

stereotype _____

_____

_____

_____

halo effect _____

_____

_____

_____

observational methods _____

_____

_____

_____

rating scale _____

_____

_____

_____

personality inventory _____

_____

_____

_____

MMPI _____

_____

_____

empirical construction _____

_____

_____

_____

California Psychological Inventory _____

_____

_____

_____

projective test _____

_____

_____

_____

Rorschach Test _____

_____

_____

_____

Thematic Apperception Test (TAT) _____

_____

_____

_____

"Barnum effect"* _____

_____

_____

_____

consistency paradox _____

_____

_____

_____

aggregated score _____

_____

_____

_____

interactionism _____

_____

_____

_____

*Indicates term used in Critical Discussion

_____ 1. Freud's major contribution to our understanding of personality is probably
    a. the recognition that unconscious needs and conflicts motivate much of our behavior
    b. the recognition that sexual conflicts cause most personality disturbances
    c. his definition of psychosexual stages
    d. his definition of defense mechanisms

_____ 2. Social-learning theorists believe that
    a. reinforcement is not necessary for learning
    b. much human learning is vicarious
    c. reinforcement is crucial for performance of learned behavior
    d. all of the above

_____ 3. Personal dispositions, behavior, and situational variables form an interlocking chain with each component reciprocally influencing the others. This statement describes
    a. psychic determinism
    b. interactionism
    c. the consistency paradox
    d. attitude-behavior reciprocity

_____ 4. In Freud's theory of personality the
    a. ego obeys the reality principle
    b. id is the "executive" of the personality
    c. superego mediates between the demands of the id and the ego
    d. ego obeys the pleasure principle

_____ 5. Social-learning theorists focus on several "person variables" that determine what an individual will do in a particular situation. These do _not_ include
    a. competencies
    b. subjective values
    c. traits
    d. cognitive strategies

_____ 6. Longitudinal studies indicate that individual differences in temperament (for example, general mood and activity level) are largely
    a. produced by mothers' different ways of handling babies
    b. innate and tend to persist into adulthood
    c. patterned by cultural and subcultural expectations
    d. developed gradually from birth to about age 20

_____ 7. What can we conclude about the relationship of body build to personality?
    a. There is a surprisingly strong relationship between body build and specific personality characteristics.
    b. Our physique determines specific personality characteristics because it is inherited.
    c. Physique has some influence on personality because of others' reactions to it and because of limitations it imposes.
    d. All of the above.

_____ 8. Although cultural and subcultural measures impose some personality similarities, an individual personality is never completely predictable from a knowledge of the group in which the person was raised because
    a. individuals differ in their inherited characteristics
    b. a given culture is not applied uniformly to all of its members
    c. individuals have different life experiences
    d. all of the above

_____ 9. The personality inventory called the MMPI
    a. is based on the method of empirical construction
    b. only works if those who take it answer truthfully
    c. is based on factor analysis
    d. was originally designed as a college admission test

_____ 10. Which of the following is _not_ a criticism of the TAT or the Rorschach?
    a. Little research has been done.
    b. Ability to predict behavior is poor.
    c. Interpretation of responses is too subjective.
    d. Test reliability is poor.

_____ 11. The halo effect typically causes problems in
    a. the Sixteen Factor Personality Questionnaire
    b. the MMPI
    c. rating scales
    d. personality inventories

_____ 12. In Carl Rogers' theory of personality, one's self-concept
    a. influences one's perception of the world
    b. consists of unsymbolized feelings
    c. is similar to Freud's ego-ideal
    d. always conforms closely to reality

13. The phenomenological approach includes several theories that emphasize
    a. innate needs for approval
    b. defenses against anxiety
    c. parent-child relationships
    d. subjective experience

14. Two dimensions found consistently in factor-analytic studies of personality are
    a. responsible-undependable and calm-anxious
    b. introversion-extraversion and stability-instability
    c. cooperative-negativistic and adventurous-cautious
    d. intellectual-unrefined and goodnatured-irritable

15. The basic concept of any projective test is the presentation of a stimulus that is deliberately ambiguous, to encourage the subject to
    a. reveal hidden psychopathology
    b. display creativity
    c. reveal his or her personality
    d. accept the tester's interpretations

16. A social-learning theorist would *not* accept _____ as a reason for the apparent consistency of our friends' behavior.
    a. our own presence in the situations when we see our friends
    b. our "implicit personality theories"
    c. stable personality traits
    d. constant physical qualities of people, such as voice tone

17. According to Freud
    a. defense mechanisms defend against repression
    b. repression reduces anxiety
    c. individuals are similar in their balance of id, ego, and superego systems
    d. all of the above

18. We are more likely to find consistency of behavior across situations if we
    a. use projective tests
    b. make repeated observations
    c. define traits in global terms
    d. use personality inventories

19. _____ theories assume that people vary on a number of continuous dimensions or scales.
    a. Humanistic
    b. Psychoanalytic
    c. Trait
    d. Social-learning

20. One criticism of trait theory is that it ignores
    a. behavior
    b. situational factors
    c. aggression
    d. genetic influences

KEY TO SELF-QUIZ

1. a	6. b	11. c	16. c
2. d	7. c	12. a	17. b
3. b	8. d	13. d	18. b
4. a	9. a	14. b	19. c
5. c	10. a	15. c	20. b

CLASS EXERCISE

A PROJECTIVE TEST

Introduction

The Rorschach Test, introduced by Hermann Rorschach in 1921, consists of a series of complex inkblots. Subjects are asked to tell what they see in each inkblot, and their responses are then scored and interpreted by experienced testers (see pp. 444–46 of the text).

In this demonstration we will use an inkblot like those used in the Rorschach Test. The exercise is designed to demonstrate that people looking at the same blot will see different things. No attempt at interpretation will be made by your instructor.

Procedure

Your instructor will ask six volunteers, preferably three men and three women, to leave the room. While they are out of the room, write below what the blot looks like to you. They will be called in one at a time and will be asked to relate what the blot looks like to them or what it makes them think of. You are to write each student's response in the space provided on p. 199.

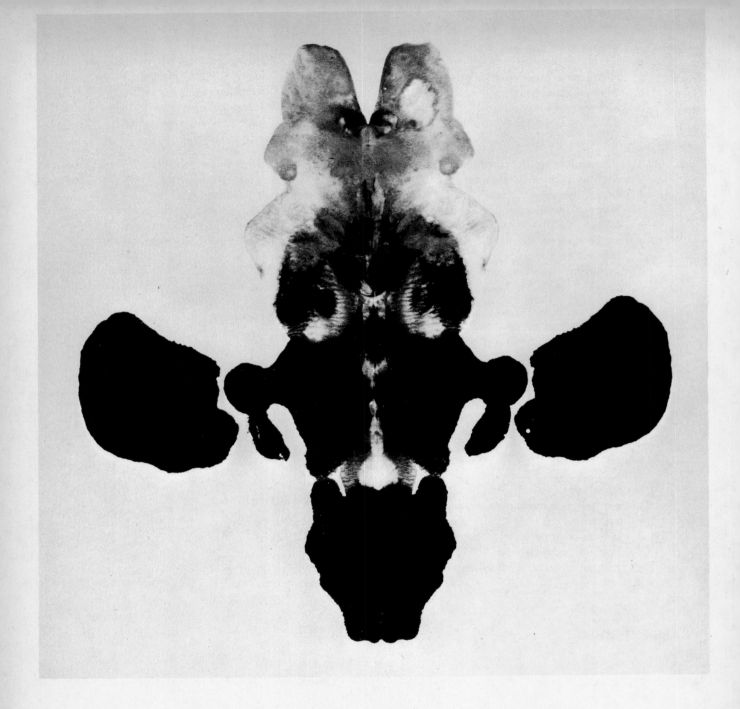

Your own impression:

Student 5:

Student 1:

Student 6:

Student 2:

Questions for Discussion

1. Were there differences in the responses of the six subjects? If so, can you think why?

2. Although the sample used was small, did there seem to be sex differences in perception?

3. Do you think people "project" aspects of their personality in responding to such a blot?

Student 3:

4. What are the advantages of using stimuli as unstructured as this to assess personality? The disadvantages?

5. How does this test differ from the Thematic Apperception Test?

6. Would it be easy to derive objective scoring methods for a test of this type?

Student 4:

14
Stress and Coping

LEARNING OBJECTIVES

14-1. Be able to describe the three general ways in which stress has been defined.

14-2. Understand how the primary and secondary appraisals of an event determine the degree of stress experienced.

14-3. Be able to describe the three stages of the general adaption syndrome.

14-4. Be familiar with the various psychological reactions to a stressful situation. Be able to discuss Freud's theory of anxiety and the research on learned helplessness.

14-5. Be able to discuss the relationship between stressful life events and illness, including studies of stress-resistant individuals.

14-6. Be familiar with the effects of predictability and controllability on the severity of stress. Be able to cite studies (drawn from various sections of the chapter) where the subject's ability to control a stressor influenced the results.

14-7. Distinguish between problem-focused coping and emotion-focused coping, giving examples of each.

14-8. Be able to describe Freud's concept of repression and the six defense mechanisms that aid repression.

14-9. Explain how the defense mechanisms of rationalization and intellectualization differ from rational and intellectual thinking. Show how reaction formation and projection would differ in their defense against an undesirable trait.

14-10. Be familiar with the research on stress-induced ulcers and on the relationship between personality characteristics and heart disease.

1. Researchers have defined *stress* in three different ways: as a *response*, a *stimulus,* and a *transaction* between the demands of the environment and the individual's ability to deal with them. When researchers investigate the pattern of physiological and psychological reactions that occur when people encounter difficult situations,

   response   they are studying stress as a _____ .

2. When we speak of an individual as being in a state of stress, we are emphasizing the

   response   _____ aspect of stress.

3. The *emergency response* is an innate pattern of physiological responses that occurs

   response   automatically when an organism perceives a threat. The emergency _____ is also called the *fight-or-flight reaction* because it prepares the organism to attack or to flee.

4. An innate pattern of physiological responses that prepares the organism to fight or

   fight-or-flight   flee is called the emergency response, or the _____ – _____ – _____ response.

5. Rapid heart rate and respiration, elevated blood pressure, muscle tension, and dry-

   flight   ness of throat and mouth are part of the fight-or-_____ reaction. These physiological responses are regulated by the *autonomic nervous system* under the control of the *hypothalamus.*

6. The innate physiological responses that prepare the organism to deal with an emer-

   nervous   gency are regulated by the autonomic _____ system under the

   hypothalamus   control of the _____ . While these responses are valuable in helping a person deal with a physical threat, they are not very adaptive for dealing with many modern-day sources of stress. (The text describes the physiological changes that occur when a stressful event continues over an extended period of time—a pattern of reactions called the *general adaptation syndrome*.)

7. The psychological responses to stress include *cognitive impairment* and emotions such as *anxiety, anger, apathy,* and *depression.* If you worried about an examination so much that you cannot recall well-learned facts, then you realize that one

   impairment   response to stress is cognitive _____ .

8. The *primary* emotional response to a situation appraised as stressful is *anxiety.* By anxiety, we mean that unpleasant emotion characterized by such terms as "worry,"

   primary   "apprehension," "tension," and "fear." While anxiety is the _____ emotional response to a stressful situation, another common response is *anger.*

9. Anger often occurs in response to a stressful situation that involves *frustration*—the inability to obtain a desired goal. A person who is blocked from obtaining a desired

   frustration   goal experiences f_____ , may feel angry, and may display *aggression* toward the source of frustration.

10. If Tommy kicks his older sister when she takes his ball away from him, he is dis-

    aggression   playing _____ toward his sister as the source of frustration.

11. When a frustrated person directly attacks the frustrating object or person, we say he or she is displaying *direct* aggression. If, after Tommy's sister takes the ball away

direct
is not

from him, he kicks her, he is displaying _____ aggression. If he kicks the door instead, he (*is/is not*) displaying direct aggression.

12. If we cannot satisfactorily express our aggression against the source of stress, we may shift, or *displace,* the aggression toward an innocent person or object. Sandra, who is angry with her father, pulls the cat's tail. She is probably exhibiting

displaced

_____ aggression.

13. The football player who has caught and then dropped a pass stamps the ground.

displaced

This is an example of _____ aggression.

14. Sometimes, when frustrated, we may simply act indifferent or attempt to withdraw from the situation—that is, we may react with *apathy*. Ann, who has been told that she cannot attend a movie with her friends, does not display active aggression but

apathy

goes to her room and sulks. Her behavior could be described as _____ , which is the opposite of aggression.

15. People react differently to stressful situations. While a common response is aggres-

displaced, apathy

sion, either direct or _____ , another response is _____ . Perhaps the person whose efforts (aggressive or otherwise) to satisfy his or her needs were never successful may have *learned* to be helpless, or apathetic, when faced with stressful situations.

16. The concept of *learned helplessness* grew out of some experiments with dogs. The dogs were placed in a situation in which they were helpless to avoid an electric shock. Later, when they could easily avoid shock by means of a simple response, the dogs made no attempt to make the avoidance response; they had learned to be

helpless

h_____ .

17. By being placed in a situation where nothing they did could avoid shock, the dogs

learned, helplessness

l_____ to be helpless; this learned _____ generalized to subsequent situations where avoidance was possible.

learned helplessness

18. The concept of _____ _____ may explain why some people react with apathy when faced with stressful situations.

19. Instead of focusing on the response aspect of stress, some researchers have studied environmental circumstances (such as floods, earthquakes, or imprisonment) that make unusual demands on the person's ability to cope. When we focus on stressful

stimulus

environmental circumstances, we are emphasizing the (*stimulus/response*) aspect of stress.

20. Divorce, death of a loved one, and loss of a job are life events that require major adjustment. Studying the relationship between such events and the risk of subse-

stimulus

quent illness focuses on stress as a _____ .

21. However, while some life events (such as divorce and bereavement) are stressful for everyone, less dramatic experiences (taking an examination, arguing with a spouse) are stressful for some people but not for others. This suggests that describing stress

is not

as a stimulus (*is/is not*) sufficient.

22. In addition, responses to a stressful event can be influenced by psychological factors. One person may respond to a painful medical procedure with anxiety and physiological indications of stress, whereas another may not. This suggests that

response
describing stress as a _____ is not sufficient.

stimulus **23.** The *transactional approach* views stress as neither a _____ nor

response
a _____ , but as a *transaction*—or relationship—between the person and the environment that *taxes* or *exceeds the person's resources*. To understand stress, we need to know how the individual appraises a situation in terms of his or her *well-being* and *resources for coping*.

24. From a transactional perspective, stress reflects a relationship between a person and

resources
the environment that is appraised by the person as taxing his or her _____ for coping.

25. Mark and David are scheduled to present a public debate. Mark feels confident in his abilities as a public speaker, but David does not. According to a transactional view, David is apt to experience stress because he appraises the situation as

taxing (*or* exceeding)
_____ his resources.

26. Two critical processes that determine the stressfulness of the person-environment

appraisal
transaction are *cognitive appraisal* and *coping*. Cognitive ap_____ is the process of evaluating an event with respect to its significance for a person's *well-being*. Coping is the process by which the person attempts to manage the demands of the stressful situation.

cognitive **27.** The first part of the _____ appraisal, the *primary appraisal*, asks, What does this situation mean to me? Am I okay or in trouble? In other words, the primary appraisal evaluates the situation with respect to the individual's

being
well-_____ .

appraisal **28.** If the primary _____ evaluates the situation as stressful (i.e., a threat to the person's well-being), then the *secondary appraisal* asks, What, if anything, can I do about it?

primary **29.** The _____ appraisal evaluates the degree of threat, and the secon-

coping (*or* dealing)
dary appraisal evaluates the individual's resources for _____ with the situation. Obviously, the two processes are interrelated, because if the person believes his coping resources are adequate, the situation is appraised as less stressful.

appraisal **30.** The transactional approach to stress emphasizes cognitive _____

responses
rather than simply stimuli or _____ .

31. The process by which a person attempts to manage the demands of a stressful situa-

coping
tion is called c_____ , and it takes two forms. One focuses on the problem that is causing stress: the individual evaluates the situation and does something to change or avoid it. This is called *problem-focused* coping.

32. Jerry realizes that he is about to fail a course required for graduation. He arranges with the professor for tutoring to help him prepare for the final exam. This ap-

problem
proach would be _____-focused coping.

33. Another way of handling a stressful situation attempts to reduce anxious feelings without dealing directly with the situation. This is called *emotion-focused coping*. If Jerry reduces his anxiety by refusing to acknowledge the possibility of failing, he

emotion   is using _____-focused coping.

34. Another way to handle his concern about failing the course would be to deaden anxiety with alcohol, tranquilizers, or marijuana. These actions, which do nothing

emotion-focused   to solve the problem, would be forms of _____ - _____

coping.

emotion   **35.** People often use a combination of _____ -focused and

problem (*either order*)   _____ -focused strategies in dealing with stressful situations.

36. If you reduce anxiety by refusing to acknowledge the possibility of failing a course,

emotion   even though the signs are clear, you are using a(n) _____ -

focused strategy. You are also *distorting reality*; you are not altering the objective situation, just changing the way you think about it.

37. Freud used the term *defense mechanisms* to refer to ways of reducing anxious feel-

reality   ings by distorting _____ in some way. He believed that they are

unconscious processes.

emotion   **38.** Defense mechanisms are (*emotion/problem*)-focused strategies for handling anxiety.

reality   They all involve some distortion of _____ .

mechanisms   **39.** Freud believed that defense m_____ are (*conscious/*

unconscious   *unconscious*) processes.

defense   **40.** Some _____ mechanisms occur often enough to have been given

mechanism   names. According to Freud the basic, and most important, defense _____

is *repression*, in which impulses or memories that are too anxiety-producing or pain-

ful are *excluded* from *conscious awareness.*

awareness   **41.** In repression, anxiety-producing thoughts are excluded from conscious _____ .

42. A young woman feels intensely hostile toward her mother. But because such feel-

ings are totally inconsistent with her concept of herself as a loving daughter, they

would cause anxiety if she were aware of them. Consequently, her feelings of

repressed   hostility are re_____ and banished from memory.

43. A young boy was partially responsible for his brother's death. As an adult he has

no memory of the events surrounding the tragedy. This is another example of

repression   _____ .

defense mechanism   **44.** Repression is the basic _____ _____ ,

but Freud believed it is seldom completely successful. The repressed impulses

threaten to break through into consciousness; thus, the individual becomes anxious

(although unaware of the reason) and uses some additional defense mechanisms to

keep the partially repressed impulses from awareness.

45. The text discusses six additional defense mechanisms that may be used to aid repression. They help keep anxiety-producing thoughts from awareness by distorting

reality _____ in some way. They include (1) rationalization, (2) reaction formation, (3) projection, (4) intellectualization, (5) denial, and (6) displacement.

46. Assigning logical reasons or plausible excuses for what we do impulsively is known as *rationalization.* The statement, "I'd have been here on time but my alarm clock

rationalization didn't go off," might very well be a _____ .

47. A young boy refuses to share his candy with his younger sister and gives as the reason, "If I give her some candy, it will only make her teeth decay." If the boy is giving a "good" reason but not the "true" reason for not sharing, he is using the

rationalization defense mechanism of _____ .

rationalization **48.** In _____ , we give "good" reasons but not "true" reasons for our behavior.

49. In *reaction formation* we *conceal a motive* from ourselves by giving strong expression to its *opposite.* The mother who unconsciously resents the demands and restrictions that result from having a child may be excessively fussy and particular in her care of the child. She conceals her real feelings through the mecha-

formation nism of reaction_____ .

50. Concealing a motive by giving strong expression to its opposite describes the de-

reaction formation fense mechanism known as _____ .

51. Mrs. Z, once an alcoholic but now a teetotaler, is an ardent prohibitionist and engages in a personal crusade to convert everyone from drinking any kind of alcoholic beverage. She may be displaying a defense mechanism called

reaction formation _____ .

52. In *projection*, we protect ourselves from recognizing our own *undesirable* qualities by assigning them in an exaggerated amount to other people. If a man says, "You can't trust people any farther than you can throw them," he may be untrustworthy himself and may be attempting to keep himself from acknowledging this trait by

projection using the mechanism of _____ .

projection **53.** In the defense mechanism known as _____ , we attribute to others traits we find undesirable in ourselves.

54. Sally is overly critical but does not readily acknowledge this as one of her traits. She is overheard saying that her roommate is a very critical person. Sally is attributing to another individual an undesirable trait that she herself possesses. This illus-

projection trates the mechanism of _____ .

55. In projection, we protect ourselves from recognizing our own

undesirable _____ qualities by assigning them in an exaggerated amount to other people.

56. *Intellectualization* is an attempt to gain *detachment* from an emotionally threatening situation by dealing with it in abstract, intellectual terms. A young man watches his mother slowly die from cancer. In talking about her death to a friend he focuses on the medical details of her condition and treatment. He is using

intellectualization   intell_____ to defend against very stressful emotions.

detachment   **57.** In intellectualization the person tries to gain de_____ from an emotionally threatening situation by dealing with it in abstract,

intellectual   _____ terms.

58. When a situation is too unpleasant to face, an individual may deny that it exists.

mechanism   This defense _____ is called *denial*.

59. Parents of a fatally ill child may refuse to admit that anything is seriously wrong. Because they cannot tolerate the pain that acknowledging reality would produce,

denial   they resort to the defense mechanism of _____ .

60. Denial is similar in some respects to Freud's basic defense mechanism, which is

repression   _____ .

61. However, in denial, the individual defends against an external threat by refusing to

reality   acknowledge some disturbing aspect of _____ ; whereas repression refers to an individual's defending against an internal threat by banishing anxiety-

conscious   producing impulses or memories from _____ awareness.

62. Let's review. The defense mechanism whereby we assign logical or plausible excuses

rationalization   for what we do is known as _____ .

63. Individuals who attribute to others qualities that they find undesirable in them-

projection   selves are engaging in _____ .

64. When we try to detach ourselves from an emotionally threatening situation by dealing with it in abstract, intellectual terms, we are using

intellectualization   _____ as a defense mechanism.

65. Concealing a motive by giving strong expression to its opposite is known as

reaction formation   _____ _____ .

anxiety   **66.** All of these mechanisms are ways of protecting oneself against _____
reality   by distorting _____ to some extent. They may be used as aids to
repression   the basic defense mechanism of re_____ , which
blocks the anxiety-producing feelings completely from awareness.

67. An additional defense mechanism discussed in the text is *displacement*. In displacement, a motive whose gratification is blocked in one form is *displaced* or directed into a different, more *socially acceptable* channel. If one's hostile impulses are expressed in boxing or wrestling, this is an example of

displacement   dis_____ . Sexual impulses that cannot be expressed directly may be expressed indirectly in such creative activities as art and music.

displacement

This is another example of _____ .

68. Freud felt that displacement was the most satisfactory way of handling blocked aggressive and sexual impulses, because it allowed these impulses to be expressed

acceptable

indirectly in more socially _____ forms.

69. To the extent that defense mechanisms help a person through difficult times until he or she can learn more *mature* and *realistic* ways of coping with

anxiety

_____ -producing situations, they contribute to satisfactory adjustment.

70. If, however, the individual continues to rely upon defense mechanisms so that he

mature

or she is never forced to learn more m_____ and realistic ways of behaving, then such mechanisms would constitute a barrier to satisfactory adjustment.

TERMS AND CONCEPTS

cognitive appraisal _____

_____

_____

_____

coping _____

_____

_____

_____

fight-or-flight response _____

_____

_____

_____

general adaptation syndrome _____

_____

_____

_____

objective anxiety _____

_____

_____

_____

neurotic anxiety _____

_____

_____

_____

defense mechanism _____

_____

_____

_____

frustration-aggression hypothesis _____

_____

_____

_____

displaced aggression _____

_____

_____

_____

learned helplessness _____

_____

_____

_____

emotion-focused coping _____

_____

_____

_____

problem-focused coping _____

_____

_____

_____

repression _____

_____

_____

_____

rationalization _____

_____

_____

_____

reaction formation _____

_____

_____

_____

projection _____

_____

_____

_____

intellectualization _____

_____

_____

_____

denial _____

_____

_____

_____

displacement _____

_____

_____

_____

behavioral medicine _____

_____

_____

_____

psychosomatic disorder _____

_____

_____

_____

Type A behavior _____

_____

_____

_____

biofeedback* _____

_____

_____

_____

relaxation training* _____

_____

_____

_____

cognitive behavior therapy* _____

_____

_____

_____

psychoimmunology _____

_____

_____

_____

*Indicates term used in Critical Discussion

_____ 1. One example of a defense mechanism as a helpful coping device is the use by doctors of the mechanism of
   a. repression
   b. displacement
   c. intellectualization
   d. rationalization

_____ 2. Freud was one of the first theorists to focus on the importance of anxiety. He
   a. differentiated between objective anxiety and neurotic anxiety
   b. viewed neurotic anxiety as synonymous with fear
   c. felt objective anxiety stemmed from an unconscious conflict
   d. all of the above

_____ 3. "Scapegoating" as an outcome of frustration illustrates a response called _____ aggression.
   a. direct
   b. frustrated
   c. instrumental
   d. displaced

_____ 4. Margaret is anxious about the talk she has to give in class tomorrow. She goes out for a beer. Margaret is displaying
   a. reaction formation
   b. intellectualization
   c. emotion-focused coping
   d. neurotic anxiety

_____ 5. The common element in defense mechanisms is
   a. primitivation
   b. self-deception
   c. covert aggression
   d. displacement

_____ 6. When subjects respond to a post-hypnotic suggestion, they sometimes feel so embarrassed that they _____ the behavior.
   a. repress
   b. rationalize
   c. project
   d. displace

_____ 7. The Type A characteristic found to be the most significant predictor of heart disease is
   a. impatience
   b. competitiveness
   c. hostility
   d. self-doubt

_____ 8. The defense mechanism that best serves its function of reducing anxiety while still allowing some gratification of the unacceptable motive is
   a. displacement
   b. rationalization
   c. intellectualization
   d. reaction formation

_____ 9. In Freud's view, defense mechanisms "defend" by
   a. keeping certain impulses out of awareness
   b. gratifying the id's impulses
   c. strengthening the superego
   d. all of the above

_____ 10. Studies of wartime prisoners show that a common reaction to frustrating conditions of long duration from which there is no hope of escape is
   a. scapegoating
   b. fantasy
   c. apathy
   d. stereotyping

_____ 11. In the experiment in which rats were wired to a shock device with only one rat able to avoid the shock in response to a warning signal,
   a. all rats developed severe gastric lesions
   b. the greater the feedback to the rat in control, the more ulceration it developed
   c. the rat in control developed less ulceration than the rats that could not avoid shock
   d. gastric lesions were observed only at near-fatal levels of shock intensity

_____ 12. According to the general adaptation syndrome, the body's first response to a stressor is
   a. resistance
   b. exhaustion
   c. countershock
   d. shock

_____ 13. The _____ approach views stress as a relationship between the person and the environment that taxes or exceeds the person's resources.
   a. social-learning
   b. cognitive
   c. transactional
   d. psychoanalytic

14. The unconscious mechanism by which we assign exaggerated versions of our own undesirable qualities to other people is called
   a. displacement
   b. projection
   c. reaction formation
   d. undoing

15. The same stressful event can be perceived quite differently by two people, depending on
   a. the reactivity of their nervous systems
   b. what the situation means to them
   c. their susceptibility to asthma and other psychosomatic illnesses
   d. whether repression is part of their psychological make-up

16. A person who shows a reaction formation is one who
   a. assigns his or her undesirable qualities to others
   b. completely blocks from awareness an anxiety-producing impulse
   c. conceals a motive by strongly expressing its opposite
   d. develops repetitive and ritualistic behavior

17. The body's reaction to a stressor that continues over time is described by the
   a. emergency response
   b. transactional model
   c. general adaptation syndrome
   d. all of the above

18. Freud believed that neurotic anxiety resulted from a(n)
   a. unconscious conflict between id impulses and ego constraints
   b. exaggerated fear of some part of the environment
   c. realistic fear of the environment
   d. conscious fear of failing to live up to society's standards

19. People who exhibit Type A behavior are much more likely than Type B individuals to
   a. stick to a diet
   b. have good family relationships
   c. enjoy vacations from work
   d. suffer a heart attack

20. Which of the following does *not* reduce the effects of stress?
   a. being unable to predict when a stressful event will occur
   b. having control over the duration of a stressful event
   c. having friends who share the worry but are supportive
   d. feeling competent about one's own abilities

KEY TO SELF-QUIZ

20. a	15. b	10. c	5. b
19. d	14. b	9. a	4. c
18. a	13. c	8. a	3. d
17. c	12. d	7. c	2. a
16. c	11. c	6. b	1. c

INDIVIDUAL EXERCISES

REACTIONS TO FRUSTRATION

Introduction

People react differently to stress and frustration. The text discusses some of the immediate reactions to, and ways of coping with, frustrating situations. This exercise should help you analyze your own responses to frustration.

Procedure

1. Think back over the past two months and list any occasions on which you were frustrated either by other people or by circumstances. Some of these events may be trivial (for example, you were late to class because you failed to awake in time or your car wouldn't start); others may be major disappointments (for example, you failed a test in an important course or were rejected by someone you love). If you can't recall any frustrations during the past two months, you

lead a blessed life or are good at repressing unpleasant experiences. Whatever the reason, keep going back in time until you have listed five to ten frustrating experiences. Write down a few phrases to identify each episode. Don't read further until you have recalled at least five or more events.

2. Now think about each event and try to recall your immediate reactions (for example, anger, tension, feelings of helplessness) and your method of coping with your feelings (for example, tried to forget about the situation, went out for a milkshake and pizza, went to a movie, sought the comfort of friends, took some action to remedy the situation). You may have had more than one reaction to each situation; if so, list all your reactions.

3. Examine your list of reactions. Do you discern a characteristic way of handling frustration?

4. As a final step, keep a record for the coming week, listing any frustrating situations and your reactions as they occur.

Questions for Discussion

1. Was it difficult to recall past reactions to frustration? If so, why do you think this is the case?

2. Did you notice any difference in reactions recorded for earlier events and those recorded for the past week? If so, what factors might contribute to this difference?

3. Does your increased awareness of your reactions to frustration make it easier to change the way you respond?

RATIONALIZATION

Complete each of the following sentences with the first answer that comes to mind. Work quickly without pondering your responses. No one else need see them.

1. My grades would be higher if _____
_____
_____

2. I would feel more comfortable in social situations if
_____
_____
_____

3. I would be more popular with the opposite sex if
_____
_____
_____

4. I would have done better in my last exam in this course if _____
_____
_____

5. I would have achieved more honors and recognition for extracurricular activities if _____
_____
_____

6. Sometimes my grades are lower than they should be because _____
_____
_____

7. I could work better if _____
_____
_____

8. I do not engage in many extracurricular activities because _____
_____
_____
_____

9. I would have more friends if_____
_____
_____

10. I could manage my finances better if _____

_____

_____

_____

Someone else looking at your answers might discern some evidence of rationalization—the tendency we all have to give "rational" and "good" explanations rather than "true" reasons. (See pp. 474–75 in the text for some examples of rationalization.) Examine each of your answers carefully and objectively, as if you were an outside observer. Do you find any evidence of rationalization—instances where the reasons you give are not exactly the real ones? In which, if any, areas of your life are you more likely to use this defense?

15
Abnormal Psychology

LEARNING OBJECTIVES

15-1. Know the four criteria that may be used in defining abnormality, as well as the characteristics that are considered indicative of normality.

15-2. Understand the advantages and disadvantages of classifying abnormal behavior into categories. Be familiar with the DSM-III system of classification, including the variables covered in an individual diagnosis and some of the major categories.

15-3. Be able to describe four types of anxiety disorders and show how their symptoms either express anxiety directly or reflect attempts to control anxious feelings.

15-4. Be able to explain the development of phobias from the standpoint of psychoanalytic, behavioral, and cognitive theories.

15-5. Be able to describe the three major affective disorders and to compare psychoanalytic, behavioral, and cognitive theories of depression.

15-6. Be familiar with the evidence indicating that genetic and biochemical factors play a role in affective disorders.

15-7. Know the defining characteristics of schizophrenia and give examples of each.

15-8. Be familiar with the research on the causes of schizophrenia; be able to discuss the probable contributions of genetic, biochemical, social, and psychological factors.

15-9. Understand the role of vulnerability and stress in the development of mental disorders; describe how studies of children at risk for schizophrenia are investigating these two factors.

15-10. Be able to define personality disorders; know the defining characteristics and probable causes of antisocial personalities.

1. This chapter discusses a variety of *abnormal* behaviors. But what do we mean by

abnormal

abnormal? The word itself, ab_____ , means "away from the norm." So one definition of abnormality is any behavior that is *statistically infrequent* or deviant from the norm.

2. But this definition is not completely satisfactory. People who are very gifted intel-

infrequent

lectually or unusually well adjusted deviate from the norm in the sense of being statistically (*frequent/infrequent*), yet we would not consider them abnormal.

3. A second method of classifying behavior as normal or abnormal is by determining whether the behavior is in accord with *society's standards.* Anthropological studies have revealed, however, that what is considered normal in one society may be considered abnormal in another. Therefore, this definition of abnormality, which really constitutes a *social* definition, also has its limitations. For example, homo-sexuality is considered normal behavior in some cultures, but in other cultures it

abnormal

is considered _____ .

statistical

4. A definition of abnormality in terms of st_____ frequency is not satisfactory because some very desirable traits may fall outside the normal

social

range. Likewise, we cannot be content with a _____ definition of abnormality, since the standards of normality and abnormality vary from one culture to the next or even from time to time within the same culture.

5. A third definition of abnormality is based on *maladaptiveness of behavior.* Behavior is abnormal if it is *maladaptive*; that is, if it has adverse effects either for the indi-vidual or for society. According to this definition a man who is so fearful of en-closed places that he cannot enter an elevator or a windowless room would be

maladaptive

considered abnormal because his behavior is mal_____ ; it has adverse effects for him.

6. A woman whose anger explodes in assaultive attacks on others would also be considered abnormal by this definition, because her behavior has adverse effects

society

for s_____ .

7. A fourth criterion looks at abnormality from the viewpoint of people's subjective feelings—their *personal distress*—rather than their behavior. According to this criterion a person who functions very effectively at his or her job and whose behavior appears quite normal to observers, may still be considered

abnormal

_____ if the individual feels acutely miserable most of the time.

8. A fourth definition looks at abnormality in terms of the individual's personal

distress

_____ rather than his or her behavior.

9. Our four definitions of abnormality take into account statistical

frequency, society

f_____ , the standards of _____ , maladaptiveness

behavior, distress

of _____ , and personal _____ . In most in-stances all four criteria are used in diagnosing abnormality.

abnormality

10. Normality is even more difficult to define than _____ . Some of the characteristics discussed in the text as possessed to a *greater degree* by normal individuals than by those diagnosed as abnormal include an *efficient perception of reality, self-knowledge,* and *self-acceptance,* ability to *control one's behavior* and to *form affectionate relationships,* and *productivity.* These characteristics do not distinguish sharply between the mentally healthy and the mentally ill; they are

greater

simply traits that the normal person possesses to a _____ degree than one diagnosed as abnormal.

11. Each person's behavior patterns and emotional problems are unique. However, enough similarities exist for mental health professionals to classify cases into categories. The classification of abnormal behavior used most often in this country is the *Diagnostic and Statistical Manual of Mental Disorders,* Third Edition, which is abbreviated DSM-III. DSM-III classifies abnormal behavior, or mental

disorders

d_____ , into a large number of categories and subcategories. The text discusses four of the major categories: anxiety disorders, affective disorders, schizophrenia, and personality disorders.

DSM

12. Anxiety disorders form one of the major categories of _____-III. All of us feel anxious at times. But when a person lives each day in a state of high tension, is apprehensive, and overacts to mild stresses, he or she is diagnosed as suffering from *generalized anxiety.* Generalized anxiety is one type of anxiety

disorder, DSM-III

_____ , as listed in _____-_____ .

anxiety

13. A person suffering from generalized _____ may also experience *panic attacks*—sudden episodes of overwhelming apprehension or terror accompanied by physiological symptoms of fear.

14. When people feel tense and anxious much of the time without being able to specify

generalized

exactly what they are afraid of, they are suffering from _____

anxiety

_____ . When they have sudden episodes of over-

panic

whelming terror, they experience _____ attacks and are diagnosed as having a *panic disorder.*

anxiety, disorder

15. Generalized _____ and panic _____ are two diagnoses included under the broader DSM-III category called

anxiety

_____ disorders. Another is *phobic disorders.*

16. *Phobias* are *excessive fears* of certain objects or situations in the *absence of real danger.* Jane is so fearful of closed places that she will never take the elevator to her ninth-floor office but insists on climbing the stairs instead. She has a

phobia

_____ .

17. Tom is so fearful of fire that he cannot stay in a room in which there is a fire burning in the fireplace. Since Tom's fear is excessive in a situation in which there is no

phobia

real danger, it is another example of a _____ .

absence   **18.** Phobias are excessive fears in the _____ of real danger. Some phobias may be maladaptive responses that are learned, while others may develop as a defense against impulses that the individual feels may become dangerous. The text discusses both of these possibilities.

19. A person with a phobia is not usually diagnosed as having a phobic

disorder   dis_____ unless the fears seriously interfere with his or her daily life.

20. David is so fearful of snakes that he refuses to go hiking. He probably (*would/*

would not   *would not*) be considered to have a phobic disorder.

21. Beth is so fearful of being in public places (a condition called *agoraphobia*) that she refuses to leave the house. She probably would be diagnosed as suffering from

phobic disorder   a _____ _____ .

22. Fear of being alone in an unfamiliar setting or in public places, called

agoraphobia   ag_____ , is the most common phobia for which people seek professional help.

generalized   **23.** So far we have discussed three types of anxiety disorders: _____

panic, phobic   anxiety, _____ disorders, and _____

(either order)   disorders. A fourth subcategory is *obsessive-compulsive disorders.*

compulsive   **24.** An *obsessive-*_____ disorder may take three forms: (1) *obsessive thoughts,* (2) *compulsive acts,* and (3) a *combination* of obsessive thoughts and compulsive acts. You might guess that a person with

obsessive   _____ thoughts has persistently unwelcome, disturbing thoughts and that a person with a compulsion has an irresistible urge to repeat a

act   certain stereotyped or ritualistic _____ .

25. *Obsessive thoughts* frequently involve aggressive or sexual impulses that are quite unacceptable to the conscious feelings of the person who has them. Because these unacceptable impulses would cause great anxiety if the person acknowledged them as his or her real feelings, they are repressed and appear as

obsessive   _____ thoughts that the individual experiences as not being really his or her own.

impulses   **26.** Obsessive thoughts thus involve unacceptable _____ that the person cannot acknowledge as his or her own.

27. A young mother had frequent thoughts of murdering her two small children. She professed nothing but love for them and maintained that "these awful thoughts that pop into my head" had nothing to do with her real feelings. In this case

obsessive   _____ thoughts protected the mother from the anxiety she would feel were she to acknowledge these impulses as her own.

28. *Compulsive acts* are stereotyped or ritualistic acts that are designed to protect the individual from feelings of anxiety or guilt. A young boy who suffered guilt feelings whenever he masturbated felt compelled to scrub his hands many times a

compulsive

day. In this case the _____ act served to relieve his feelings of guilt.

29. Obsessive thoughts and compulsive acts thus serve to protect the individual against

anxiety, obsessive-

compulsive

_____ or guilt. They are characteristic of an _____- _____ disorder.

DSM

generalized anxiety

panic

phobic

obsessive-

compulsive

30. Let's review. Anxiety disorders are a major diagnostic category of _____-III. They include (1) _____ _____ disorders in which the individual feels tense and apprehensive most of the time; (2) _____ disorders that involve sudden episodes of overwhelming apprehension; (3) _____ disorders, in which excessive fears are focused on particular objects or situations; and (4) _____- _____ disorders, in which ritualistic acts serve to ward off anxiety-producing impulses.

31. *Affective disorders,* another major diagnostic category, are disturbances of *affect,* or mood. The person may be severely *depressed, manic* (wildly elated), or may

depression

affect

alternate between periods of mania and d_____ . These changes of mood, or _____ , are often so extreme that the individual requires hospitalization.

disorders

depressed

manic, depressed
(either order)

32. People suffering from affective _____ may be either severely _____ or elated. Or they may alternate cyclically between _____ and _____ states, with a period of normal behavior in between. This pattern is called a *manic-depressive* disorder.

manic-depressive

33. One type of affective disorder is a _____- _____ disorder. The text discusses several theories that attempt to explain affective disorders.

34. *Schizophrenia* is the label applied to another group of serious mental disorders (the DSM-III category is listed as schizophrenic disorders, but schizophrenia is the more commonly used term.) Whereas affective disorders are characterized by disturb-

affect

ances of mood, or _____ , schizophrenia is characterized by disturbances of *thought*.

35. A person suffering from schizophrenia may speak in a jumble of words and phrases that seem unrelated. This "word salad" reflects the disturbance of

thought

_____ that is characteristic of schizophrenia.

schizophrenia

36. The thought disturbances that are characteristics of schizo_____ seem to reflect difficulty in *"filtering out" irrelevant stimuli.* Whereas normal individuals are able to selectively focus attention, people suffering from schizo-

irrelevant

phrenia appear unable to filter out _____ stimuli; they are responsive to many stimuli at the same time and have difficulty focusing

attention

at_____ on the relevant ones.

filtering	37. The thought disturbances observed in cases of schizophrenia seem to stem from a difficulty in _____ out irrelevant stimuli.
schizophrenia	38. Another common symptom of sch_____ *is withdrawal from reality.* The individual tends to withdraw from interaction with others and becomes absorbed in his or her inner thoughts and fantasies.
reality	39. In some cases this withdrawal from _____ progresses to the point where the person is completely unresponsive to external events, remaining silent and immobile for days at a time.
withdrawal	40. The disturbed thought processes and _____ from reality characteristic of schizophrenia may be accompanied by *delusions* and *hallucinations.*
delusion	41. Delusions are *false beliefs* that are maintained despite contradictory evidence or experience. Patient X thinks that he is God and has returned to earth to save us. He is evidently experiencing a _____ , since he is maintaining a false belief.
beliefs	42. Whereas delusions are false _____ , hallucinations are false sensory perceptions—that is, sense experiences occurring in the absence of appropriate external stimuli.
hallucination	43. Patient Y hears voices talking to her and threatening her that no one else hears. She is probably experiencing a _____ .
beliefs perceptions (*or* experiences)	44. Delusions are false _____ , whereas hallucinations are false sensory _____ .
thought stimuli, reality delusions hallucinations	45. We have mentioned several signs of schizophrenia. These include disturbed _____ processes, which may reflect difficulty in filtering out irrelevant _____ ; withdrawal from _____ ; false beliefs, or _____ ; and false sensory perceptions, or _____ . Another characteristic of schizophrenia is a *disturbance of affect*; the individual's affect, or emotion, is inappropriate to the thoughts being expressed or the situation being experienced.
affect	46. Patient Z smiles as he describes the death of a friend. Since the emotion is inappropriate to the thoughts being expressed, this indicates a disturbance of _____ .
affect	47. Although disturbed thought processes constitute one of the major signs of schizophrenia, there may also be disturbances of _____ . The text discusses some of the social, psychological, and biological factors that may lead to schizophrenia and points out that the label probably includes a *group* of disorders, which may turn out to have different causes.
DSM-III, anxiety	48. We have discussed three major categories of mental disorders as listed in _____-_____ . These include (1) _____

disorders, which are characterized by anxiety or attempts to control it;

affective

(2) _____ disorders, which are characterized by extreme

schizophrenia

changes in mood; and (3) _____ , characterized by thought disturbances and withdrawal from reality. A fourth category of abnormal behavior is called *personality disorders.* This category includes a wide variety of disorders that are often *longstanding patterns of maladaptive behavior* rather than reactions to conflict or stress.

disorders

49. Personality _____ are often longstanding patterns of

maladaptive

_____ behavior. *Antisocial personality,* for example, is a form of personality disorder in which the individual has a lifelong history of socially deviant behavior.

antisocial

50. One type of personality disorder is the _____ personality (also called psychopathic personality). The chief characteristic of individuals diagnosed as antisocial personalities is a *lack of conscience.* They have no sense of morality or concern for others; their behavior is determined entirely by their own needs.

conscience

51. The chief characteristic of individuals with antisocial personalities is a lack of _____ . They cannot tolerate frustration and seek immediate gratification of their needs, regardless of the welfare of others.

antisocial

52. "I want what I want when I want it" sums up the behavior of the individual with a(n) _____ personality.

prison

53. The characteristics of antisocial personalities frequently bring them into conflict with the law. They are likely to be found in a (*prison/hospital*). The text discusses some of the biological and psychological factors that may be responsible for the antisocial personality.

affective

54. A concept helpful in understanding the development of mental disorders is *vulnerability and stress.* For example, in depression (which is classed as a(n) _____ disorder) inherited biochemical abnormalities may predispose an individual to extreme mood changes.

vulnerable

55. This inherited predisposition may make the person vul_____ to depression when faced with stressful life events.

56. The kind of stressful events that depressed patients report precipitated their disorder are usually within the range of normal life experiences—experiences most people can handle without becoming abnormally depressed. Thus, the concept of

vulnerability

_____ is helpful in understanding why some people develop depression but others do not when confronted with a particular stressful experience.

57. Vulnerability to depression (due to biochemical abnormalities or certain traumatic childhood experiences) makes an individual more likely to develop an affective dis-

stress

order when confronted with _____ in later life.

58. Similarly, while evidence indicates a genetic predisposition for schizophrenia, most children of schizophrenic parents do not develop the disorder. Genetic and environmental factors undoubtedly interact to produce schizophrenia. This points up the

vulnerability, stress

importance of the concept of _____ and _____ in understanding mental disorders.

59. Let's review. The four criteria used in defining abnormal behavior include:

frequency

a. statistical _____

social

b. _____ standards or norms

behavior

c. maladaptiveness of _____

personal

d. _____ distress

60. See if you can identify four types of anxiety disorders.

generalized anxiety

a. Continual tension and anxiety: _____ _____
disorders

panic

b. Sudden episodes of intense terror: _____ disorders

phobic

c. Excessive fears in the absence of danger: _____
disorders

obsessive-

d. Persistently disturbing thoughts or urges: _____ -

compulsive

_____ disorders

61. Among the more severe mental disorders that often require hospitalization are

affective

_____ disorders, characterized by disturbances of

schizophrenia (*or* schizophrenic disorders)

mood, and _____ , characterized by withdrawal from reality and disturbed thinking.

62. Longstanding patterns of maladaptive behavior, such as antisocial personality, are

personality disorders

classified as _____ _____ .

TERMS AND CONCEPTS

DSM-III _____

_____

_____

_____

psychosis _____

_____

_____

_____

neurosis _____

_____

_____

_____

hallucination _____

_____

_____

_____

delusion _____

_____

_____

_____

anxiety disorder _____

_____

_____

_____

generalized anxiety _____

_____

_____

_____

panic attack _____

_____

_____

_____

simple phobia _____

_____

_____

_____

social phobia _____

_____

_____

_____

agoraphobia _____

_____

_____

_____

obsession _____

_____

_____

_____

compulsion _____

_____

_____

_____

obsessive-compulsive disorder ____

_____

_____

_____

prepared conditioning _____

_____

_____

_____

benzodiazepines _____

_____

_____

_____

affective disorder _____

_____

_____

_____

depression _____

_____

_____

_____

parasuicide* _____

_____

_____

_____

manic depression _____

_____

_____

_____

manic-depressive disorder _____

_____

_____

_____

biogenic amines _____

_____

_____

_____

schizophrenia _____

_____

_____

_____

autism _____

_____

_____

_____

dopamine hypothesis _____

_____

_____

_____

personality disorder _____

_____

_____

_____

antisocial personality _____

_____

_____

_____

*Indicates term used in Critical Discussion

_____ 1. A person who exhibits compulsive rituals, such as continual hand washing, would be classified as suffering from a(n) _____ disorder.
   a. anxiety
   b. personality
   c. schizophrenic
   d. affective

_____ 2. The dopamine hypothesis attempts to explain the symptoms of
   a. depression
   b. schizophrenia
   c. panic disorders
   d. agoraphobia

_____ 3. Normal people are characterized in the text as possessing a series of traits to a greater degree than individuals diagnosed as abnormal. Which of the following is *not* one of these characteristics of the psychologically healthy individual?
   a. self-esteem and acceptance
   b. social conformity
   c. productivity
   d. self-knowledge

_____ 4. A major defining characteristic of personality disorders is that they
   a. are longstanding patterns of maladaptive behavior
   b. reflect a lack of contact with reality
   c. are comparatively easy to treat
   d. are frequently short-term responses to stress

_____ 5. Reduced reinforcement has been proposed as a causal factor in
   a. schizophrenia
   b. antisocial personalities
   c. depression
   d. alcoholism

_____ 6. An abnormality in the metabolism of the neurotransmitter _____ has been proposed as an underlying cause of schizophrenia.
   a. amphetamine
   b. serotonin
   c. norepinephrine
   d. dopamine

_____ 7. Which of the following statements is *not* true of individuals diagnosed as schizophrenics? They
   a. occupy about half of all neuropsychiatric hospital beds
   b. often experience hallucinations
   c. exhibit multiple personalities
   d. are characterized by thought disorders

_____ 8. Each of the criteria for defining abnormal behavior has both advantages and drawbacks. The only useful criterion in some instances, for example, is
   a. personal distress
   b. adaptiveness of behavior
   c. social standards
   d. statistical frequency

_____ 9. The person diagnosed as an antisocial personality
   a. typically comes from a home marked by intense conflict or disturbed relationships
   b. is best characterized by "lovelessness" and "guiltlessness"
   c. has been said to have an overreactive autonomic system
   d. suffers from anxiety attacks.

_____ 10. Studies of the family background of schizophrenics have found that
   a. schizophrenics are more likely than normals to have lost a parent early in life
   b. disturbed home life is much more common for schizophrenics than normals
   c. no single pattern of family interaction leads to schizophrenia
   d. all of the above

_____ 11. The college student described in the text as fearful of many things, including leaving his dorm room, represents a
   a. typical college student
   b. phobic disorder
   c. affective disorder
   d. schizophrenic disorder

_____ 12. It has been hypothesized that class differences in the incidence of schizophrenia result from
   a. differences in diagnoses

b. a downward drift to a lower class due to lack of skills
c. the stress of living in poverty
d. all of the above

_____13. The woman described in the text as spending most of her waking hours checking the doors and windows and taking showers is displaying
a. generalized anxiety
b. an obsessive-compulsive disorder
c. a phobic disorder
d. autistic behavior

_____14. Biochemical abnormalities found in the blood or urine of schizophrenic patients
a. may be either a cause or a result of their problem
b. are called psychotomimetic substances
c. have been shown to cause certain symptoms
d. probably have no relationship to schizophrenia

_____15. Which one of the following is *not* listed as a major diagnostic category in DSM-III?
a. personality disorders
b. affective disorders
c. anxiety disorders
d. neurotic disorders

_____16. Brian has felt too terrified to leave his apartment, even to walk to the corner mailbox, for the past year. He is probably suffering from
a. depression
b. an obsessive-compulsive disorder
c. agoraphobia
d. schizophrenia

_____17. Psychoanalytic theories of depression interpret depression as
a. akin to learned helplessness
b. a result of reduced reinforcement
c. anger turned inward
d. all of the above

_____18. Phobias are often irrational and difficult to extinguish. This may be because they are a form of _____ learning.
a. prepared
b. operant
c. vicarious
d. one-trial

_____19. A person whose pacing, shouting, and general disorientation fit our popular notion of a "raving maniac" is probably
a. displaying generalized anxiety
b. in an acute manic episode
c. an antisocial personality
d. suffering from an obsessive-compulsive disorder

_____20. The chronic tension of a person with generalized anxiety is often interrupted by periods of
a. comparative relaxation
b. loss of contact with reality
c. acute panic
d. extreme withdrawal

KEY TO SELF-QUIZ

1. a	6. d	11. b	16. c
2. b	7. c	12. d	17. c
3. b	8. a	13. b	18. a
4. a	9. b	14. a	19. b
5. c	10. d	15. d	20. c

INDIVIDUAL EXERCISE

CLASSIFYING ABNORMAL BEHAVIOR

Descriptions of individuals displaying various kinds of abnormal behavior are given below. In each instance, attempt to classify the disorder on the basis of the behavioral symptoms, using the descriptions in Chapter 15 as a guide. Remember that the *anxiety disorders* include generalized anxiety, panic, phobic, and obsessive-compulsive disorders.

The *affective disorders* include depression, manic episodes, and a cyclical alternation between the two moods known as a manic-depressive disorder. Most people who have manic episodes also experience periods of depression, so they are usually diagnosed as suffering from a manic-depressive disorder. Antisocial personality is a *personality disorder.* When appropriate, give the major diagnostic category followed by the subcategory: for example, anxiety disorder–phobic disorder.

It is important to remember that clinical cases in real life show a wide variety of symptoms and seldom fit as neatly into categories as do our hypothetical cases. The correct diagnoses are given on p. 288 of the Appendix.

CASE 1

John, a patient at the state mental hospital, appears to be happy and elated. He frequently makes humorous remarks, laughs at them himself, and is successful in making others laugh too. In expressing his thoughts, he jumps from one topic to another without following any particular course. If, while he is talking about his family, the psychologist suddenly interjects a comment about the weather, John immediately switches his conversation to the weather or any other topic the psychologist introduces. Furthermore, he is hyperactive. He is either drumming with his fingers, playing with a pencil, or engaging others with his rapid talk. There is no deterioration of intellectual and emotional faculties, however. His present state will probably be followed by a period of depression.

CASE 2

Jack has been hearing the same voice for several months, which makes derogatory accusations about his being a sexual pervert. This same voice often commands him to do such things as throw furniture out of the window. His speech is monotonous except when he is talking about his troubles, at which time it becomes quite animated and vehement. His sentence structure is often shattered and his statements are usually incoherent, because they consist of a sequence of apparently unconnected words. An example of his "word-salad" is "The pipe tail on the bed, the TV said, a brown came out of the lawn, the flowers are board walk." He also coins new words such as "lapicator," which he said was an important chemical that will be used to purify the world.

CASE 3

Jane has been referred to a psychiatrist by her local physician, who can find nothing physically wrong with her. She complains, however, of feeling tense and apprehensive most of the time; she has difficulty sleeping and experiences frequent headaches. Minor stresses that she once handled with ease, such as driving in traffic or presenting a paper in class, now make her extremely nervous. In addition, she has moments of terror during which she feels that something dreadful is about to happen to her. Jane has no clear idea of the source of her fears.

CASE 4

Margaret has become increasingly fearful of leaving the house by herself. She insists that her mother or sister accompany her when she goes to the store or even walks as far as the corner mailbox. The thought of being in a crowd so terrifies her that she no longer attends concerts or church (activities she once enjoyed) regardless of whether someone accompanies her. Her life is confined within the four walls of her home.

CASE 5

Bill is an extremely orderly, clean, and stubborn person. He expects everything in the house to be spotless at all times. He insists that every chair, napkin, ashtray, and book be in its proper place. His wife loves him but finds it very difficult to keep the house in the rigid order he demands. He tends to have some time-consuming rituals connected with dressing and personal care, such as arranging his toilet articles in a particular order, rinsing his face exactly five times after shaving, laying out all of his clothes in a fixed sequence and making sure that he puts them on in that order.

CASE 6

Ralph is a highly impulsive person who has difficulty making plans or sticking to a job for any length of time. He has been fired from several jobs because he was caught stealing or because of frequent absences due to periodic drinking and gambling sprees. He always blames his employer for his dismissal and will not admit that his own behavior is responsible for his poor job history. Women tend to find him charming and personable, but they soon tire of his irresponsible behavior, frequent financial sponging, and general lack of consideration. His quick temper and disregard for social regulations have brought him into frequent brushes with the law, but he usually manages to charm his way out and has never been convicted of a crime. He appears to feel little guilt or anxiety regarding his behavior.

CASE 7

Following the breakup of her engagement to Fred, Martha has become very despondent. She shows little interest in her job (which previously she found stimulating and exciting) and often calls in sick. She spends a great deal of time alone in her room, sitting idly by the window or listening to the radio. When friends call to invite her out she usually refuses, pleading illness or fatigue. She complains that she feels continually tired, has to force herself to undertake such simple tasks as getting dressed or fixing a meal, and cannot concentrate enough to read a newspaper or magazine. Tears flow at the slightest provocation, and she feels worthless and inadequate. Her condition does not improve after several months have passed.

Questions for Discussion

1. Which of the symptoms shown by these individuals are common (in less extreme form) among mentally healthy people?

2. Which individuals exhibit behavior that would be called psychotic?

3. In what way does the antisocial personality differ from individuals suffering from other mental disorders?

16
Methods of Therapy

LEARNING OBJECTIVES

16-1. Be familiar with the historical background and current trends in the treatment of abnormal behavior.

16-2. Be able to specify the backgrounds and professional roles of the different specialists involved in psychotherapy.

Be able to describe the following approaches to psychotherapy, including the therapist's techniques and the patient's or client's experiences that are presumed to yield improvement.

16-3. Psychoanalysis.

16-4. Behavior therapy.

16-5. Person-centered therapy.

16-6. Cognitive behavior therapy.

16-7. Be familiar with the techniques, advantages, and disadvantages of group therapy and family therapy. Understand what is meant by an eclectic approach to therapy.

16-8. Be able to discuss the difficulties involved in evaluating the success of psychotherapeutic techniques. Know the factors, common to the various psychotherapies, that may be most important for behavior change.

16-9. Be familiar with the techniques, advantages, and disadvantages of the three forms of biological therapy; be able to describe the major classes of psychotherapeutic drugs.

16-10. Be familiar with the variety of community resources being explored as techniques for enhancing mental health.

1. What can be done to help people who are seriously disturbed emotionally or who show signs of abnormal behavior? One method of treatment is *psychotherapy.* If you know that "therapy" means treatment, you can guess that psychotherapy is

psychological   treatment by _____ methods.

2. The use of psychological methods for treating abnormal behavior is called

psychotherapy   _____ . This is in contrast to *biological therapy*, which uses drugs, electroconvulsive therapy, and brain surgery to treat some types of abnormal behavior.

psychotherapy   3. The professionals involved in the practice of psycho_____ include *psychiatrists, clinical* or *counseling psychologists, psychiatric social workers,* and, in hospitals, *psychiatric nurses.*

4. A psychiatrist is the only member of this group with an M.D. degree. Since the only person who can assume *medical* responsibility for a patient is a physician, this is

psychiatrist   one function of the _____ .

5. Some psychiatrists are psychoanalysts and follow the therapeutic methods formulated by Freud, but most psychiatrists are not trained in psychoanalysis. They use

biological   other methods of psychotherapy and may also use bio_____ therapies, such as drugs.

6. A psychoanalyst is usually a psychiatrist, but a psychiatrist is not usually a

psychoanalyst   _____ .

7. The clinical psychologist has a Ph.D. degree in psychology and has special training in the fields of diagnostic testing, psychotherapy, and research. Clinical psycholo-

medical   gists are not trained in medicine, however, and cannot assume m_____ responsibility for their patients.

clinical   8. Counseling psychologists receive training somewhat similar to that of cl_____ psychologists, although they usually deal with less serious problems—such as problems of social adjustment or educational goals.

9. Psychiatric social workers have a Master's or Ph.D. degree in social work with special training in interviewing, compiling case histories, and carrying treatment procedures into the home and community. Neither psychiatric social workers nor clinical or counseling psychologists have medical training, however, and therefore they

cannot   (*can/cannot*) assume medical responsibility for their patients.

10. You will remember that psychoanalysis was discussed as a theory of personality. We will now consider psychoanalysis as a method of psychotherapy. One of the basic techniques of this method is called *free association:* the patient is told to say, without selection or editing, everything that enters his or her mind. In order to bring repressed thoughts into awareness, the psychoanalyst asks the person to talk, to ramble, not to think too much about what he or she is saying, and not to sup-

free association   press anything. This is the technique of _____ _____ .

11. One word will be associated, through past experience, with other words. For instance, if the persons says "father," the word "stern" may come to mind. If this type of association is allowed to continue freely, without censorship, repressed

free
thoughts and feelings may enter awareness through the technique of _____
association _____ .

free association **12.** The technique of _____ _____ assumes that as people continue to talk without editing their words, they will utter thoughts and feelings that are associated with their problems and that these will give the analyst, and eventually the patient, the information necessary to understand and work through the problems.

13. Thoughts, feelings, and impulses of which a person is unaware are assumed to be repressed into the unconscious. The psychoanalyst uses the technique of free association to help the person bring to conscious awareness that which is

unconscious
un_____ .

14. People often repress thoughts and feelings that make them feel uncomfortable. It is natural, therefore, to *resist* their recall during psychoanalysis. You might guess that

resistance
one of the tasks of the analyst is to help people overcome their _____ance, so that they can deal with these unconscious thoughts and feelings.

15. Patient C is late for her appointment and when she does show up, she states that she cannot recall something she wishes to share with the analyst. This is an example

resistance
of _____ . That is, consciously the patient wishes to recall, but unconscious blocks hinder recall. And the fact that she was late for her appoint-

resistance
ment might also be interpreted as _____ .

16. In order to help Patient C to overcome resistance and to better understand herself, the psychoanalyst will make *interpretations* of her behavior. The analyst may, for instance, call the patient's attention to her resistance to treatment by pointing out to her that she was late for her appointment and that she cannot recall what she

interpretation
wishes to share with the therapist. Psychoanalysts use _____
to help people overcome resistance to treatment and to help them understand themselves better.

17. The psychoanalyst helps people understand some of the deeper meanings of their free associations as well as their dreams by helping them make interpretations. For instance, a man may recall the manifest content of a nightmare he had the previous night, but he cannot understand the dream's latent content—what the dream means or implies. With the help of the analyst, however, he may be able to make an

interpretation
_____ of what the dream really means.

resistance **18.** It is not unusual for a person to have some _____ to therapy, since symptoms are often less painful than the reality of some of the person's conflicts and feelings. To help the individual deal with what has been repressed, the

free, interpretations
analyst may use _____ association and make _____
of the deeper meanings of the person's associations and dreams.

19. On a conscious level the person wishes to solve his or her problems and feel better.

resistance

But on an unconscious level, the person may show _____ to therapy by coming late for appointments and by frequent blocking of what he or she wishes to relate to the analyst.

20. During psychotherapy people often *transfer* to the analyst emotional reactions they have had to other people important to their lives. This tendency is called

transference

tr_____ence. By analyzing these reactions, which often are not appropriate to the actual relationship of the analyst and the patient, the analyst gets clues to the patient's difficulties.

21. If a woman acts toward an analyst in the way she used to act toward her father or mother or some other significant person in her life, we would call this a manifesta-

transference

tion of _____ .

22. Sometimes a patient acts in a hostile manner toward the analyst when the latter has

transference

provided no reason to do so. This is interpreted as _____ , since the patient is responding emotionally toward the analyst as though the analyst were someone else.

23. In the permissive atmosphere of the therapist's office it is sometimes possible for a patient to relive a past situation that had strong emotional aspects and to express this emotion *freely,* as he or she had been unable to do in the original situation. This process, called *abreaction,* often brings the patient some relief from tension. If a woman relives a situation in which her father treated her unfairly and freely expresses the anger that she could not express then, she is experiencing

abreaction

_____ .

emotion   24. A free expression of _____ that was felt but not expressed in an earlier

abreaction

situation is known as _____ .

25. At the time of his father's funeral Peter suppressed his feelings of anguish because they might be regarded as unmanly. Now that Peter is in therapy and relating the experience to an uncritical listener, the former suppressed feelings are expressed and he sobs freely. We would say Peter is now experiencing what psychoanalysts

abreaction

call _____ .

freely   26. Abreaction is like catharsis in that pent-up feelings are _____ly expressed in a permissive setting.

abreaction   27. A form of emotional cleansing, called _____ by psychoanalysts, sometimes takes place in therapy; by itself, it does not eliminate the causes of conflict, though the patient may feel some relief from tension.

28. When people understand the roots of their conflicts, they have achieved *insight.* For instance, Sue now understands the relationship between some of her current problems and some early life experiences. In other words, she has achieved some measure

insight

of _____ into her difficulties.

29. Stan now understands that he forms an immediate dislike of anyone in a supervisory capacity over him because the first authority figure in his life, his father, continually bossed and belittled him. We would say that Stan now has some

insight

_____ into his hatred for authority figures.

30. As a patient gains insight, he or she goes through a process known as *working through*. In this process, the person examines the same conflicts over and over again as they have appeared in a variety of situations throughout life, and learns to face

Working them in a more mature way. _____ through is part of the process of learning to face reality.

31. Since the patient will often face his or her conflicts over and over again outside the

working through therapist's office, it follows that the _____ _____ process will continue in many situations in everyday life.

psychotherapy **32.** Psychoanalysis is a method of _____ therapy that focuses on unconscious conflicts. A quite different form of psychotherapy is *behavior therapy*, which is based on learning theory. The assumption behind this kind of therapy is that if

unlearned *maladaptive behavior* is *learned,* it can also be un_____ by having the person learn new or more appropriate responses in place of the maladaptive responses.

33. Whereas psychoanalysis is concerned with understanding how one's past conflicts

behavior influence behavior, behavior therapy focuses on the actual b_____ itself.

34. For example, behavior therapists view anxiety as a learned response to certain situations, rather than as the result of unconscious conflicts (which is the

psychoanalytic _____ view). Since anxiety is a maladaptive response, the behavior therapist would try to have the person learn a more appropriate response to the situation.

35. Behavior therapists attempt to have the person learn more appropriate responses to

maladaptive, behavior replace mal_____ ones. One technique used by _____ therapists is called *systematic desensitization*: a maladaptive response is weakened by strengthening an incompatible, or *antagonistic*, response. Since it is difficult to be relaxed and anxious at the same time, relaxation is a response that is

antagonistic an _____ to anxiety.

desensitization **36.** In the technique of systematic _____ a person is systematically desensitized to an anxiety-producing situation by learning to relax in response to that situation.

systematic **37.** The behavior therapist starts the procedure of _____ desensitization by having people list the sorts of situations that are anxiety producing for them. The situations are ranked in a sort of *hierarchy* from least to most anxiety provoking. Such a list is called an *anxiety hierarchy* because the situations are

most ranked from the least to the _____ anxiety provoking.

38. When a behavior therapist ranks from low to high those situations that a particular

anxiety person finds anxiety producing, he or she is establishing a(n)_____ hierarchy.

hierarchy **39.** Once the anxiety _____ is established, the individual is trained in a procedure of muscle relaxation. We noted that relaxation is a response that is

antagonistic _____ to anxiety.

anxiety hierarchy

anxiety

40. The person is instructed to relax while visualizing or imagining the least anxiety-provoking situation in his or her _____ _____ . If the individual remains relaxed and appears not to be anxious, the therapist proceeds to the next situation in the _____ hierarchy.

41. Therapy continues in this manner until the situation that originally provoked the most anxiety now elicits only relaxation. Thus, the individual has learned to respond

relaxation

with _____ to situations that initially produced a response of anxiety.

densensitization

42. While this method of systematic _____ through imagined scenes has proved effective in reducing anxiety, it is *less* effective than desensitization through actual encounters with the anxiety-producing situations.

43. Thus, if you want to overcome your anxiety about speaking in public, giving speeches before progressively larger audiences while practicing relaxation techniques

more

would be (*more/less*) effective than imagining speech situations while relaxing.

behavior

strengthening

44. Systematic desensitization is a technique used by _____ therapists in which a maladaptive response is weakened by _____ an incompatible, or antagonistic, response. Relaxation is one response that is

antagonistic

_____ to anxiety; another is an approach or *assertive*, response.

45. Some people feel anxious in social situations because they do not know how to assert themselves—to "speak up" for what they feel is right or to "say no" when others take advantage of them. In *assertiveness training* the therapist helps the per-

assertive (*or* approach)

son practice _____ responses that might be used in situations where the individual tends to be passive.

46. Two methods used by behavior therapists to help the individual substitute adaptive

systematic

responses for maladaptive ones are _____ desensitization and

assertiveness

_____ training. The text discusses some additional behavior therapy methods that are based on learning principles. These include positive reinforcement of adaptive responses, extinction of maladaptive ones, modeling adaptive behavior, and learning to regulate, or control, one's own behavior.

behavior

47. Initially, behavior therapists focused on modifying maladaptive _____ and were not concerned with *cognition*—the individual's thoughts, expectations, and interpretation of events. Recently, however, behavior therapists have paid increased attention to the role of *cognitive factors* in determining behavior.

48. *Cognitive behavior therapy* is the general term for treatment methods that use behavior modification techniques but also incorporate procedures designed to

cognitions

change maladaptive beliefs, or cog_____ .

behavior

49. Cognitive _____ therapists attempt to help people control disturbing emotional reactions (such as anxiety and depression) by teaching them more effective ways of interpreting and thinking about their experiences. They assume that changing maladaptive beliefs will help to change maladaptive

behavior

_____ .

234   CHAPTER 16

50. A therapist who attempts to help a depressed woman change her self-critical negative thoughts and to become more assertive as well, would be called a

cognitive behavior therapist

_____ _____ _____ .

51. A fourth approach to psychotherapy that differs from psychoanalysis, behavior

cognitive

therapy, and _____ behavior therapy includes the *humanistic therapies*, which focus on the individual's natural tendency toward *growth* and *self-actualization*.

52. The humanistic therapist does not interpret a person's statements and behavior (as

psychoanalyst

would a _____) or try to modify behavior (as would a

behavior therapist

_____ _____). Instead, the therapist tries to facili-

growth

tate the individual's own tendency toward _____ and self-actualization.

actualization

53. Self-_____ refers to the realization, or actualization, of an individual's *potentials*. The job of the humanistic therapist is to help the

potentials

individual realize his or her _____ .

humanistic

54. One of the most widely used h _____ therapies was developed by *Carl Rogers*: it is called *person-centered therapy*. Rogers assumes that the patient can work out his or her own problems if the therapist provides the right psychological atmosphere.

centered

55. The person-_____ therapist neither instructs the

person to free associate nor interprets the individual's statements as would a(n)

psychoanalyst

_____ . Instead the therapist attempts to under-stand the individual's feelings, to see things from the individual's point of view, and to *clarify* these feelings without judging or elaborating them.

clarify

56. The person-centered therapist tries to understand and _____ the person's feelings. As the therapist accepts the individual and his or her feelings

accept

without judgment, the individual begins to acc_____ himself or herself.

person-centered

57. In _____ -_____ therapy, the therapist accepts and clarifies the views of the person so that the individual gradually learns to under-stand and accept himself or herself.

person-centered

58. An assumption basic to _____ -_____ therapy is that each individual has the capacity to deal with his or her problems; the therapist's task

growth

is simply to facilitate the individual's natural tendency toward _____

self-actualization

and _____ -_____ .

59. Person-centered therapists believe that individuals can work out their own problems;

accept, clarify

the therapist's task is to _____ , understand, and cl_____ the individual's viewpoint.

60. Let's review. We have discussed four approaches to psychotherapy; see if you can identify them in terms of their techniques.

psychoanalytic

a. Uses free association to arrive at unconscious conflicts: _____ therapy.

person- centered	b. Tries to understand and clarify the patient's viewpoint: _____- _____ therapy.
behavior	c. Uses learning principles to modify behavior: _____ therapy.
cognitive behavior	d. Tries to change maladaptive beliefs: _____ _____ therapy.

61. Since most emotional problems stem from difficulties in relating to other people, it makes sense sometimes to practice therapy in *groups*. Such therapy is called, appropriately enough, gr_____ *therapy.*

group

62. When therapy is carried out with a therapist and more than one client, we call it _____ therapy. Group therapy saves time, gives the individual the feeling that his or her problems are not unique—that others are "in the same boat"—and provides opportunities to learn better ways of interacting with other people. All the methods of psychotherapy that we have discussed have been used, often in modified form, in group therapy.

group

63. *Encounter groups* are a popular offshoot of group therapy. The main difference is that en_____groups are aimed at teaching people how to relate more openly to one another rather than at solving emotional problems or treating behavior disorders.

encounter

64. Encounter _____, also known as *T-groups* or *sensitivity groups,* emphasize learning how to express one's feelings more openly. They may help people achieve a better understanding of how to interact with others, but they are not designed to treat emotional problems or behavior _____.

groups

disorders

65. T-groups and sensitivity groups are other names for _____
_____.

encounter
groups

66. Psychotherapy is the treatment of abnormal behavior or emotional disorders by psych_____ means. *Biological therapies* use physiological methods such as *electroconvulsive therapy, psychosurgery,* and *drugs* to modify emotions and behavior.

psychological

67. Electroconvulsive therapy, which is one type of _____ therapy, is sometimes used to relieve severe depression. Psychosurgery, a controversial procedure in which certain nerve fibers in the limbic system or hypothalamus are destroyed, has also been used to treat severely depressed and suicidal individuals.

biological

68. The most successful biological _____, however, has been the use of drugs to modify behavior.

therapy

69. *Antianxiety drugs*, commonly known as tranquilizers, are often prescribed to treat anxiety disorders or to help people cope during difficult periods in their lives. This is one type of _____ therapy.

biological (*or* drug)

70. *Antipsychotic drugs,* such as reserpine and chlorpromazine, have proved effective in relieving the symptoms of schizophrenia. They help schizophrenic patients reestablish contact with reality, making them more amendable to treatment by psychological means, or _____.

psychotherapy

71. Two classes of drugs used in the treatment of mental disorders are
_____ and _____ drugs.

antianxiety, antipsychotic
(either order)

72. Another group of drugs, called antidepressants, help to elevate the mood of de-
depressed individuals. They energize rather than tr_____ , apparently
by affecting the amount of certain neurotransmitters in the brain.

tranquilize

73. The most successful biological therapy has been the use of _____ to modify
behavior. Drugs that are effective in reducing anxiety are called _____
drugs; those that are effective in alleviating the symptoms of schizophrenia are
called _____ drugs; those that elevate the mood of depressed
individuals are called _____ drugs.

drugs

antianxiety

antipsychotic

antidepressant

74. While drug therapy has been helpful in treating many types of mental disorders,
there are limitations. Drugs can produce undesirable side effects, and they may
alleviate symptoms without requiring the individual to face the problems that are
contributing to maladaptive _____ . Since the attitudes and
response patterns that have developed over a lifetime cannot be suddenly changed
by taking a drug, psychotherapy is usually needed along with _____ therapy.

behavior(s)

drug

TERMS AND CONCEPTS

psychiatrist _____

_____

_____

_____

psychoanalyst _____

_____

_____

_____

clinical psychologist _____

_____

_____

_____

counseling psychologist _____

_____

_____

_____

psychiatric social worker _____

_____

_____

_____

psychiatric nurse _____

_____

_____

_____

psychotherapy _____

_____

_____

_____

psychoanalysis _____

_____

_____

_____

free association _____

_____

_____

interpretation _____

_____

_____

_____

transference _____

_____

_____

_____

abreaction _____

_____

_____

_____

insight _____

_____

_____

_____

working through _____

_____

_____

_____

behavior therapy _____

_____

_____

_____

systematic desensitization _____

_____

_____

_____

anxiety hierarchy _____

_____

_____

_____

assertiveness training _____

_____

_____

systematic reinforcement _____

_____

_____

_____

modeling _____

_____

_____

_____

self-regulation _____

_____

_____

_____

cognitive behavior therapy _____

_____

_____

_____

humanistic therapy _____

_____

_____

_____

person-centered therapy _____

_____

_____

_____

group therapy _____

_____

_____

_____

encounter group _____

_____

_____

_____

marital therapy _____

_____

_____

_____

family therapy _____

_____

_____

_____

eclectic approach _____

_____

_____

_____

hello-goodbye effect _____

_____

_____

_____

spontaneous remission _____

_____

_____

_____

placebo response* _____

_____

_____

_____

double-blind procedure* _____

_____

_____

_____

biological therapies _____

_____

_____

_____

electroconvulsive therapy _____

_____

_____

_____

psychosurgery _____

_____

_____

_____

*Indicates term used in Critical Discussion

antianxiety drugs _____

_____

_____

_____

antipsychotic drugs _____

_____

_____

_____

antidepressant drugs _____

_____

_____

_____

_____

_____

_____

_____

_____ 1. Free association and interpretation are important techniques in
   a. behavior therapy
   b. person-centered therapy
   c. psychoanalysis
   d. assertive training

_____ 2. In the use of behavior therapy for the relief of snake phobias the most effective approach was
   a. symbolic modeling
   b. live modeling with participation
   c. desensitization
   d. positive reinforcement

_____ 3. A consensus regarding the effectiveness of psychotherapy is difficult to reach. Nevertheless some things do seem clear. Which of the following is *not* one of them?
   a. Only those patients treated by the psychotherapy most appropriate to their problems show much improvement.
   b. Psychotherapies do help patients.
   c. All psychotherapies share common features, such as a warm relationship in a special setting.
   d. There is little evidence, except for phobias and specific anxieties, that one form of therapy produces better results than another.

_____ 4. The "basic rule" of _____ is to say everything that enters your mind, without selection or editing.
   a. interpretation
   b. transference
   c. abreaction
   d. free association

_____ 5. A psychotherapist who maintains an eclectic approach might include _____ in the treatment of an anxiety disorder.
   a. tranquilizers and relaxation training
   b. a discussion of the patient's history
   c. education techniques
   d. any of the above

_____ 6. The text offers several suggestions for bettering your emotional well-being. Which of the following is *not* one of them?
   a. Seek always to solve your own problems, turning to professionals only as a last resort.
   b. Discover occasions that provoke emotional overreaction, so as to be able to guard against it.
   c. Learn to accept your feelings as something natural and normal.
   d. If emotional expression is blocked by circumstances, learn to seek permissible outlets.

_____ 7. During the past 20 years the emphasis in treatment of the mentally ill has shifted from
   a. person-centered therapy to psychoanalytic therapy
   b. somatotherapy to psychotherapy
   c. professionals to amateurs
   d. hospital treatment to community treatment

_____ 8. When systematic desensitization is used as a therapeutic technique.
   a. maladaptive responses are weakened or eliminated by strengthening antagonistic responses
   b. anxiety is increased to effect an alteration in behavior
   c. the patient is placed in a restricted environment with no anxiety-provoking stimuli
   d. modification of behavior depends on the patient's understanding of unconscious motives

_____ 9. An important concept in psychoanalysis is transference. This refers to the tendency of patients to
   a. transfer emotional responses to the therapist
   b. transfer their own responsibilities to the therapist
   c. show reduced resistance as therapy progresses
   d. free associate less freely as therapy progresses

_____ 10. Carl Rogers has described what he believes to be a consistent pattern of change in encounter groups. Which of the following is *not* characteristic of such groups? Members
   a. initially tend to be confused and frustrated
   b. often begin the expression of their feelings with negative comments about others
   c. express their feelings openly at the beginning
   d. become impatient with defensiveness, by the final session

_____ 11. Behavior therapists believe that insight is
   a. a worthwhile goal
   b. not sufficient for behavior change

c. not necessary for behavior change

d. all of the above

_____12. The first advocate of humane treatment of the mentally ill was

a. Clifford Beers

b. Hippocrates

c. Phillippe Pinel

d. Sigmund Freud

_____13. The course of improvement during psychoanalytic therapy is commonly attributed to three main experiences of the patient. Which of the following is *not* one of these?

a. insight

b. abreaction

c. transference

d. working through

_____14. The purpose of person-centered therapy is to _____ the individual's feelings.

a. direct

b. clarify

c. judge

d. elaborate on

_____15. In recent studies described in the text, former drug addicts, prison inmates, and college students have all

a. been found to suffer depressive episodes

b. functioned as psychotherapists

c. been relieved of phobias by modeling techniques

d. been found to need assertive training

_____16. Some of the problems of assessing cure in psychotherapy are seen in the "hello-goodbye effect," in which

a. therapists see the patients' problems as more severe when they enter therapy than when they leave

b. patients exaggerate their problems at the beginning of therapy

c. patients try to minimize their problems at the beginning of therapy

d. patients exaggerate any of their problems that still remain at the end of therapy

_____17. The text discusses several factors, common to the various psychotherapies, that may be more important than specific techniques in producing behavior change. Which of the following is *not* one of them?

a. an interpersonal relationship of warmth and trust

b. desensitization

c. transference

d. reinforcement of adaptive responses

_____18. For Carl Rogers, an important element of a therapeutic relationship is

a. therapist who shows empathy and warmth

b. abreaction

c. the "shaping" of behavior

d. transference

_____19. Electroconvulsive therapy is currently used successfully with

a. a wide variety of mental problems

b. most psychoses

c. severely depressed patients

d. no one

_____20. The most successul biological therapy is

a. psychosurgery

b. electroconvulsive therapy

c. insulin-shock therapy

d. drug therapy

KEY TO SELF-QUIZ

20. d	15. b	10. c	5. d
19. c	14. b	9. a	4. a
18. a	13. c	8. a	3. a
17. c	12. b	7. d	2. b
16. b	11. d	6. a	1. c

INDIVIDUAL EXERCISE

FREE ASSOCIATION

Introduction

This is a very simple exercise, but it will give you a better feeling for what goes on in therapy and a better understanding of why certain kinds of therapy take so long.

The main technique in psychoanalytic therapy is free association. The therapist instructs the client to say whatever comes into his or her mind. There should be no attempt to censor any material that comes to consciousness—it should all be verbalized, no matter how irrelevant, unimportant, or embarrassing it may seem.

Equipment Needed

None required, but if a tape recorder is available it would be useful.

Procedure

The technique of free association appears to be very simple. It is, however, harder to do than it might seem. In order to get some idea of what it is like, first go to a place in which you know you will not be disturbed or overheard; go to any lengths you feel necessary in order to find such a place. Some students have waited until they were at home and their family was away. Then, when you are *sure* that you are alone and no one else can hear you, try to follow the rules for free association. Say everything *aloud* in a clear tone.

If possible, it would be instructive to tape record your free associations so that you can analyze them later.

Questions for Discussion

1. Was it easy to do? If not, why do you think it was not?

2. Can you imagine what it would be like to do this in the presence of another person?

3. How long do you think it would take you to be able to do this in the presence of another person?

4. Can you trace some of the cues that made one thought lead to another?

17
Social Information Processing

LEARNING OBJECTIVES

17-1.   Be able to define social psychology in terms of its two major emphases.

17-2.   Be able to describe the three tasks that we, as informal scientists, perform in constructing our intuitive theories of human behavior. Give examples of the kinds of biases that influence our judgments at each stage.

17-3.   Understand schematic processing. Show how it can lead to errors in processing social information, using the primacy effect as an example.

17-4.   Be able to explain how stereotypes can be self-perpetuating and self-fulfilling.

17-5.   Be familiar with the three criteria we use to infer causality, the distinction between dispositional and situational attributions, and the fundamental attribution error.

17-6.   Be able to show how the principles of schematic processing and attribution also apply to the process of self-perception.

17-7.   Be able to define attitudes as distinct from beliefs and behavior.

17-8.   Be familiar with the research on consistency among beliefs, among attitudes, between beliefs and attitudes, and between attitudes and behavior.

17-9.   Be able to explain the results of induced-compliance experiments in terms of self-perception theory, cognitive dissonance theory, and impression management theory.

17-10. Be familiar with the factors that determine interpersonal attraction, including the data on physical attractiveness.

1. *Social psychology* is the study of *social interaction*: how we think, feel, and act in the presence of other people, and how our thoughts, feelings, and actions are influenced by others. How we think or act in a given situation depends on the way we perceive and interpret the behaviors and motives of those around us, that is, the

   social   way we *process social information.* Thus, in studying _____ inter-

   process   action, we need to know how people _____ social information.

2. For example, the way you respond to a new acquaintance depends on the initial impression you form of him or her. And forming impressions involves processing

   social   _____ information.

3. In attempting to understand ourselves and other people we construct our own *intuitive theories* of human behavior; and these intuitive theories will, in turn,

   social information   influence the way we process _____ _____ .

   theories   4. In constructing our intuitive _____ of human behavior, we face the same basic tasks as a scientist does in constructing theories: first, we *observe* or *collect data*; second, we try to *detect covariation*—that is, to determine what goes with what; and third, we attempt to *infer cause and effect*—to evaluate what causes what.

5. Our informal, intuitive theories of human behavior are often correct. If they were not, social interaction would be chaotic. But we also make a number of systematic errors in arriving at social judgments. These errors can occur at any one of the

   data   three stages of theory construction: collecting _____ , detecting

   covariation, cause   _____ , and inferring _____ and effect.

6. In addition, our theories can actually shape our perceptions of the data, distort our estimates of what goes with what, and bias our evaluations of cause and effect. In other words, our intuitive theories of human behavior can interfere with accurate

   social information   _____ _____ processing.

7. One variable that can cause errors at the first stage of theory construction, the stage

   data   of _____ collection, is the *vividness* of the information. We tend to pay attention to and recall information that is *vivid* rather than pallid.

8. You watch a TV news program showing a policeman roughly handling a protester who is blocking the entrance to a nuclear power plant. Later you read a newspaper account that describes the police as doing a courteous and careful job of managing an unruly crowd of antinuclear protesters. The dramatic TV scene influences your perception and memory of the event more than the pallid, but more accurate, newspaper description; you write a letter to the police chief complaining about police

   vividness   brutality. This demonstrates that _____ of information can cause errors in data collection.

   data   9. Even if we could collect _____ in a systematic and unbiased way, our perceptions of the data can still be biased by our expectations and preconceptions of what the data should look like.

10. As noted in earlier chapters, our memories of people, objects, and events are often simplified representations of our original perceptions. These simplified

representations

rep_____ or memory structures are called *schemata* (plural of *schema*). They help us to process information, but they can also bias our perceptions of the data.

11. Rather than forming separate memories of every person, object, or event, we form mental representations of *classes* of people, objects, and events. These mental

schemata

representations are called _____ .

12. For example, we have schemata for different kinds of people. If you think of an extravert as someone who is sociable, outgoing, and talkative, this is your

schema

_____ (*singular*) for an extravert.

13. If the word "doctor" brings to mind a middle-aged male who is knowledgeable,

schema

efficient, and somewhat aloof, this is your _____ for a doctor. *General person-schemata* such as these are sometimes called *stereotypes*.

memory

14. Schemata are simplified representations in _____ based on earlier perceptions of people, objects, and events. They help us process social information. Instead of having to perceive and remember all of the details of each new person, object, or event, we can note that it is like one of our preexisting schemata and encode or remember only its most prominent features.

information

15. Schemata help us process social _____ , but because they constitute simplifications of reality, they can lead to errors. This is particularly evident in forming impressions of people when meeting them for the first time.

16. Suppose you meet a tall, muscular young man and are told that he is a quarterback on his college football team. Your initial impression will be influenced by your

stereotype

general person-schema, or _____ , for college athlete or football player.

17. When you talk with him you discover that he is a premedical student, has a wide range of intellectual interests, and plays the cello. Your initial impression, based

person-schema

partly on your general _____–_____ for athlete, is gradually replaced by a more specific schema for this particular person.

18. As we get to know people better, we replace general and abstract schemata with a

specific

more _____ schema for that person.

19. Nevertheless, research on impression formation indicates that the first information

impression

we have about a person has the greatest impact on our overall imp_____ of that person. This is known as the *primacy effect*.

20. At first meeting, Linda strikes you as attractive, well-groomed, soft-spoken, and very much in control of her emotions. Several days later you observe her looking disheveled and screaming at her children. If you still think of Linda as well-groomed and controlled (and consider her later behavior to be an atypical reaction to unusual

primacy

stress), you are demonstrating the _____ effect.

much

21. Primacy effects refer to the tendency to give too (*much/little*) weight to the initial information we receive about a person.

22. Agnes did very well on her first psychology test but poorly on later tests; Mark received a low score on his first test but improved markedly on subsequent tests. The instructor still thinks of Agnes as a better student than Mark. The instructor is

primacy

biased by _____ effects.

23. The tendency to stick to our initial impression of a person and to ignore later con-

primacy effect

tradictory information is called the _____ _____ . It appears to be primarily a consequence of the way we process schemata.

24. In forming our first impressions of a person, we actively search in memory for the

schemata

person schema or _____ (*plural*) that best matches the incoming information. At some point to make a decision—this person is "friendly" (or whatever). We then assimilate any further information to that schema and dismiss discrepant information as not representative of the "real" person.

25. Thus, schemata can influence what we observe or remember about a person. They can lead to errors at the first stage in our attempt to construct theories of human

data

behavior—namely, the stage of _____ collection.

stereotypes

26. General person-schemata, or _____ , are actually miniature theories of covariation. The stereotype of an extravert or a college football player, for example, is a theory of what particular traits or behaviors go with certain other traits or behaviors. Deciding what goes with what, or detecting

covariation

_____ , is our second task as an informal scientist.

27. Our third task in constructing our intuitive theories of human behavior is inferring

effect

cause and _____ . We observe a particular behavior and must decide to which of many possible causes the action should be attributed. The process by which we attempt to explain the behavior of other people is called *attribution*.

attribution

28. If, while observing a person's behavior, we attempt to interpret it—to infer the causes of the individual's actions—we are engaged in the process of

at_____ .

29. To what do we *attribute* the individual's behavior? We may attribute it to forces or

attribute

pressures in the environment, or we may _____ it to the individual's own personality and attitudes.

30. If we decide that something about the person is primarily responsible for the behavior, we are making a *dispositional attribution*. (A person's beliefs, attitudes, and personality characteristics are sometimes called dispositions.) If we decide that some external force (such as money, threats, or social pressure) is primarily respon-

attribution

sible for the behavior, then we are making a *situational* _____ .

31. A young man stands on a street corner giving an eloquent speech in support of a bill to legalize prostitution. To what do we attribute his behavior? To the fact that he fervently believes in legalized prostitution? That he or his wife is a prostitute and they need more money? That he is being paid to give the speech? That he is fulfilling an assignment for his public-speaking class? If you attribute his behavior to

dispositional — either of the first two possibilities, you are making a _____ attribution. If you attribute his actions to either of the last two possibilities, you

situational attribution — are making a _____ _____ .

32. We make a dispositional attribution when we infer that the cause of behavior lies

personality — in the individual's attitudes or _____ characteristics.

33. We make a situational disposition when we attribute the cause of behavior to some

external (*or* environmental) — _____ force.

34. The attribution process refers to our attempts to infer the causes of an individual's

behavior — _____ .

35. Research shows that there are some systematic biases in our attributions; we tend to give too much weight to personality variables as determinants of behavior and to underestimate the situational factors that caused the person to behave as he or

dispositonal — she did. That is, we tend to give too much importance to (*dispositonal/situational*) factors.

36. In one study subjects heard an individual give a speech either favoring or opposing racial segregation. They were informed in advance that the speaker had been *told* which side of the issue to take and the specific arguments to use. Despite this knowledge, the subjects inferred that the speaker believed to some degree the point of

dispositonal — view he or she was arguing. This illustrates our bias toward _____ attributions.

37. Because another person's behavior is such a dominant aspect of any situation we

situational — observe, we tend to weigh it too heavily and to underestimate _____ factors that may have led the individual to act as he or she did. This tendency to

dispositional — give too much weight to _____ factors and too little to

situational — _____ variables is known as the *fundamental attribution error.*

38. *Self-perception theory* suggests that in interpreting our own behavior we sometimes play the role of an outside observer in deciding whether our actions were deter-

dispositional — mined by our attitudes and feelings (a(n)_____ attribution) or

situational — by the pressure of the circumstances (a(n) _____ attribution).

39. Consider the following experiment. College students were given some dull, repetitive tasks to perform, and after completing them were bribed to go into the waiting room and tell the next subjects that the tasks had been fun and interesting. For some of the students the bribe was only $1; for others it was $20. Later the students were asked their actual opinion of the tasks. The students who had been paid only

tasks — $1 said they had, in fact, enjoyed the _____ ; those who had been paid $20 found them dull, as did a control group of subjects who were not asked to talk to the next subjects.

perception

40. Self-_____ theory assumes that the subjects looked at their behavior of saying that the tasks were fun and had to solve an attribution problem: "Why did I say this?"

attribution

did not

41. The subjects paid $20 could easily make a situational _____ : "Anyone would have done it for that sum; that's why I said the tasks were fun." These subjects (*did/did not*) change their attitudes about the tasks.

dispositonal

attitudes

42. The subjects paid $1 found it more difficult to justify their behavior in terms of situational influences: "No one would say the tasks were fun for only $1; I must have enjoyed them." These subjects thus made a(n)_____ attribution which influenced their _____ about the task.

error, dispositional
situational

43. Note that the $1 bribe actually was sufficient to persuade the subjects to say that the tasks were fun. Hence these subjects committed the fundamental attribution _____: they made a (*situational/dispositional*) attribution where they should have made a (*situational/dispositional*) one.

perception

44. Self-_____ theory explains the results of this experiment by assuming that people infer what their attitudes must be by observing their behavior. *Cognitive dissonance theory* provides a different explanation for the same results.

dissonance

45. Cognitive _____ theory assumes that people strive for consistency between their attitudes and their behaviors. When people engage in behavior they do not believe in, they will be uncomfortable because their behavior is not

consistent

con_____ with their attitudes.

attitudes

dissonance

46. Cognitive dissonance theory assumes that people want their behaviors to be consistent with their _____. The feeling of inconsistency that occurs when people engage in behavior they do not believe in is called cognitive _____ .

dissonance (*or* inconsistency)

behavior

47. People seek to resolve this _____ , and one way is to change their attitudes so they are consistent with their _____ .

48. When a student in the above study tells another person that the tasks were interesting when actually he or she considered them dull, this behavior is inconsistent with the person's true attitude. Hence, we would expect this situation to produce

cognitive

_____ dissonance.

49. The students who were paid $20 have a good reason for making the false statements. They can justify their behavior ("I did it for the money"), so there is no

attitudes

"dissonance pressure" for them to change their _____ about the tasks.

50. The students who were paid only $1 cannot justify their behavior by convincing themselves that they made false statements for the money. They thus experience

cognitive dissonance

consistent

_____ _____ until they change their attitudes to be more _____ with their behavior. They decide they must have enjoyed the tasks.

51. Thus, we have two different theories about the way behavior influences attitudes:

cognitive dissonance
_____ _____ theory assumes that inconsistency between behavior and attitudes motivates people to change their attitudes;

self-perception
_____-_____ theory assumes that people do not *change* their attitudes but infer what their attitudes must be by observing their own

behavior
_____ . A third theory, *impression management theory*, proposes that subjects in the above study were motivated to make a good impression on the experimenter. The text describes this theory and goes on to discuss additional research on consistency among beliefs, among attitudes, between beliefs and attitudes, and between attitudes and behavior.

52. The final section of this chapter is concerned with interpersonal attraction, the factors that influence whether people will be *attracted* to each other. These include *physical appearance, proximity, familiarity,* and *similarity.* All of these factors help

attracted
determine whether two people will be _____ to each other.

53. Although people usually do not rate physical attractiveness as important in their liking of others, studies indicate that appearance is more important than personality characteristics or similar interests in determining whom college students choose to date. And people tend to attribute more positive personality characteristics to photographs of attractive individuals than they do to photos of unattractive indi-

appearance
(*or* attractiveness)
viduals. Despite what we prefer to believe, physical _____ is an important determiner of liking.

54. College students are more likely to form friendships with individuals who live on their dormitory floor than with other dormitory residents. This indicates that

proximity
p_____ is another important determiner of interpersonal attraction.

55. One reason that proximity creates liking is because it increases familiarity. We tend to like people and situations we have encountered before. Two important deter-

proximity, familiarity
miners of liking are _____ and _____ .
A third is similarity.

similar
56. We tend to form friendships with people who are _____ to us in social class, educational level, and interests and who share our attitudes and values.

57. However, even if your roommate is quite different from you in attitudes and values, you may like him or her better at the end of the year than a new acquaintance who

familiarity
is more similar to you. In this instance, _____ is a more important determiner of interpersonal attraction than similarity.

58. The variables that influence whether two people will like each other include

physical, proximity,
familiarity,
similarity
_____ appearance, _____ , f_____ , and s_____ . The text discusses the process by which relationships move from liking toward the greater closeness and intimacy of love.

TERMS AND CONCEPTS

schema _____

_____

_____

_____

schematic processing _____

_____

_____

_____

stereotype _____

_____

_____

_____

primacy effect _____

_____

_____

_____

scripts _____

_____

_____

_____

sex typing* _____

_____

_____

_____

gender schema* _____

_____

_____

_____

androgynous individual* _____

_____

_____

_____

implicit personality theories _____

_____

_____

attribution problem _____

_____

_____

_____

dispositional attribution _____

_____

_____

_____

situational attribution _____

_____

_____

_____

fundamental attribution error _____

_____

_____

_____

self-perception theory _____

_____

_____

_____

cognitive dissonance theory _____

_____

_____

information-processing biases _____

_____

_____

*Indicates term used in Critical Discussion

cognitive consistency _____

_____

_____

_____

impression management theory _____

_____

_____

_____

expectancy-value theory _____

_____

_____

_____

need-complementarity hypothesis _____

_____

_____

_____

social penetration _____

_____

_____

_____

_____ 1. Which one of the following illustrates the application of a *general person-schema*?
   a. When you give your paycheck to the bank teller, you assume that she will not steal it.
   b. When you learn that the president will be appearing on television, you anticipate that he will be wearing a plaid suit.
   c. When you hear a speech by a politician, you make a fundamental attribution error.
   d. You readily change your opinions about a certain minority group when a member of that group joins your fraternity.

_____ 2. Self-perception theory relates behavior and attitude change by a rather surprising proposal; it claims that we
   a. base our interpretations of others' behavior on what we would do in similar circumstances
   b. assume that situational forces are very powerful and attribute too little effect to our own motives
   c. try to behave according to the way that we feel but are often unsuccessful
   d. infer our attitudes by observing our own behavior as if it were that of someone else

_____ 3. If subjects are instructed to remember as much information as they can about a stimulus person, they remember *less* than if they are told to try to form an impression of the person. This illustrates the effect of
   a. primacy
   b. schematic processing
   c. impression management
   d. attribution processes

_____ 4. A *schema* is
   a. an erroneous causal attribution
   b. a determinant of interpersonal attraction
   c. an organized reconstruction of perceptions held in memory
   d. consistency between attitudes and behaviors

_____ 5. Studies of the attribution process investigate
   a. the conditions necessary for changing stereotypes
   b. the permanence of interpersonal attraction
   c. inconsistencies between beliefs, attitudes, and behaviors
   d. how we interpret the behaviors of others

_____ 6. When we receive mixed information about a person, we tend to base our impression on the information that is
   a. favorable
   b. received first
   c. unfavorable
   d. received last

_____ 7. Subjects who observed students solving a series of problems attributed greater intelligence to the students who
   a. performed consistently throughout the test
   b. missed problems at the beginning but improved as the test progressed
   c. did best at the beginning of the test
   d. performed best on the last few problems

_____ 8. Research shows that physical appearance is important in determining
   a. whether blind dates like each other
   b. whether 5-year-old children are popular with their peers
   c. adults' predictions of a child's personality
   d. all of the above

_____ 9. If one of your friends recommends a book that all of your other friends disliked, you might conclude that the book is not worth reading by using the criterion of
   a. consistency
   b. consensus
   c. discounting
   d. distinctiveness

_____ 10. Conrad Conservative delivers a speech in favor of legalizing all forms of sexual behavior between consenting adults. George hears the speech and makes the *dispositional* attribution that Conrad is
   a. homosexual
   b. being paid to say this
   c. distorting his true feelings to win votes
   d. telling the audience what they want to hear

_____ 11. Ellen thinks, "I'm driving so fast; I guess I am really anxious to get there." This is an example of
   a. cognitive dissonance
   b. the criterion of consensus
   c. the primacy effect
   d. self-attribution

12. According to the theory of cognitive dissonance, when we engage in behavior we do not believe in, there is pressure to
    a. dismiss the behavior as an aberration
    b. experience guilt feelings
    c. alter the belief
    d. change reference groups

13. Which of the following best summarizes the data on marriage and personal similarities?
    a. Married couples develop similar tastes.
    b. Complementary traits are more important than similar attitudes.
    c. People like those similar to them.
    d. Opposites attract.

14. The "attribution problem" refers to the question of why
    a. one theory wins out over another
    b. primacy effects are so powerful
    c. reference groups are so powerful
    d. a person performs any action

15. When subjects were asked to perform a dull task and then were paid to tell the next person that the task was really fun and interesting, _____ later stated that they really did enjoy the task.
    a. only subjects who were paid $1
    b. only subjects who were paid $20
    c. neither group of subjects
    d. both groups of subjects

16. A dispositional attribution would be appropriate if a person's actions were motivated by a
    a. financial reward
    b. social norm in favor of the action
    c. belief in the correctness of the action
    d. threat of punishment

17. Mack is crazy about Bonnie but she remains cool toward him. Which of Mack's actions would be *least* likely to attract Bonnie?
    a. spend less time with her since absence makes the heart grow fonder

b. let her know that he likes her
    c. try to develop a personality that is more like hers, since likes attract
    d. try to look more physically attractive

18. When we attempt to interpret human behavior, we look to see whether certain effects tend to go with certain suspected causes. This is referred to as
    a. detecting covariation
    b. evidence of primacy effects
    c. social perception
    d. emphasizing the individual's phenomenology

19. Social psychologists typically study attitudes as one component of a three-part system. This system includes _____ components.
    a. cognitive, affective, and behavioral
    b. belief, stereotypes, and perception
    c. dispositional, situational, and attitudinal
    d. likes, dislikes, and feelings

20. Suppose you think, "I believe that most homicides are committed with guns, so gun control must be a good idea." What does this show?
    a. "wishful thinking" on your part
    b. your desire for consistency between your beliefs and your attitudes
    c. the effect of media persuasion on changes in values
    d. application of the covariance rule

KEY TO SELF-QUIZ

20. b	15. a	10. a	5. d
19. a	14. d	9. b	4. c
18. a	13. c	8. d	3. b
17. a	12. c	7. c	2. d
16. c	11. d	6. b	1. a

INDIVIDUAL OR CLASS EXERCISE

Introduction

As discussed in the text (p. 588), physical attractiveness is an important determiner of interpersonal attraction. Why is physical attractiveness so important? Part of the reason is that people hold a schema, or stereotype, about the physically attractive person, believing that he or she has a cluster of other desirable characteristics. Some of the early research on this phenomenon was reported in an article with the provocative title "What Is Beautiful Is Good."* In this study, male and female subjects were presented with photographs of men and women from a college yearbook and asked to rate the pictured individuals on a number of traits. The photographs had been judged previously as very attractive, average, or unattractive. Compared to the unattractive individuals, the attractive individuals were rated as being more sensitive, kind, interesting, strong, poised, sociable, outgoing, exciting, and sexually warm and responsive. They were also rated as having higher status and as being more likely to get married, to have a successful marriage, and to be happy. The only exception to this rosy portrait was that the more attractive individuals were rated as being slightly, but not significantly, less likely to be good parents than neutral or unattractive individuals.

The purpose of this exercise is to try to replicate some aspects of the study described above, but under less controlled conditions.

Materials Needed

Obtain photographs of six individuals of college age, all of the same sex. Two of the individuals should be judged as very attractive physically, two as average, and two as relatively unattractive. If possible, the photographs should be of just the individual's face and not show background details that might influence judgments about the person. Label the six photographs from A to F in a random order that is unrelated to the attractiveness–unattractiveness dimension (e.g., label the two very attractive photographs B and F, the two average photographs A and D, and the two unattractive photos C and E).

Procedure

Ask friends to participate as subjects in your study. Try to run at least two or three subjects, more if time permits. Use

*Dion, K., Berscheid, E., and Walster, E. (1972) What is beautiful is good. *Journal of Personality and Social Psychology*, 24:285–90.

the data sheet on the following page for each subject (to simplify the procedure you can make xerox copies of the data sheet).

Have each subject rate every photograph on the ten personality traits listed on the data sheet, using the rating scale at the top of the data sheet. Go through the photographs in order from A to F and be sure that your subject rates every personality trait for every photograph. When you are finished with a subject, every box of the data sheet should contain a single number.

Treatment of Data

1. Add the ratings in each column of your data sheet to get a total score for each photograph.

2. Compute the average total score for each photograph over all subjects. You will have six averages, one for each photograph.

3. Compute the average total score for the two photographs of very attractive individuals, for the two intermediate photos, and for the two unattractive photographs.

Questions for Discussion

1. Did the photographs of very attractive individuals have a higher total score on personality traits than the photos of unattractive individuals?

2. Do your data indicate that some personality traits were more influenced by physical attractiveness than others?

3. Do you think that male and female subjects were differentially influenced by the physical attractiveness of the individuals they rated?

4. Do your results suggest that a physical-attractiveness stereotype exists and that its content is compatible with the "What is beautiful is good" thesis?

5. If you were to do a more carefully controlled study, what changes would you make in the procedure?

DATA SHEET

RATING SCALE

5 Very high on trait
4 Above average
3 Average
2 Below average
1 Very low on trait

Personality trait	Photographs					
	A	B	C	D	E	F
Outgoing						
Conscientious						
Sensitive						
Imaginative						
Sociable						
Interesting						
Kind						
Intelligent						
Poised						
Sexually responsive						

18
Social Influence

LEARNING OBJECTIVES

18-1. Be able to distinguish among the three basic processes of social influence.

18-2. Be able to discuss the research on social facilitation and explain the findings in terms of drive level and cognitive factors.

18-3. Understand how the concept of deindividuation explains mob behavior, including the variables assumed to contribute to and result from this hypothetical state.

18-4. Be familiar with the factors that determine whether a bystander will intervene in an emergency situation. Be able to differentiate between "pluralistic ignorance" and "diffusion of responsibility."

18-5. Be able to discuss the Asch studies on social norms and conformity; understand the factors that lead to conformity and those that reduce it.

18-6. Be able to describe the Milgram studies on obedience to authority and the four factors that contributed to the high obedience rates.

18-7. Understand the circumstances that undermined obedience and produced rebellion in the MHRC study.

18-8. Be familiar with the factors that must be present for a minority to influence the majority.

18-9. Be able to give three reasons why mass media persuasion is not more effective.

18-10. Know what is meant by identification with a reference group. Be familiar with the findings of the Bennington study.

1. Social psychologists study the way an individual's thoughts, feelings, and behaviors are influenced by others, and they have identified three basic processes of social

influence   in_____ : *compliance, internalization,* and *identification.*

2. In compliance, the person publicly conforms to the wishes of the influencing source but does not change his or her private beliefs or attitudes. A boy eats spinach because his mother tells him to but continues to dislike spinach. This is an example of

compliance   _____ .

3. In compliance the individual conforms publicly but does not change his or her

private   _____ belief or attitudes. In the second process of social

influence   _____ , internalization, the individual changes his or her beliefs, attitudes or behaviors because he or she genuinely believes in the validity of the position advocated by the influencing source.

4. You decide to give up smoking after reading—and believing—a report warning that

internalization   smoking causes cancer and heart disease. This is an example of _____ .

compliance,   5. The first two processes of social influence are _____ and

internalization (*either order*)   _____ . In the third process, identification, the

behaviors   person changes his or her beliefs, attitudes, or _____ in order to identify with, or be like, an influencing source that is respected or admired.

6. A teenage girl takes up smoking in order to be like a group of older girls she ad-

identification   mires. This is an example of _____ .

7. The three basic processes of social influence are compliance, internalization, and identification. List each term next to its key ingredient.

compliance   a. Change behavior but not attitude: _____

internalization   b. Believe in the position: _____

identification   c. Wish to resemble the influencing source: _____

8. Even if there is no intention to persuade, the presence of other people can influence our behavior in a number of ways. For example, if you are running with a group you are apt to run faster than when running alone. The fact that you run

faster   _____ when others are present is called *social facilitation.*

9. One study found that college students completed more multiplication problems when working in a group than when working alone. This is another example of

social   _____ facilitation.

10. Even if other people are only watching us (an *audience*) rather than performing the

facilitation   same task (*coactors*), we tend to work faster. Thus, social _____

audience   occurs in the presence of an au_____ as well as with coactors.

social facilitation	**11.** The effect of coactors or an audience on performance is called _____ _____ .
audience, coactors	**12.** While the performance of simple or well-learned tasks is facilitated by the presence of either an _____ or _____ , performance on more complex tasks may be impaired.
social	**13.** Subjects learn a simple maze faster but a complex maze more slowly in the presence of an audience than when alone. This shows that whether _____ facilitation occurs depends on the nature of the task.
facilitation, task	**14.** Subjects memorize easy word lists faster but difficult word lists more slowly when others are present. This is another example of the fact that the occurrence of social _____ depends on the complexity of the _____ .
level	**15.** Apparently the presence of others raises the individual's drive level, and studies have shown that increased drive _____ energizes the dominant responses of an organism.
incorrect	**16.** With a simple task or one that is well learned the dominant response is likely to be correct. With more complex tasks or behavior just being learned there are many possible responses; the dominant response is apt to be (*correct/incorrect*).
drive level	**17.** The effects of an audience on performance is hypothesized to result from increased _____ _____ . Whether the performance is facilitated or impaired depends on whether the dominant response is likely to be the correct one.
better	**18.** James is a very skillful skater. We would expect him to perform (*better/worse*) before an audience than when skating alone.
impaired	**19.** Howard is just learning to skate. His performance would probably be (*facilitated/impaired*) by the presence of an audience.
audience drive level complexity (*or* difficulty)	**20.** The presence of coactors or an _____ presumably raises the individual's _____ _____ . Whether performance will be facilitated by this increase in drive level depends on the _____ of the task.
more	**21.** Feelings of competition or concerns about being evaluated are the main variables that raise drive level when others are present. Thus, we would expect an audience of "experts" to have (*more/less*) effect on a person's performance than an audience of "novices." The text discusses several competing theories that attempt to explain social facilitation.
facilitation	**22.** Social _____ is one way the presence of other people can influence our behavior. Another example of social influence is mob behavior. People in crowds often show more impulsive, unruly, or destructive behavior than when alone. The psychological state that has been hypothesized to account for mob behavior is called *deindividuation*.

Deindividuation	**23.** Deindi_____ is a feeling that one has lost one's *personal identity* and merged anonymously into the group. It is hypothesized to account for _____ behavior.
mob (*or* crowd)	
personal	**24.** A feeling of loss of _____ identity in a group situation is called
deindividuation	_____ . The text discusses the conditions that contribute to deindividuation and some of the consequences that result from it.
	25. So far we have discussed two ways in which the presence of other people can influence our behavior: _____ _____ and
social facilitation	
deindividuation	_____ .
people	**26.** The presence of other _____ also influences the way we react to an emergency situation. You are more apt to come to the aid of a stranger in distress when you are the only bystander than if others are present.
less	**27.** The presence of other observers makes it (*more/less*) likely that you will intervene in an emergency situation in two main ways: (a) by defining the situation as a *nonemergency* and (b) by *diffusing the responsibility* for acting.
	28. Suppose you are sitting in a theater and think you smell smoke; you even imagine you see wisps of smoke coming from behind the curtain. But everyone else appears to be unconcerned. You might take action if you were alone. But the presence of other people who remain calm serves to define the situation as a
nonemergency	_____ .
	29. Suppose that while walking down a crowded street, you observe a woman fall to the pavement, striking her head severely. In this case it is difficult to define the situation as a nonemergency, but the presence of other people diffuses the
responsibility	_____ for acting. If you were alone you might go to her aid. But in a crowd you do not feel responsible. You assume that someone else will take care of her.
	30. Two factors that help explain why bystanders fail to intervene are defining the
nonemergency, responsibility	situation as a _____ and diffusion of _____ .
more	**31.** One factor that will *increase* the probability of an individual's helping in an emergency is having watched someone else help in a similar situation. If you pass a car with a flat tire and notice that someone has stopped to help, you will be (*more/less*) likely to stop and help the next disabled driver you pass.
	32. Just as we rely on other people in helping to define an ambiguous situation as an
nonemergency	emergency or non_____ , so too we rely on others to provide guidelines for appropriate behavior in particular situations; these guidelines are called *social norms*.
norms	**33.** Social _____ are consensual agreements about the appropriate ways to
situations	behave in particular _____ .

34. In the market we wait in line behind those who have arrived ahead of us at the checkout counter. Waiting our turn is an example of a(n) _____ norm. Failing to comply with this norm usually evokes disapproval from others.

social

35. We push our cart forward (rather than backward) as we collect our purchases, and we do not stop to dance in the aisles. Our behavior is governed by a set of _____ _____ about how to behave in a market.

social

norms

36. Social norms are consensual _____ about the _____ ways to behave in particular situations. Usually people conform to social norms with little awareness of external pressure to do so.

agreements

appropriate

37. Although people usually conform to social norms (*with/without*) awareness of external pressures to do so, experiments demonstrate that the need to agree with our peers does exert a powerful influence.

without

38. In one experiment, in which the correct answer to a simple perceptual task was obvious, subjects changed their response to agree with an incorrect answer given by the group. Thus, pressure to conform to the opinion of one's p_____ does influence behavior.

peers

39. In this experiment the subjects did not actually change their beliefs about the correct answer to the perceptual task, they simply conformed to the answer given by their peers. As we noted earlier, this process of social influence is called _____ .

compliance

40. When an individual conforms to the wishes of an influencing source but does not change his or her private beliefs or attitudes, the process is called _____ . When a source obtains compliance by setting an example, it is called *conformity*. When a source obtains complaince by wielding authority, it is called *obedience*.

compliance

41. Conformity to social norms and obedience to _____ are taught from early childhood; they are essential for communal life.

authority

42. A study by Milgram demonstrated that people would obey an experimenter's orders to deliver strong electric shocks to an innocent victim. Even though the subjects were distressed and objected, they continued to obey the experimenter's instructions. This demonstrates that _____ to authority is strongly instilled in our society.

obedience

43. A number of factors contributed to the high obedience rates found in the study by _____ . For one thing, by answering the advertisement and agreeing to participate, the subjects had implicitly contracted to cooperate and see the job through to completion; refusing to continue thus violates a strong _____ norm.

Milgram

social

44. Secondly, several *buffers* distanced the subjects from the consequences of their aggressive acts. (The victim was in a separate room and could not be seen or communicated with.) Later experiments found that the more direct the person's experi-

buffers	ence with the victim—that is, the fewer the b_____ between the person and the consequences of his or her act—the less the obedience.
	45. Since the shock was generated by a machine, rather than in person, the shock generator served as an additional _____ .
buffer	
	46. If the subjects had been instructed to hit the victim with their fists instead of pushing a shock button, obedience rates would have (*increased/decreased*).
decreased	
	47. In modern warfare, acts of violence can be committed by guided missiles activated hundreds of miles from the scene of destruction. Thus, in current wars buffers often remove aggressors from the c_____ of their acts.
consequences	
	48. Most people vastly underestimate the obedience rates found in studies such as Milgram's, illustrating that we tend to underestimate the degree to which (*external/internal*) forces influence behavior.
external	
	49. As you may recall from Chapter 17, this is known as the fundamental _____ error.
attribution	
	50. Obedience to authority is a form of _____ . But in everyday life most sources of influence try to obtain change that the individual believes in so that the change will be sustained after the source has departed. As noted earlier, when an individual changes his or her attitudes or behaviors because he or she believes in the validity of the position advocated by the source, the process is called _____ .
compliance	
internalization	
	51. The goal of parents, educators, politicians, and advertisers is to persuade, not to coerce; they try to mold our attitudes and beliefs. In other words, their goal is _____ , not just compliance. The text discusses several factors (such as the credibility of the influencing source) that promote internalization.
internalization	
	52. The third process of social influence, in which we change our attitudes or behaviors in order to be like a source we admire, is called _____ .
identification	
	53. If we respect or admire other individuals or groups we may follow their norms and adopt their beliefs, attitudes, and behaviors in order to be like, or to _____ with, them.
identify	
	54. Any group to which we refer in deciding how to act or how to interpret events and social issues is called a *reference* group. Reference _____ influence our attitudes and behavior, either through the use of social rewards and punishments, or by providing us with a frame of reference for interpreting events.
groups	
	55. Since our families have certain attitudes about the world and provide us with a frame of reference for interpreting events, they would be considered a _____ group.
reference	

56. The society in which we live also prescribes certain attitudes and behaviors that are considered "correct" and punishes us with social disapproval (or worse) when we stray from them. Thus, society would be another _____ _____ .

reference group

57. Any group that influences us, either through the use of social rewards and _____ or by providing a frame of _____ for interpreting events, is called a reference group.

punishments, reference

58. We "refer" to such groups in order to evaluate our beliefs, attitudes, and _____ . If we seek to be like them, we are said to *identify* with them.

behaviors

59. An aspiring young swimmer admires the members of the local college swim team and attempts to model her behavior after theirs. The swim team is a _____ group with which she id_____ .

reference

identifies

60. If we seek to be like a reference group, we are said to _____ with that group.

identify

61. Most of us identify with more than one reference group, and this often leads to conflicting pressures on our beliefs, attitudes, and _____ .

behaviors

62. College students often find that the attitudes of their classmates differ on a number of issues from those of their parents. These differences between the peer reference group and the family _____ _____ may lead to conflict.

reference group

63. Studies have shown that students become more politically liberal during their college years, moving away from the conservative views of their parents. If the students revert to their former conservatism after graduation, then the changes in attitude would be considered a temporary id_____ .

identification

64. Often, however, the more liberal attitudes acquired in college are maintained in later life, largely because we seek new friends and spouses who share our attitudes and these constitute new _____ groups.

reference

65. If new views, originally adopted through identification with a reference group, are sustained and become part of our beliefs, then we can say that identification leads to _____ .

internalization

TERMS AND CONCEPTS

compliance _____

_____

_____

_____

internalization _____

_____

_____

_____

identification _____

_____

_____

_____

social norms _____

_____

_____

_____

social facilitation _____

_____

_____

_____

deindividuation _____

_____

_____

_____

pluralistic ignorance _____

_____

_____

_____

diffusion of responsibility _____

_____

_____

_____

social impact theory* _____

_____

_____

_____

fundamental attribution error* _____

_____

_____

_____

reference group _____

_____

_____

_____

*Indicates term used in Critical Discussion

_____ 1. Margaret dislikes opera but purchases a season ticket because her mother persuades her to do so. This is an example of
   a. deindividuation
   b. identification
   c. compliance
   d. a social norm

_____ 2. Obedience to authority can be undermined if the individual is with a group whose members
   a. provide social support for dissent
   b. are part of his or her reference group
   c. show pluralistic ignorance
   d. diffuse the responsibility

_____ 3. According to Newcomb, the changes observed in the political attitudes of most Bennington College students over their four years of attendance reflected
   a. a deliberate choice between reference groups
   b. the changes in their parents' political attitudes
   c. "brainwashing" by liberal professors
   d. compliance without true attitude change

_____ 4. A *reference group* is any group that
   a. consists of individuals with whom we identify
   b. regulates its members through the use of social reward and punishment
   c. provides us with an interpretation of events and social issues
   d. all of the above

_____ 5. Asch's studies on conformity, in which a subject was asked to judge the length of a line after pseudosubjects had intentionally misjudged it, have since been replicated and extended. Which of the following statements is *not* true about this research?
   a. In the basic study about 3/4 of the subjects conformed on at least one trial.
   b. If even one confederate broke with the majority, conformity dropped sharply.
   c. Conformity was reduced by a nonconforming confederate only when the confederate gave the correct answer.
   d. Subjects in the basic study conformed about 1/3 of the time (that is, on 1/3 of the critical trials).

_____ 6. "Pluralistic ignorance" refers to the fact that
   a. few of us know what to do in a real emergency
   b. most people are simply not attentive enough to notice the signs of an emergency
   c. the presence of other people diffuses the responsibility for action
   d. collective inaction in a group convinces each member that no emergency exists

_____ 7. Psychologists studying the influences of reference groups have noted that
   a. individuals must belong to the reference group if its influence is to be effective
   b. most individuals identify with a single reference group
   c. reference groups serve to both regulate behavior and interpret events for their members.
   d. all of the above

_____ 8. Milgram's compliance studies not only utilized a phony "shock machine" but shock us with their results. We can take some comfort, however, from the finding that
   a. once the "learner" no longer answered at all, few subjects continued the shocks
   b. the obedience rate dropped when subjects were made to feel more responsible for their actions
   c. none of the subjects continued to administer shocks when the experimenter left the room and gave instructions by telephone
   d. all of the above

_____ 9. Which of these is an example of a *social norm*?
   a. Murder is against the law.
   b. You face the cash register when you pay for your purchases.
   c. People generally perform better when others are present.
   d. Normal people are unlikely to end up in jail.

_____ 10. What is *coaction*?
   a. two organisms working together on a task
   b. a group of organisms observing a single organism
   c. an increase in performance due to the presence of others
   d. pressure to conform to the norm

_____11. Social facilitation includes
    a. the effects of noise and crowding
    b. obedience and conformity
    c. coaction and audience effects
    d. buffers and etiquette

_____12. What kinds of behaviors show social facilitation?
    a. simple, well learned behaviors
    b. complex or newly learned behaviors
    c. behaviors performed in social isolation
    d. all of the above

_____13. Recent studies of social facilitation effects in humans show that
    a. lower levels of drive energize dominant responses
    b. the effects are most evident when tasks are difficult
    c. the effects do not necessarily depend upon competition or concern about evaluation
    d. the presence of others leads to deindividualization of responses

_____14. The feeling that one has lost personal identity and has merged anonymously into the group is called
    a. bystander apathy
    b. coaction
    c. deindividuation
    d. conformity

_____15. According to Diener's theory, antecedent conditions lead to deindividuation by
    a. causing a high arousal level
    b. producing a state of reduced self-awareness in the individual
    c. reducing ability to plan rationally
    d. lessening concern about evaluation by others

_____16. In one study, college women were told to deliver electric shocks to another woman who was supposedly in a learning experiment. What happened?
    a. None of the women complied with the experimenter.
    b. Deindividualized women delivered more shocks to the learner than did individuated women.
    c. Women wearing large name tags gave the most shocks to the learner they believed to be "nice."

    d. Women who were dressed in coats and hoods refused to shock the learners.

_____17. When Kitty Genovese was murdered, the bystanders who failed to call the police were probably influenced by
    a. deindividuation
    b. diffusion of responsibility
    c. pluralistic ignorance
    d. apathy

_____18. Sometimes groups of people behave in destructive ways that no single individual in the group would likely behave. How can this "mob behavior" be explained?
    a. Persons in the crowd have been deindividuated.
    b. Members may be influenced by strongly held beliefs and the charisma of a group leader.
    c. Group members feel they are less likely to be caught and punished when they act in a mob.
    d. All of the above

_____19. Studies of bystander intervention show that when other people
    a. are present, we are more likely to intervene
    b. respond to an emergency, we are less likely to do so
    c. are not present, we will assume more responsibility for intervening
    d. are present but do not respond, we are more likely to intervene

_____20. In Milgram shock experiments, the level of compliance drops significantly when the subject is
    a. told that the "learner" is of the same sex
    b. moved closer to the experimenter
    c. told that the study is part of a university research program
    d. in the same room as the "learner"

KEY TO SELF-QUIZ

1. c	6. d	11. c	16. b
2. a	7. c	12. a	17. b
3. a	8. b	13. c	18. d
4. d	9. b	14. c	19. c
5. c	10. a	15. b	20. d

INDIVIDUAL OR CLASS EXERCISE

CONFORMITY TO RULES

Introduction

In order to function effectively and to provide for the safety and welfare of its people, any society must establish certain rules and regulations governing behavior. Social psychologists are interested in the factors that produce conformity to society's rules. The purpose of this exercise is to investigate some of the variables that influence motorists' conformity to the rule requiring them to stop at a stop sign.

Equipment Needed

Clipboard and pencil

Procedure

Select a four-way stop intersection (marked by stop signs, not a traffic light) with a moderate flow of traffic. It should be an intersection where you can watch the traffic from all four directions without being too conspicuous.

For a 45-minute period observe each car that approaches the intersection and record the information specified on the data sheet on p. 270. You will need to decide first whether the car (1) comes to a full stop at the intersection, (2) slows down but does not make a complete stop, or (3) makes little or no attempt to slow down. You should spend a few minutes observing the cars before starting your recording period in order to get an idea of how to classify the various degrees of "stopping." Exclude from your records those cards that are forced to stop because they were either behind another car or blocked by cross traffic.

After deciding on the appropriate conformity category, note the sex of the driver, approximate age (under or over 25), and whether or not the driver is traveling alone. Place a tally mark in the appropriate box on the data sheet. For example, if the driver was a female, over 25, traveling with two children, and she made no attempt to slow down, you would place a tally mark in the bottom row in the box to the far right. If the driver was a male, under 25, traveling alone, and he came to a full stop, your tally mark would go in the top box of the extreme left-hand column. Obviously, if the car does not stop you will have to make some quick judgments as to age, sex, and companion.

Treatment of Data

Either you may analayze only your own data or the instructor may collect the data sheets from the entire class and provide you with the class totals in each category for your analysis.

1. Compute the overall percentage of individuals who made a full stop (that is, those who were rated as falling in conformity category 1).

    _____%

2. Compute the percentage of males who made a full stop, and do the same for females.

    males _____%
    females _____%

3. Compute the percentage of individuals under 25 who made a full stop, and do the same for those over 25.

    under 25 _____%
    over 25 _____%

4. Compute the percentage of times a full stop was made when the driver was alone, and the percentage when he or she was accompanied by one or more riders.

    alone _____%
    accompanied _____%

			Conformity categories		
			1 Full stop	**2** Considerable slowing but not full stop	**3** Little or no slowing
Alone	Under 25	Male		*1*	
		Female			
	Over 25	Male			
		Female			
With others	Under 25	Male			
		Female			
	Over 25	Male			
		Female			

Questions for Discussion

1. Do most people comply with the regulation requiring a full stop at stop signs?

2. Does the degree of compliance or conformity depend on the age and sex of the drivers? Is compliance influenced by whether or not the driver is alone?

3. In calculating our percentages, only conformity category 1 was considered. Do we gain any additional information by examining the percentage of drivers that fell in categories 2 and 3?

4. What other variables besides those recorded in this study seemed to predict conformity behavior? For example, did you get the impression that factors such as type or condition of the car or the apparent socioeconomic status of the driver were related to conformity?

5. How accurate do you think your judgments were concerning stopping behavior and the other variables? Would it have been worthwhile to have had several judges rather than a single observer making ratings?

6. If you were to make a large-scale study of this type of conformity behavior, what changes would you make in the research procedure?

Appendix III: Statistical Methods and Measurement

LEARNING OBJECTIVES

A-1.   Be familiar with the presentation of data in the form of frequency distributions, frequency histograms, and frequency polygons. Understand why such presentations are termed descriptive statistics.

A-2.   Be able to define the measures of central tendency called mean, median, and mode. Understand how and why these differ from each other for a skewed distribution.

A-3.   Be familiar with the measures of variation termed range and standard deviation. Be able to state what information such measures provide that measures of central tendency do not.

A-4.   Be able to explain the basis on which one makes a statistical inference about a population based on a sample.

A-5.   Be able to describe a normal curve. Know the approximate percentages of cases falling within ±1, 2, and 3 standard deviations of the mean.

A-6.   Know what is meant by scaling data and be familiar with scaling using standard scores.

A-7.   Understand why the specialized standard deviation termed the standard error of the mean is used.

A-8.   Be able to explain what a finding of statistical significance tells you about the difference between two means. Understand the use of the critical ratio and its relationship to the 5-percent level of significance.

A-9.   Be familiar with the computation of the product-moment correlation coefficient. Be able to describe the general relationship between a scatter diagram and a computed r.

A-10. Be able to interpret various values of a correlation coefficient, including the meaning of a positive vs. negative sign. Be able to demonstrate, with an original example, why correlation does not imply cause-and-effect relationships.

1. If we administer a test to 1,000 students and enter their scores in a notebook, we will be recording information about the test results in the form of *raw* scores. The

raw   scores are called _____ because these are the data as they were collected; they have not been changed in any way.

2. The number a person receives on any measure (height, weight, a test, and so on) is

raw   called a _____ score because it has not been manipulated in any way—it remains just as it was collected.

3. Raw data become comprehensible if they are presented in the form of a *frequency distribution*. If we follow a common procedure, we may list each possible score and record next to it the number of people who made that score. In this way the raw

distribution   data are rearranged as a frequency _____ .

4. Whenever we take raw data and arrange them so that we can tell how many people

frequency distribution   made each possible score, we have a(n)_____ _____ .

5. Since we cannot keep 1,000 raw scores in mind at any one time, it would be convenient if we could *describe* these scores more simply. There are a number of ways to describe (or summarize) frequency distributions; all of them, so long as they merely *describe* the distribution, are classified as *descriptive statistics*. Whenever we use a number (for example, an average) to describe a distribution, we are using a

descriptive   _____ statistic.

6. A professor, who has given a test to a large class, wishes to compute the average score in order to describe how well her students as a whole have performed. The

descriptive statistic   professor is using a(n) _____ _____ .

7. Anyone who describes a distribution of scores by the use of summarizing or simpli-

descriptive statistics   fying scores is using _____ _____ .

8. One descriptive statistic, used often, is the *mean*; it is nothing more than the familiar arithmetic average. In order to determine the *mean* of a distribution of scores, one merely sums (that is, adds up) all the scores and *divides* by the *number* of scores. If you sum the raw scores and divide by the number of scores, you have

mean   computed the_____ .

9. John has taken eight tests during a semester, each of which counts equally toward his final grade. To get an idea of how well he has done, he sums the scores received

mean   on the tests and divides the sum by eight. He has computed a _____ grade.

10. In order to compute a mean, one sums all the raw scores and divides by the

number   _____ of scores.

11. Another descriptive statistic is called the *median*. The *median* is defined as the middle score of the distribution. This statistic is obtained by arranging all the scores from low to high and counting in to the middle from either end. The middle score

median   is the _____ score. If the number of cases is even, one simply averages the

median   cases on either side of the middle. For instance, with 10 cases, the _____ is the average of the fifth and sixth scores when they are arranged from low to high.

12. Put another way, if we find the score that divides the distribution in half, we have

median   found the _____ .

13. The *mode* is the score that appears most *frequently* in the distribution. We find the mode by merely examining the distribution; it requires no computation. Whenever we are talking about the score that occurs most frequently, we are talking about the

mode   _____ .

frequently   **14.** The mode, then, is the score that appears most _____ in the
(*or synonym*)   distribution.

descriptive   **15.** The mean, the median, and the mode are all _____ statistics. They simply describe the distribution of scores.

16. Let us illustrate the way these three statistics may differ by using an example. Let us consider the salaries of five people. Assume that Jim earns $5,000 a year, Mary earns $10,000, Harry also earns $10,000, Bob earns $20,000, and June earns $155,000. First let us compute the *mean* salary. To make this computation, sum all

divide   the salaries and _____ by the number of salaries. (Use a separate sheet for this computation and keep it in view.)

5   **17.** When we sum the salaries of the five people, and divide by ___, we arrive at a mean
$40,000   salary of $ _____ .

18. Next find the *median* salary. The median is the salary in the middle of the distribution. Arranging the five salaries in order from high to low and counting in to the
$10,000   middle yields a median of $ _____ .

19. Finally we examine the distribution to find the *modal* salary. It is obvious that the
$10,000   *mode* of the distribution is $ _____ , since this is the salary that appears most often in the distribution.

20. It now becomes clear that these three statistics may be very different from one an-
same   other. In this particular example, the mode and median both take on the _____
larger   value, but the mean is much _____ .

21. Once we have a mean, it is often helpful to know whether the scores are all very close to the mean or whether they are spread from very low to very high. In other words, we would like to have a *measure of variation* to describe whether the scores vary a lot or just a little. One measure of variation is the *range*, which is the spread from the lowest to the highest score. For example, if the instructor says that the scores on a test went from a low of 32 to a high of 93, he or she is giving the

range   _____ of scores.

variation   **22.** The range is one measure of _____ .

23. Joyce got a 63 on a test. Her roommate asked her how well the others in the class did, and she replied that the score ran from 40 to 74. Joyce was describing the

range   variation of scores in terms of their _____ .

24. Most scores are not the same as the mean; that is, they deviate from the mean. The *standard deviation* is a frequently used measure of the amount by which scores

mean   deviate or depart from their _____ . The standard deviation is thus another

variation   measure of _____ .

25. The lowercase Greek letter σ is frequently used as an abbreviation for the standard

deviation   _____ . The formula for computing the standard deviation is as follows:

$$\sigma = \sqrt{\frac{\text{Sum of } d^2}{N}}$$

The deviation, *d*, for each score is first computed by subtracting the score from the mean. Next, the *d* for each score is squared, and then the squared deviations for all the scores are summed.

26. Statisticians use *N* as a shorthand for the number of scores. When we divide the

deviations   sum of the squared _____ by *N*, we are dividing by the number of

scores   _____ .

27. In computing the *standard deviation*, then, the first step is to determine the devia-

square   tion of each raw score from the mean. The second step is to _____ each of these deviations.

28. In the third step, sum these squared deviations and then divide by *N*. To review:

deviation   The first step is to determine the _____ of each raw score from the

square   mean. The second step is to _____ each of these deviations. Third, sum

N   the squared deviations and divide by _____ .

29. When we take the *square root* of the result of step three, we arrive at the

standard deviation   _____ _____ .

mean   **30.** To recapitulate: First, determine the deviations of the raw scores from the _____;

deviations, sum   second, square each of these _____ ; third, _____ these squared

root   deviations and divide by *N*. Finally, take the square _____ of the result to

standard deviation   obtain the _____ _____ .

31. Let us consider the following example to show how a standard deviation is calculated. For the sake of simplicity, we will use only a few scores. Suppose a test is given to five people and the scores are as follows: 11, 13, 14, 15, 17. In this case

14   the mean would be _____ . (Use a separate sheet of paper.)

32. For the score of 17, the deviation from the mean (obtained by subtracting the

9   mean from the score) is 3. Squaring this we would arrive at the number _____ .

1, 1   **33.** The deviation of the score of 15 would be _____ . Squaring this yields _____ .

0, 0   **34.** The deviation of the score of 14 would be _____ . Squaring this yields _____ .

1   **35.** The deviation of the score of 13 would be –1 (13 – 14 = –1). Squaring –1 yields __ .

–3, 9   **36.** The deviation of the score of 11 would be _____ . Squaring this yields _____ .

37. We now have the squared deviation of each of the scores. In other words, we have completed steps one and two in the sequence mentioned above and are ready to move on to step three in the computation of the standard deviation. In step three

sum, 5   we _____ the squared deviations and divide by N. In this case N equals _____ .

4   **38.** When the operations in step three are carried out, we arrive at _____ (*number*) as a result.

39. We now perform the final operation; we take the square root of the result of step

2   three. The square root of 4 is _____ .

2   **40.** Therefore the standard deviation of this distribution of scores is _____ .

standard   **41.** We have examined two *measures of variation*: the range and the _____ deviation.

variation   **42.** The range and the standard deviation are both measures of _____ . Since these two statistics merely *describe* the distribution, they are classified as

descriptive   _____ statistics.

43. We often wish to say something about large groups of people, for example, the population of China, or the population of the United States, or all college students, or all students at a particular college. The group we wish to talk about is called the *population*, whether it contains 50,000,000 or 100 people. In research, the total

population   group we wish to make our statements about is called the _____ .

44. Professor Jones wishes to find out whether English males are taller than German males. Since he wants to say something about both English males and German

populations   males, these are his _____ s.

45. It is obvious that Professor Jones will not have enough time or money to test all English and German males. Therefore he will have to be satisfied to test fewer than all of them. In a way he has the same problem that customs inspectors have. Customs inspectors want to make sure that no one brings in contraband, but they haven't time to inspect everyone's luggage. Therefore they select some of the people and inspect their baggage thoroughly. They have drawn a *sample* of the total population. A(n)_____, then, is a smaller number of cases that is drawn from the

_____.

sample

population

46. Whenever we select and test a smaller number of cases from the total population we are interested in, we have drawn a(n)_____ from the population.

sample

47. A sample should be selected in such a way that it is *representative* of the total population. Otherwise, we cannot make reasonable *inferences* about the total

_____ based solely on information obtained from the sample.

population

48. A sample that is not representative of the population will not allow us to make

reasonable _____ about the population.

inferences

49. One way of obtaining a representative sample is to select it at *random*. To do this, we can put the names of the members of the population in a hat and draw out the number we need, or use any other means of selection that will guarantee that *every person in the population has an equal chance of being chosen.* When we draw a sample in such a way that each individual in the population has an equal chance of

being chosen, we have drawn a r_____ sample.

random

50. A key feature of a random sample is that each individual in the population has an

_____ _____ of being chosen.

equal chance

51. If we collect data on a sample of 100 people in a town of 1,000 people and then make statements about the *entire* population of the town on the basis of these data, we cannot be *sure* our statements are correct. Only if we collect data on the entire

_____ of the town can we be sure that any statements based on the data will be correct for the whole population.

population

52. When we make statements about a population on the basis of a sample, we *infer* that what is true about the sample will also be approximately true for the entire population. A statement about a population based on a sample of that population is

called a(n)_____ence. We can never be completely _____ that such an inference is correct.

inference, sure (*or synonym*)

53. Another way of putting this is to say that when we make an inference about a population from a sample, we have only a certain probability that our statement is correct for the population as a whole. The probability of our statement being true

would be 100 percent only if we had data on the _____ population.

entire (*or synonym*)

54. The smaller the size of the sample, the smaller the probability of making a correct inference about the population. Since we are making inferences about the

_____ , based on *statistics* that are computed from only a

population

_____ of the population, we call this process *statistical inference.*

sample

55. When the Gallup poll interviews a small number of people and makes a pre-

diction about who will be elected President of the United States, a statistical

inference

_____ is being made.

56. Suppose a researcher is interested in the population of a particular college with 10,000 students. She goes to the college directory and takes each hundredth name,

random

thus drawing a _____ sample of the population of students at that college.

57. She tests this sample of students and, on the basis of their scores alone, she makes

population

statements about the entire _____ of the college. When she does

statistical inference

this, she is making a(n)_____ _____.

58. Suppose we gave an intelligence test to all the people in the United States and then plotted on a graph the scores and the number of people who got each score. We plot

horizontal

the number of people on the vertical axis and their scores on the hor_____ axis. In schematic form the graph would look like the illustration below.

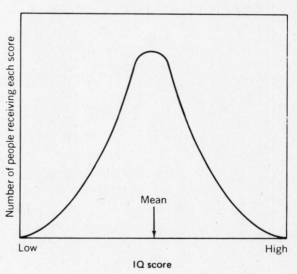

59. This graph represents a *frequency distribution* of scores. Looking at the graph, we find that there are relatively few people who got very low scores and that the num-

increases

ber of people who got any particular score (*increases/decreases*) as we move upward toward the mean. As we move past the mean to the right, there are fewer and fewer people getting the higher scores and very few getting the highest scores.

60. Note that the curve of the frequency distribution is *symmetrical* in form; that is,

above

the part of the curve below the mean is a mirror image of the part _____ the mean. Symmetry implies that for every score a fixed distance above the mean there

below

is a corresponding score the same distance _____ the mean, so that the number of people receiving each score will be the same.

frequency

61. The curve of the _____ distribution shown above not only is symmetrical in form but also is shaped very much like a bell. A frequency-distribution

bell

curve that is symmetrical and also _____-*shaped* is called a *normal curve*.

distribution

normal

62. When we plot a frequency _____ and get a curve that is

bell-shaped, we call this curve a _____ curve.

63. For a normal curve the mean, median, and mode all have the same value. There are the same number of cases below and above the middle of the distribution; for every score below the mean there is another score the same distance above the mean; and the number of cases receiving a score a given distance below the mean is matched by an equal number of cases receiving a score the same distance above the mean. In

symmetrical

other words, the two halves of the curve are _____ .

50

64. If 50 people have a score of 80 and the mean is 100, then _____ (*number*) people can be expected to have a score of 120 if the curve is a normal curve.

65. If we actually administered the Stanford-Binet intelligence test to all the people in the United States, we would find that the frequency distribution of scores would take the form of a normal curve. The *mean* of the scores would be 100 and the *standard deviation* would be 16. The standard deviation, as you will remember, is a

variation

measure of var _____ .

66. Statisticians often talk about a score as being one or more standard deviations away from the mean. If the mean of the scores on an intelligence test is 100 and the standard deviation is 16, a score of 84 would be said to be one standard deviation

below

_____ the mean.

67. One of the properties of the normal curve is that *68 percent* of all the cases in the distribution will have scores that lie between one standard deviation below and one above the mean. The normal curve is so defined that this will *always* be true. If a

68

distribution of intelligence test scores fits a normal curve, ____ percent of the cases will have scores between one standard deviation below the mean and one standard

above

deviation _____ the mean. This characteristic of the normal curve is shown in the illustration below, in which new labels have been added to the normal curve with which you are already familiar.

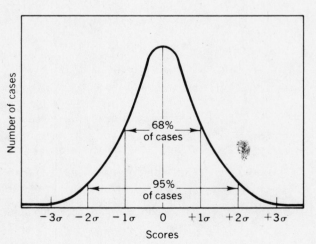

68. As you already know, the Greek letter σ is the abbreviation for standard deviation.

below

Thus –1σ means one standard deviation _____ the mean.

84

69. Referring again to the intelligence test with a mean of 100 and a standard deviation of 16, the score that is one standard deviation below the mean is _____ (*number*).

116   **70.** The score that is one standard deviation above the mean would be _____ .

71. Therefore, if we group all the people with scores between 84 and 116 on the intelligence test, we will have _____ percent of the population.

68

72. If we look again at the normal curve on p. 278, we see that 95 percent of the population have scores that lie between *two* standard deviations below the mean and two standard deviations above the mean. To go back to the intelligence test with a mean of 100 and a standard deviation of 16, 95 percent of the population

132   will have scores between 68 and _____ .

73. If 68 percent of the population have scores that lie between one standard deviation below the mean and one standard deviation above the mean on the normal curve,

34   then it follows that _____ percent of the population have scores between one standard deviation below the mean and the mean itself.

74. In other words, in our example, 34 percent of the population have scores between

100   84 and _____ .

75. If 95 percent of the population have scores between two standard deviations below the mean and two standard deviations above the mean, then 47.5 percent of the population have scores between two standard deviations above the mean and the mean itself. In our example, then 47.5 percent of the population have scores

132   between 100 and _____ .

76. Again looking at our illustration of the normal curve, we can see that almost all of the people (over 99 percent) have scores that lie between three standard deviations

above   below the mean and three standard deviations _____ the mean. Thus for

three   practical purposes virtually all of the scores fall between minus and plus _____ standard deviations from the mean.

77. To use our example once more, we would expect that practically all the people who took the intelligence test (mean = 100, standard deviation = 16) would have scores

52, 148   between _____ and _____ .

78. As a quick example of how one can use the concept of the standard deviation on the normal curve, let us suppose that Susan had a score of 148 on the intelligence test. Knowing the mean and the standard deviation of that test, Susan can be sure

three   that she has earned one of the very highest scores, since her score is _____ standard deviations above the mean. In other words, she knows how her score compares with those from the population at large.

Note: The Appendix in the text can be only an introduction to the subject of statistics. In turn, this programmed unit can be only an introduction to that material. You have learned about some of the basic terms and techniques of statistical analysis, but several concepts that are treated in the text have not even been mentioned in this program. You should, however, find it easier to master the text treatment if you have understood the concepts presented here.

TERMS AND CONCEPTS

frequency distribution _____

_____

_____

_____

mean _____

_____

_____

_____

median _____

_____

_____

mode _____

_____

_____

_____

skewed distribution _____

_____

_____

_____

range _____

_____

_____

_____

standard deviation _____

_____

_____

population _____

_____

_____

_____

sample _____

_____

_____

_____

statistical inference _____

_____

_____

_____

normal distribution _____

_____

_____

standard score _____

_____

_____

_____

standard error of the mean _____

_____

_____

_____

statistical significance _____

_____

_____

_____

critical ratio _____

_____

_____

_____

product-moment correlation (*r*) _____

_____

_____

_____

SELF-QUIZ

_____ 1. Descriptive statistics
    a. include the analysis of variance
    b. provide a shorthand notation for summarizing a large number of observations
    c. exclude measures of variation
    d. allow us to learn about a population by studying small samples

_____ 2. Suppose scores on test A have a mean of 20 and a standard error of the mean of 1, while scores on test B have a mean of 25 and also have a standard error of the mean of 1. Can we depend on the difference between the two means, that is, is it significant?
    a. Yes, since the critical ratio is high.
    b. No, the difference is not significant.
    c. Maybe, since the critical ratio is close to the significance level.
    d. We cannot tell from these data.

_____ 3. The curve that results from a large number of chance events occurring independently is a _____ curve.
    a. standard
    b. normal
    c. random
    d. chance

_____ 4. What two measures of central tendency are identical for this distribution: 1, 1, 3, 4, 6?
    a. mean and mode
    b. mode and median
    c. mean and median
    d. all of the above

_____ 5. Suppose you take a midterm and a final in this course. Will you be able to tell on which one you do better when there are different numbers of questions? If the midterm has a mean of 50 with a standard deviation of 10, the final has a mean of 120 with a standard deviation of 20, and your scores are 55 and 135, you will have
    a. done better on the final
    b. done worse on the final
    c. stayed the same on the final
    d. failed the course

_____ 6. It should always be remembered that correlation
    a. does not measure linear relationships
    b. cannot show statistical significance
    c. does not yield causal relationships
    d. all of the above

_____ 7. A measure of variation
    a. is the range
    b. tells us how representative the mean is
    c. is the standard deviation
    d. all of the above

_____ 8. A correlation of $r = -2.0$ indicates that
    a. the relation between x and y has a negative slope of two
    b. an error has been made in computing the correlation coefficient
    c. x tends to increase with increases in y
    d. x tends to decrease with increases in y

_____ 9. If we wished to know whether the average of a distribution is typical of the scores within it, we would look at the _____ for a simple indicator but would compute the _____ if we wished a more sensitive measure.
    a. range, standard deviation
    b. range, standard score
    c. mean, standard deviation
    d. mode, critical ratio

_____ 10. The most widely used graph form for plotting data grouped into class intervals is the
    a. frequency distribution
    b. symmetrical distribution
    c. frequency histogram
    d. normal distribution

_____ 11. A standard score is
    a. based on the standard deviation
    b. offers a way of scaling the data
    c. tells us how one score compares to the others in a distribution
    d. all of the above

_____ 12. The conventional rule of thumb for an acceptable level of statistical significance is _____ percent, that is, we are willing to risk a chance result occurring _____ in 100 decisions.
    a. 1, once
    b. 2, twice
    c. 5, five times
    d. 10, ten times

13. If a normal distribution has a mean of 100 and a standard deviation of 5, we know that
    a. 68 percent of the scores fall between 95 and 105
    b. 95 percent of the scores fall between 85 and 115
    c. approximately half of the scores fall between 80 and 120
    d. the range of scores is 75 to 125

14. A correlation of $r = -.80$
    a. is significant
    b. means that increases in x are accompanied by decreases in y
    c. means that increases in x are accompanied by increases in y
    d. makes the relationship between x and y unclear

15. The median is
    a. obtained by adding the scores and dividing by the number of cases
    b. that part of the scale where most cases occur
    c. the score with the highest frequency
    d. the middle score in a distribution

16. We can have confidence in a statistical inference if the
    a. sample is significant
    b. effect is large relative to the sampling error
    c. population is normal
    d. all of the above

17. If a general round of wage increases were to be combined with a reduction of extremely high incomes, the
    a. mean income would tend to go up
    b. distribution of income would become more skewed

    c. median would tend to go down
    d. distribution of income would become less skewed

18. Since the standard error of the mean is a special case of the standard deviation, it tells us about the distribution of the *population* made up of *sample means.* For example, we know that if a sample has a mean of 50 and a standard error of the mean of 5, the population mean almost certainly falls in the range of
    a. 45–55
    b. 40–60
    c. 35–65
    d. 30–70

19. The _____ is very useful, in that it gives us a mathematical way of stating the degree of relationship between two variables.
    a. correlation coefficient
    b. coefficient of correlation
    c. product-moment correlation
    d. all of the above

20. In order to make a judgment about a population without testing all members of it, we
    a. draw a random sample for testing
    b. examine the normal distribution
    c. develop a standard score
    d. examine the standard error of the scores

KEY TO SELF-QUIZ

1. b	6. c	11. d	16. b
2. a	7. d	12. c	17. d
3. b	8. b	13. a	18. c
4. c	9. a	14. b	19. d
5. a	10. c	15. d	20. a

INDIVIDUAL EXERCISES

Introduction

Although a mastery of statistical techniques requires time and training, the basic notions of statistics can be understood by those with a minimum of mathematical background. The following exercises use simple data in order to make computations easy. These exercises are designed to illustrate how the formulas work rather than to provide skill in their use; you should attempt the exercises only after you have read Appendix III in the textbook. (The

answers to these exercises are given in the Appendix of this Study Guide, p. 289.)

FREQUENCY DISTRIBUTION

Eleven applicants for a job made the following scores on a test of relevant skills:

25   53   42   64   38   43   56   36   38   48   47

Complete the table below by counting the scores in each class interval; then plot the diagram.

Frequency Distribution

Scores on test	Number of applicants making these scores
20-29	_____
30-39	_____
40-49	_____
50-59	_____
60-69	_____

FREQUENCY DIAGRAM

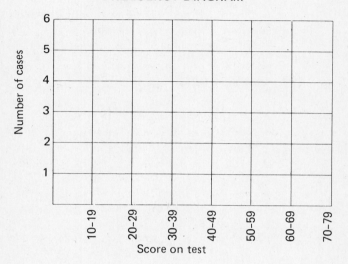

Questions

1. What is the class interval?

2. Is the distribution symmetrical?

MEASURES OF CENTRAL TENDENCY

Questions

3. Determine the *median* score for the above data by arranging the scores in order and finding the *middle* case (that is, the 6th from either end of 11).

    Median = _____

4. Calculate the *mean* for the above data by adding the *raw scores* and dividing by the number of scores.

    Mean = _____

5. Under what circumstances do the mean and median differ?

6. If the person getting the high score of 64 had in fact gotten a score of 75, how would it have affected the mean and the median?

MEASURES OF VARIATION

Consider the following weekly earnings reported by five part-time taxicab drivers:

Driver	Weekly earnings
A	$50
B	$60
C	$70
D	$80
E	$90

Questions

7. What is the *range* of weekly earnings? _____

    The *mean?* _____

8. Compute the *standard deviation* by completing the following table.

Driver	Weekly earnings	Deviation from mean (d)	Deviation squared (d^2)
A			
B			
C			
D			
E			

Sum of d^2 = _____

$\dfrac{\text{Sum of } d^2}{N}$ = _____

Standard deviation = $\sqrt{\dfrac{\text{Sum of } d^2}{N}}$ = _____

STANDARD ERROR OF THE MEAN

The more cases that enter into the computation of a mean, the more confidence we have that our obtained mean represents the total group from which our sample has been drawn.

Suppose that we draw successive samples of increasing size in order to measure some psychological characteristic, such as speed of reaction, among college students. How does our confidence increase with the size of the sample?

Suppose that the means of our reaction-time measurement fluctuate around 150 milliseconds (0.150 seconds), with standard deviations around 15 milliseconds. Where does the true mean reaction time fall?

These problems will be dealt with as you answer Questions 9 and 10.

Sample size	Mean reaction time (milliseconds)	95 percent confidence limits	
		Lower limit (mean less 2.0 × standard error)	Upper limit (mean plus 2.0 × standard error)
25	150		
100	150		
400	150		

Thus far nothing has been said about the true mean of the population. Setting the confidence limits as we have, we may infer that the true mean lies within our confidence limits 95 percent of the time.

SIGNIFICANCE OF A DIFFERENCE

Suppose that we are comparing the mathematics scores of boys and girls in the fourth grade, with the following results:

	Number of cases (N)	Mean	Standard error of mean (σ_M)
Girls	50	72.0	0.4
Boys	50	70.5	0.3

Questions

Do the girls score significantly higher than the boys? To find out, we compute a *critical ratio,* but first we have to find the *standard error of difference,* according to the following formula.

11.   The formula for the standard error of difference is

$$\sigma_D = \sqrt{\sigma_{M_1}^2 + \sigma_{M_2}^2}$$

where σ_{M_1} and σ_{M_2} are the standard errors of the means for girls and boys. Work out this formula using the data above.

$$\sigma_D = \sqrt{(\qquad)^2 + (\qquad)^2} =$$

$$\sqrt{(\qquad)} = \underline{\hspace{2cm}}$$

Questions

9.   Let us compute the *standard error of the mean,* assuming different numbers of cases (persons) in our sample. Complete the following table, using the formula:

$$\text{Standard error of the mean } (\sigma_M) = \frac{\text{Standard deviation } (\sigma)}{\sqrt{N}}$$

Number of cases (N)	$\sqrt{N}$	Standard deviation (σ)	Standard error of mean (σ_M)
25	5	15	
100	10	15	
400	20	15	

Note that the standard error of the mean decreases as N increases. How can we convert this into some kind of statement about the true mean?

10.   *Confidence limits.* We can state that with repeated measurements we can expect our means to fall within the range from -2.0σ to $+2.0\sigma$ in 95 percent of the cases. Using the table at the top of the right-hand column, determine the confidence limits for the mean reaction times of the three different sample sizes.

12. Compute the critical ratio, using this formula:

$$\text{Critical ratio} = \frac{\text{Difference between means}}{\sigma_D} =$$

$$\frac{(\quad) - (\quad)}{(\quad)} = \underline{\quad\quad}$$

13. If the absolute size of the critical ratio is over 2.0, we usually call the difference *significant*. In our example, is there a significant difference between the mathematics scores of boys and girls?

COEFFICIENT OF CORRELATION

Job applicants were given a test of sales ability before being hired. Then their scores were compared with subsequent performance on the job (as shown in the table below).

14. The degree of relationship between scores and sales is expressed by the *coefficient of correlation*. What is the product-moment correlation between the applicants' test scores and earnings? Complete the computations indicated in the table on p. 286 and copy your result here:

$r = $ _____ .

15. On the basis of this correlation, what can be said about the cause-and-effect relations between test scores and sales performance?

	Applicant				
	Anderson	Brown	Cook	Dodge	East
Test score	50	60	70	80	90
Sales (in thousands of dollars)	$60	$80	$90	$70	$100

COMPUTATION OF PRODUCT-MOMENT CORRELATION (r)
(Correlation between a sales test and later sales in thousands of dollars)

Applicant	Scores on the sales test and computation of σ_x			Sales success and computation of σ_y			Cross-products used in computing r
	Test score (x)	Deviation from mean (dx)* (mean = 70)	(dx)^2	Sales score (y)	Deviation from mean (dy)* (mean = $80)	(dy)^2	Product of deviations (dx) (dy)
Anderson							
Brown							
Cook							
Dodge							
East							
	Sum (dx)^2 = $\dfrac{\text{Sum }(dx)^2}{N}$ = $\sigma_x = \sqrt{\dfrac{\text{Sum }(dx)^2}{N}}$ =			Sum (dy)^2 = $\dfrac{\text{Sum }(dy)^2}{N}$ = $\sigma_y = \sqrt{\dfrac{\text{Sum }(dy)^2}{N}}$ =			Sum (dx) (dy) =

*Subtract mean from score: respect the sign of the difference.

Coefficient of correlation, $r = \dfrac{\text{Sum }(dx)\,(dy)}{N\,\sigma_x\,\sigma_y}$

$$= \frac{(\qquad)}{(\qquad) \times (\qquad) \times (\qquad)}$$

$$= \frac{(\qquad)}{(\qquad)}$$

$$= \underline{\qquad\qquad\qquad}$$

Appendix to Study Guide

Note. This Appendix includes answers to exercises and problems presented in the *Study Guide.* The student should not read this material until reference is made to it in the text of the *Guide.*

CHAPTER 11 (P. 166) MEASURING MOTIVATION

Score your completed sentences as follows:

P . . . . if your response indicates a positive, humorous, or hopeful attitude

C . . . . if your response indicates conflict, antagonism, pessimism, emotional disturbance

N . . . . if your response is neutral, that is, not clearly positive or conflictful

Examples of how your responses should be scored:

Men _____ .

P . . . . are friendly, are easy to get along with, are nice, are good sports, are considerate, are fun at a party, are good friends, are O.K.

C . . . . are a pain in the neck, get on my nerves, can't be trusted, bother me, give me a headache, think they are superior, are rude, are stupid.

N . . . . are human beings, are taller than women, are stronger than women, are the opposite sex, are the same sex.

Count the total number of P, C, and N scores. Your instructor may ask you to write these on a slip of paper so that he or she can determine the distribution of results for the entire class. (You may then complete the table on p. 288 and determine the median score.) You need not identify yourself. Compute your score by adding 50 to the number of C responses and subtracting the number of P responses. Any omissions (incompleted sentences) are not scored.

Score	Number of students	Score	Number of students
96–100		46–50	
91–95		41–45	
86–90		36–40	
81–85		31–35	
76–80		26–30	
71–75		21–25	
66–70		16–20	
61–65		11–15	
56–60		6–10	
51–55		1–5	

Median score

CHAPTER 12 (P. 180) INDIVIDUAL DIFFERENCES

The unscrambled sentences are as follows:

1. The good that men do lives after them.
2. Don't shoot until you see the whites of their eyes.
3. The most valuable thing in the world is the free human mind.
4. Tell your yarn and let your style go to the devil.
5. It is only at rare moments that we live.
6. Do not blame me too much for not knowing all the answers.
7. The greatest of faults is to be conscious of none.
8. It is better to understand a little than to misunderstand a lot.
9. The worst use that can be made of success is boasting of it.
10. Better a witty fool than a foolish wit.
11. First love is only a little foolishness and a lot of curiosity.
12. The power of laughter is astonishing.
13. Money cannot cure unhappiness.
14. Your reputation grows with every failure.
15. Talk to a man about himself and he will listen for hours.
16. The truth is the one thing nobody will believe.
17. My way of joking is to tell the truth.
18. It is not pleasure that makes life worth living.
19. I had rather be right than President.
20. Very simple ideas lie within the reach only of complex minds.

CHAPTER 15 (P. 226) CLASSIFYING ABNORMAL BEHAVIOR

The cases are designed to illustrate the following disorders:

Case 1 Affective disorder—manic-depressive disorder, manic episode

Case 2 Schizophrenia

Case 3 Anxiety disorder—generalized anxiety disorder with panic episodes

Case 4 Anxiety disorder—agoraphobia

Case 5 Anxiety disorder—obsessive-compulsive disorder

Case 6 Personality disorder—antisocial personality

Case 7 Affective disorder—depression

APPENDIX III: STATISTICAL METHODS
AND MEASUREMENT (pp. 283-86)

Answers to the *Individual Exercises.*

1. 10
2. No
3. Median = 43
4. Mean = 44.55
5. When the frequency distribution is not perfectly symmetrical about the mean
6. Increased the mean, no effect on the median
7. Range from $50 to $90, or $40; Mean = $70
8. Standard deviation = 14.14
9. Standard errors: for 25 cases, 3.0; for 100 cases, 1.5; for 400 cases, 0.75
10. Confidence limits: for 25 cases, 144-156; for 100 cases, 147-153; for 400 cases, 148.5-151.5
11. Standard error of difference = 0.5
12. Critical ratio = 3.0
13. Yes
14. $r = .90$
15. No definite conclusions about cause-and-effect relations can be drawn from correlational evidence. See discussion of this topic in text.

A 7
B 8
C 9
D 0
E 1
F 2
G 3
H 4
I 5
J 6